How to Stop a Hijacking

Hijackings and bombings have plagued civil aviation since 1931 and air rage incidents are on the rise. While there is aircraft and inflight training available for air marshals, other first responders receive minimal training on inflight security awareness and protocols. There are no other resources currently available to flight crews or armed first responders that specifically address inflight security and how to control threats of disturbances on airplanes.

How to Stop a Hijacking provides readers with fundamental principles on how to think more critically about onboard security threats. The aircraft cabin is an environment that poses unique security challenges, and first responders can apply security awareness and critical thinking skills to establish a safer environment in the cabin and airport for everyone onboard. The lessons in this book are driven by the central objective of teaching the reader how to counter inflight aggression and maintain tactical control of the cabin. Written by a former federal air marshal instructor, this book looks at the recent rash of air rage incidents and violence on airplanes, in addition to the real and ever-present threat of hijack or potential explosive device.

How to Stop a Hijacking is a practical guide that offers methodological and tactically proven strategies for stopping violent acts on board an aircraft inflight.

Clay W. Biles is a former US Federal Air Marshal and inflight security instructor. Biles joined the Federal Air Marshal Service in 2008 and flew more than 1 million miles on international and domestic flights. Biles resigned in 2013 and founded High Order Security, a company that assists at-risk personnel in Latin America. He lives in the San Francisco Bay Area with his wife and two children.

T0386460

How to Stop a Hijacking

Critical Thinking
in Civil Aviation Security

Clay W. Biles

CRC Press
Taylor & Francis Group
Boca Raton London

CRC Press is an imprint of the
Taylor & Francis Group, an **informa** business

Designed cover image: TBC

First edition published 2023
by CRC Press
6000 Broken Sound Parkway NW, Suite 300, Boca Raton, FL 33487–2742

and by CRC Press
4 Park Square, Milton Park, Abingdon, Oxon, OX14 4RN

CRC Press is an imprint of Taylor & Francis Group, LLC

© 2023 Clay W. Biles

ISBN: 978-1-032-37315-7 (hbk)
ISBN: 978-1-032-37300-3 (pbk)
ISBN: 978-1-003-33645-7 (ebk)

DOI: 10.4324/9781003336457

Typeset in Palatino
by Apex CoVantage, LLC

This book is dedicated to first responders in civil aviation, past, present, and future.

CONTENTS

SECTION III *Safety and Security Considerations*

SECTION IV *Tenets of Inflight Security*

SECTION V Counter-Hijack Response Strategies

CONTENTS

ACKNOWLEDGMENT

A thorough government review was performed on the manuscript—by the SSI (Sensitive Security Information) Program, within TSA (Transportation Security Administration), an Agency of the U.S. DHS (Department of Homeland Security). Such review, in accordance with the SSI Regulation at 49 C.F.R. part 1520, confirmed that the work contained no sensitive information.

INTRODUCTION

This book's main purpose is to help first responders in civil aviation like you learn how to think more critically about onboard security threats. By applying critical thinking skills to inflight security, you can establish a safer environment in the cabin for everyone on board. The aircraft cabin poses unique security challenges. Unfortunately, current training falls short for preparing you to analyze situations that may be harmless on the ground but catastrophic in the air. The lessons in this book are driven with the central objective of teaching you how to maintain tactical control of the cabin during an inflight security threat so the pilot-in-command can safely land the aircraft. The tactics outlined in this book are not new; they have been in the terrorist hijacker playbook for decades. It is time for first responders like you to understand these tactics, too. By applying the lessons within, you can learn how to be a more effective first responder and how to avoid becoming the victim of onboard violence. I hope the information within will help you think more critically about civil aviation security now and in the future. Fly safe.

Section I

The Basics of Inflight Security

Hijackings and bombings have plagued civil aviation since 1931. Individuals have used these violent acts to make political statements, to bring awareness to political causes, and for reasons of psychological abnormality. Flight attendants, special passengers (such as law enforcement officers), and other first responders in civil aviation have been on the frontlines of this inflight violence, responding when needed in order to preserve the safety of the aircraft, crew, and other passengers on board. But aircraft hijackings and bombings are extremely rare. At least, this is what the past two decades of the historical record reflect. In fact, recent trends suggest a prevalence for inflight rowdiness in the form of aggressive behavior, or *air rage*, not of suicide bombings or hijackings. But if there are any violent extremist hijackers or would-be bombers out there, hatching plans anew, we can always rely on inflight security officers like federal air marshals to keep us safe, right? *Wrong.* Unfortunately, in the United States, federal air marshals perform security on less than 1% of commercial flights. Other countries around the world have similar inflight security coverage. This means that, regardless of what airline you work or travel on, there is a high likelihood that you will find yourself on an aircraft without inflight security support. This also means that, in the face of an onboard threat, it will likely be up to you and other first responders to find a solution to keep everyone on board safe.

DOI: 10.4324/9781003336457-1

Although attempted hijackings and bombings of aircraft are rare, they pose a serious risk to an aircraft inflight. Because of these dangers, inflight security decisions are always made by anticipating the threat of a hijacking or bombing. By keeping hijack and bomb threats at the fore-front of your mind (and by implementing the tactical processes outlined in this book) when you initiate threat protocol, you will be able to more rapidly and effectively respond to inflight security threats. Two people who are seen fighting in the cabin may, at face value, appear to be engag-ing in aggressive behavior for reasons of air rage; however, a fight like this could also be a diversion in preparation for a violent hijacking. When you respond to an inflight security threat as a first responder, it is impor-tant for you to follow specific protocols in the cabin to help maintain the security of the flight deck, integrity of the aircraft, and safety of the crew, yourself, and other first responders and/or passengers. This book guides you through this decision process. Making more effective inflight secu-rity decisions can be accomplished by learning and applying the tenets of inflight security and by expanding your knowledge of threats against civil aviation. The tenets of inflight security will teach you the basics of threat hierarchy and inflight security protocols, whereas a firm under-standing of past threats to civil aviation will allow you to better predict and respond to future threats in aircraft and airports. Section I is split into four chapters: Chapter 1 gives a brief introduction to inflight secu-rity, explains basic terminology, and provides a general understanding of inflight security; Chapter 2 gives examples of threats to civil aviation and lessons on hijacker and bomber tactics and behavior; Chapter 3 will give you a brief understanding of terrorist planning and operations and will expand on aggressor behavior and tactics; finally, Chapter 4 provides information about inflight jurisdiction and the layers of aviation security, all of which will help you think more critically about inflight security. The purpose of this section is to help you form a security perspective that considers the most dangerous threats to passengers, crew, and other first responders in aircraft and airports.

1

Introduction to Inflight Security

This chapter introduces terminology to ease your communication with other first responders and introduces some basic information about inflight security to help broaden your understanding of the subject. *Inflight security* is a security discipline that is focused on maintaining the security of the flight deck, the integrity of the aircraft, and the safety of the flight crew, the first responder, the first responder's team and passengers. Australia and many other countries around the world have government-operated *inflight security programs* where individuals travel in commercial aircraft to help secure the inflight environment. In Australia, there are *air security officers* or ASOs. In the United States, there are *federal air marshals* or FAMs. Austria, Canada, Jordan, China, Israel, and Poland (among many other countries) all have their own inflight security programs and specific titles (or names) assigned to their security officials. These security officials are universally called *inflight security officers* or IFSOs. The aircraft that inflight security officers typically travel in are those that are *flagged* (belonging) to the country of the respective inflight security program that is providing the security (e.g., federal air marshals typically fly on United States-flagged aircraft). Many countries around the world either re-initiated their inflight security programs or built new ones after the September 11, 2001, coordinated hijackings. A number of the previously mentioned countries rapidly hired and trained thousands of new inflight security officers in the wake of this particular attack.

Inflight security officers receive several months of training in detecting criminal behavior; terrorist attack methods and planning; and aircraft-specific tactics. This training gives insight into criminal behavioral

DOI: 10.4324/9781003336457-2

indicators and physiological changes to the human body under stress; teaches how a terrorist or criminal organization may plan and execute an attack against civil aviation; and provides instruction on how to re-hijack an aircraft during a hijacking or bombing attempt. After formal training, inflight security officers learn more about the aviation environment by conducting surveillance on and observing the behavior of passengers in aircraft and airports around the world. This on-the-job training gives inflight security officers a heightened ability to detect potential terrorist and criminal acts by enabling them to distinguish baseline behavior from illicit (or deceptive) behavior. Frequent flyers like you will be particularly good at recognizing baseline behavior inside the aircraft environment because of your repeated exposure to it. This experience will help you better implement the topics discussed in this book and will give you an advantage in helping to detect inflight security threats.

To deter hostile acts on board an aircraft inflight, inflight security programs must reveal some information about itself. At a minimum, they must let their adversary know of the existence of their inflight security program. This is considered *deterrence*. An example of deterrence would be the public acknowledgment by the Chinese government that it has an inflight security program. This is the same thing as telling air pirates that, if they attempt to hijack or bomb a China-flagged aircraft, there is a chance that a security team could be on board to stop them. Therefore, there is *deterrence value* in having the potential on board presence of an inflight security officer (or inflight security team) known. There is a higher deterrence value in releasing information about the existence of an inflight security program and a lower deterrence value when the existence of an inflight security program is kept secret. This book could be considered a form of deterrence, since those who read it will be better prepared to thwart a hijacking or bombing attempt. By reading this book and applying the techniques and principles within, you will not only act as a more effective deterrent against hijackings and attempted bombings, but you will also be better prepared to handle the cases of air rage, inflight aggression, and other inflight disturbances that are more likely to require communication with the captain and the initiation of threat protocols.

To ease communication between first responders, a standard system of terminology should be used at all times. To begin, the *cabin* is the area inside the aircraft where passengers sit and where cabin crew members, for example, flight attendants, perform their duties. Cabins are divided by *travel class*, which denotes the quality of seating accommodations. The travel class of cabins found in commercial aircraft typically includes *first class* (highest travel class), *business class*, and *coach class* (lowest travel class). Some aircraft may have a cabin with only one type of travel class, while others may have a cabin with mixed travel class. Cabins typically contain one or more *lavatories* (or bathrooms) and may have one aisle (single-aisle) or two aisles (double-aisle); some aircraft have a mix of single- and double-aisle cabins. Aircraft typically have one *deck* (one floor) or two *decks* (two floors); aircraft may therefore be referred to as *single-decker* or *double-decker aircraft*. A cabin also typically has a *galley* (or kitchen).

All aircraft have a *forward area*. The forward area is often referred to as the *position of dominance* because of its importance as a tactical position inside the aircraft. The position of dominance is the area aft of the flight deck door and forward of the first row of seats. The *flight deck*, or cockpit, is where the pilots control the aircraft, while the person legally responsible for the safety and operation of the aircraft during its flight is the *pilot-in-command*, or *captain*.

An *aircraft hijacking*, or *air piracy*, is the unlawful seizure of an aircraft within the *special aircraft jurisdiction*, a legal term that means that all external passenger doors in the aircraft have been closed. In contrast to a hijacking, a *commandeering* is defined as the unlawful seizure of an aircraft; a commandeering can take place either in the special aircraft jurisdiction or on the ground with the doors open. Hijackers often attempt to gain *cabin compliance* as a way to control people in the cabin during a hijacking or commandeering; hijackers have historically sought to gain cabin compliance by forcing passengers and/or cabin flight crew into a position of disadvantage, that is, seated, with hands on top of the head, fingers interlaced, and faced away from the aisles.

As a first responder in civil aviation, you undoubtedly have familiarization with various makes and models of aircraft, also known as *aircraft equipment*. This is an important consideration for inflight security. Likewise, an aircraft's cabin layout, often referred to as *aircraft configuration*, is equally important to understand because it can give you an idea of where a hijacker or bomber can hide and how they might move to position themselves tactically inside of the aircraft. Important aircraft configuration considerations include the *number of aisles* (single-aisle or double-aisle); *lavatory number and location; the number of decks; number and location of emergency exits;* and *how the flight deck is accessed*.

The number of aisles in an aircraft is important because it determines how an *aggressor* (e.g., aggressive individual, hijacker, hijacker team, suicide bomber) can move inside the cabin. As noted earlier, commercial aircraft have either one or two aisles (referred to as single-aisle or double-aisle aircraft). Some aircraft have both double- and single-aisle cabins, like the Boeing 747, which has a double-aisle configuration on the lower deck and a single-aisle configuration on the upper deck. If one of the decks inside of a *double-decker* aircraft has two aisles, then the aircraft is considered to be a double-aisle aircraft. Double-aisle aircraft are also often referred to as *wide-body aircraft* and *Jumbo jet aircraft*. Another important consideration about aisles is that the majority of them are not arranged in a perfectly straight line. Most aisles appear straight, but they actually curve along the length of the aircraft cabin, following the fuselage. This curve in the aisle is more obvious on double-aisle aircraft configurations (you can see this curve by standing in the rear of a double-aisle aircraft and looking down the aisle toward the flight deck). The aisle in single-aisle aircraft is easier to navigate than the aisles in double-aisle aircraft; however, there are certain single-aisle aircraft with bulkheads that jut out into the aisle and prevent rapid movement in the cabin. An aircraft's aisle configuration should always be considered and evaluated *before* flight and any potential obstacles such as carts, bulkheads, and/or people in the aisle(s) that could prevent ease of rapid movement in the cabin should be periodically evaluated *during* flight.

It is equally important to understand how the flight deck door is positioned in relation to the aisle(s). This is important because a hijacker (or hijack team) needs to move down the aisle toward the flight deck in order to reach the forward area, breach the cockpit door, and hijack the aircraft and they typically choose the fastest path (e.g., the aisle in-line with the flight deck door) in order to perform those actions as quickly as possible. Some double-aisle aircraft, such as the Boeing 767, Boeing 777, and Boeing 787, have a flight deck door that is in-line with the left-side aisle. The importance of this *left-side dominant*, or *aisle-to-flight deck, configuration* is a topic that will be expanded upon throughout this book.

The location of emergency exits is important because there is a higher likelihood of an emergency landing on land or water during an aircraft hijacking or inflight bombing. This is one example (among many others) where finding an escape route from the aircraft cabin is an important safety consideration. Onboard safety brochures that depict an aircraft's cabin layout typically indicate the location of emergency exits. As a first responder, you should know the location of the nearest emergency exit and be ready to assist in emergency evacuations if needed. An emergency exit can also be used to ground an aircraft. If an emergency exit door is opened prior to departure, the aircraft cannot take off because it will not be capable of maintaining stable flight. An evacuation slide is heavy and bulky, and if an emergency exit is deployed prior to take-off, the aircraft will not be able to leave the ground until the slide is removed. Removing an emergency slide takes time and requires an experienced aviation mechanic, making the deployment of an emergency slide a viable option for preventing take-off and for allowing the aircraft more time on the ground where a military or law enforcement rescue/response can be attempted. If an emergency slide needs to be opened on the ground in order to deny a hijacker the ability to force a take-off of the aircraft, one should be aware of any people on the outside of the aircraft in the vicinity where the emergency slide might impact upon inflation. Ensuring that people on the ground are away from the area where an emergency slide will open is an important safety consideration because emergency slides inflate suddenly and with violent force. Although opening an emergency exit on the ground can be a useful tactic during certain inflight security situations, it is especially dangerous for people on the outside of the aircraft and should only be performed by using caution and forethought.

All aircraft are unique in some respect, but the majority of aircraft have a single deck, regardless of whether they have a *narrow-body* or wide-body. There are, however, two aircraft in common use today that have two decks (a *lower deck* and an *upper deck*): these are the Boeing 747 and the Airbus A380. As mentioned earlier, the Boeing 747 has a unique cabin configuration because it has a double aisle on the lower deck and a single aisle on the upper deck. Also, the forward area on a Boeing 747 is located on the upper deck (there is no forward area on the lower deck of a Boeing 747). The Airbus A380 has its own unique configuration; for example, the Airbus A380 has two forward areas (one on the upper deck and one on the main deck). Although the lower deck of the Airbus A380 is where the flight deck stairwell is located, the forward area of the lower deck can also be easily accessed from the upper deck stairway (which ends at the forward area of the lower deck). For these reasons, you must make special inflight security considerations when you are working or traveling in the cabin of an Airbus A380 or Boeing 747. Other special security considerations for these aircraft configurations will be explained in greater detail in the section about deployment strategies.

2

A Brief History of Threats to Civil Aviation

In order for you to better understand how to formulate an inflight security response and to be able to adapt that response to meet future threats, it is important for you to examine some of the more important aircraft hijackings and bombings that have occurred throughout history. The study of the historical record is important because it will give you an idea of the various types of rare, but extremely dangerous aggressive actions you might expect to see inflight. This is true whether the aggressor is a lone-wolf hijacker, a dedicated hijacker team, a suicidal-hijacker team, a trained hijacker pilot, or a suicide bomber. The study of this history will also poise you to better predict future methods of inflight and ground-based attacks.

Although the focus of this chapter is to review past inflight security threats, three examples of past airport attacks will also be presented. Ground-based historical snapshots of threats to civil aviation are as important to understand as inflight threats because they serve as examples for teaching lessons in criminal behavior detection and passenger profiling. After reading all of the examples presented in this chapter, you will begin to be able to recognize and predict hijack tactics on the ground and in the air. The ability to predict methods of attack is important when applying critical thinking skills in civil aviation.

DOI: 10.4324/9781003336457-3

FIRST RECORDED HIJACKING AND
FIRST LETHAL HIJACKING

The *first recorded hijacking* occurred in February 1931, in Peru. During this hijacking, a Pan Am mail plane was assaulted from the ground by a small group of three to four Peruvian revolutionaries who breached the cockpit and forced the captain to fly a specific route so that the revolutionaries could drop propaganda leaflets. Seventeen years later, the *first lethal hijacking* occurred. On July 25, 1947, three Romanian hijackers hijacked an aircraft in their attempt at receiving political asylum. Shortly after takeoff, the hijackers stood up from their seats and gained cabin compliance by threatening the crew and passengers with violence. The hijackers controlled the forward area, breached the flight deck door, and forced the pilots to divert the aircraft. As the hijacking came to a climax, one of the hijackers killed flight mechanic Mitrofan Bescioti.

FIRST RECORDED AIRCRAFT BOMBING

On November 1, 1955, a man named Jack Graham took out multiple life insurance policies on his mother prior to her flight from Denver to Seattle. Using deception and his understanding of security procedures for checked baggage, he then managed to insert a bomb into his mother's luggage which was later loaded onto his mother's flight, a Douglas DC-6B aircraft (United Airlines Flight 629). The bomb eventually detonated inside the aircraft en route to Seattle and killed all 44 passengers and crew members on board. This was recorded as the first bombing of an aircraft inflight. Graham never had the chance to cash in the insurance policy on his mother: he was sentenced to death for his crime instead.

SUSPECTED SUICIDE BOMBING
OF AN AIRCRAFT INFLIGHT

On January 6, 1960, a McDonnell Douglas DC-6B aircraft (National Airlines Flight 2511) exploded en route to Miami, Florida, from New York. The investigation remains open to this day; however, it is suspected that the explosion was a murder-suicide. Inspectors determined that Julian A. Frank, a lawyer from New York, had wounds consistent with those caused by dynamite and residue indicative of the handling of an explosive prior to its detonation; investigators suspect that Frank placed an explosive device under his seat and then detonated it. All 35 passengers and crew on board were killed as a result of the blast. If the investigators' version of events is to be believed, the tactics used by Frank included deception, a basic understanding of airport security procedures, and the surreptitious placement of an explosive device inflight. Since it is much easier for a suicide terrorist to strap an explosive device to their body and walk onto the aircraft than it is to carry it onto the aircraft and place it below their seat, the official explanation of events cannot be certain. Evidence does suggest that the destruction of the aircraft occurred because of a suicide bombing; if true, this makes this particular attack a first of its kind.

FIRST DOMESTIC HIJACKING OF AN AIRCRAFT IN THE UNITED STATES

On May 1, 1961, a passenger on a Convair 440 aircraft (National Airlines Flight 337) stood up from his seat and, using the alias "Cofresi the Pirate," locked himself in the forward lavatory and passed a note to a flight attendant that said he had a bomb. The hijacker wanted to be taken to Cuba and claimed he would "blow up the plane" if his demands were not followed. The hijacker was armed with a small pistol and claimed to have been hired to kill Fidel Castro by a Cuban diplomat. This hijacking was recorded as the first hijacking of a US aircraft in the United States. The aircraft was successfully diverted to a military base in Havana and allowed to return to the United States the following day. This hijacking was the first in a long string of hijackings to Cuba that would eventually lead to the inception of an inflight security program in the United States. During May 1, 1961, hijacking the hijacker applied tactics through deceptive means by claiming to have an explosive device inside the cabin (this claim was made in order to gain cabin compliance, control the forward area, and to aid the hijacker's breach of the flight deck and diversion of the aircraft). This example shows how powerful the threat of an explosive device can be when the claim is made inflight.

FIRST DISRUPTED HIJACKING BY A PASSENGER

On August 3, 1961, a father and son hijacker team (aged 38 and 16) stood up from their seats approximately 20 minutes before landing in El Paso, Texas (inbound from Albuquerque, New Mexico) and, armed with handguns, gained cabin compliance by threatening passengers and crew inside the Boeing 707 aircraft (Continental Airlines Flight 54). A law enforcement officer on board named Leonard W. Gilman quickly volunteered to be one of the hostages. The hijackers took Gilman hostage as they controlled the forward area aircraft and attempted to divert the aircraft to Cuba. In order to get the aircraft on the ground, the pilots told the hijackers that the aircraft needed to land in El Paso to get fuel for Cuba. Upon landing, the aircraft was met by Federal Bureau of Investigation (FBI) agents who surrounded the aircraft; FBI agents shot out the aircraft's tires while an ambulance blocked the aircraft from moving. As law enforcement officers were acting on the ground and a negotiator was talking with the hijackers, Gilman punched the older hijacker in the face, stopping the hijacking. The hijackers were subsequently charged with kidnapping and interstate transportation of a stolen craft. Luckily, nobody on board the aircraft other than Gilman and one of the hijackers was hurt (Gilman suffered a broken hand; and the hijacker, a broken nose). A lot of important lessons can be learned from the successful inflight security response initiated by Mr. Gilman; he acted in a discreet way that allowed him to get close to the hijackers (a form of surprise), and by using a strategy of speed, surprise, and aggression, Gilman was able to put a quick end to an onboard drama that had the potential for a much more violent outcome for passengers and crew. Speed, surprise, and aggression is a tactic that will be expanded on in detail in the section on deployment strategies.

HIJACKING/MURDER-SUICIDE

On May 7, 1964, a Fokker F-27 aircraft (Pacific Airlines Flight 773) mysteriously crashed into the ground in San Ramon, California. The flight was referred to as the "gambler special" because of its route between San Francisco and the casinos in Reno. The investigation into the crash ruled it to be a hijacking/murder-suicide. Francisco Paula Gonzales, a 27-year-old former Philippine sailing team member, was suspected as the culprit. Voice recordings from the cockpit suggest that Gonzales breached the cockpit and then shot the captain and the co-pilot with a Smith & Wesson .357 magnum before turning the firearm on himself. The aircraft crashed immediately afterward and all 44 passengers and crew on board were killed. Gonzales was plagued by financial problems and had reportedly planned the suicide in advance. The investigation suggested it is likely that, like other hijackers before him, Gonzales used his firearm to threaten passengers and crew members with violence to gain cabin compliance, control the forward area, and breach the flight deck. Once inside the flight deck, the suicide hijacker was able to kill the pilots and gain control of the aircraft to force a crash. Although hijackings remained rare during this time, the tactic of breaching the flight deck door during a hijacking was common, but it did not raise concerns among airlines nor calls from Congress to harden the cockpit and restrict access to the forward area. By 1964, although criminals had been targeting aircraft for hijackings and bombings for several decades, terrorist groups began to turn their attention toward aircraft as a means of political currency and as a way to make a political statement. This initiated a period of several years beginning in the mid-1960s when violent extremist terrorist groups began performing surveillance on targets in civil aviation, mostly in countries in Europe and the Middle East. This surveillance would be re-initiated by other violent terrorist extremist groups in the mid-1990s in the United States, information from which would lead to the September 11, 2001, coordinated terrorist hijackings.

HIJACKER TEAM HIJACKING

On July 23, 1968, a pilot, a military colonel and a karate teacher, all members of the Palestinian Front for the Liberation of Palestine (PFLP), hijacked a Boeing 707 aircraft (El Al Flight 426) by threatening the crew and passengers with pistols and grenades. The hijackers initiated the hijacking while the aircraft was on its way to Lod Airport (now Ben Gurion International Airport) from London Heathrow International Airport. This assembly of hijackers was unique, since it was the first time a hijacker team had used a trained hijacker pilot. The hijackers breached the flight deck, hit the captain in the head with a pistol, and demanded that the aircraft be flown to Algiers, Algeria. The hijackers also separated passengers in the cabin into two groups: Israeli and non-Israeli. After landing in Dar El Beida, Algerian officials impounded the aircraft and released the non-Israeli passengers. Negotiations ensued over the next 40 days and were eventually successful in obtaining the release of the 16 remaining prisoners.

HIJACKER TEAM HIJACKING

On August 29, 1969, two individuals armed with assault rifles and grenades hijacked a Boeing 707 aircraft (TWA Flight 840) while it was en route to Tel Aviv from Rome. A *dirty airport* in Rome was chosen for its lax security, giving the terrorist group the ability to smuggle weapons onto the aircraft. This was one of many violent hijackings during which hijackers worked in a team by using the threat of violence to control the cabin and take a position in the forward area prior to breaching the cockpit. The hijackers selected Westerners for torture by separating the passengers into groups (Westerners and non-Westerners). The hijackers had been interested in hijacking TWA Flight 840 because the Israeli Ambassador Yitzhak Rabin was supposed to be on board; however, luckily for the Ambassador, he had decided not to travel on that particular flight. When it was discovered that the Israeli Ambassador was not on board, the hijackers had the aircraft diverted to Damascus, Syria. In Damascus, the hijackers evacuated the passengers and crew and then rigged an explosive device to the nose of the aircraft. Passengers were eventually released from the aircraft after the Israeli government agreed to release 71 imprisoned Syrian soldiers; unfortunately, this showed terrorists that it was possible to have their demands met by hijacking an aircraft and led to an increase in air piracy. Luckily, no one was killed or injured during the otherwise violent hijacking of TWA Flight 840. Like others before them, the hijackers of TWA 840 were successful in hijacking aircraft because they were (1) able to quickly reach and control the forward area, (2) able to control passengers in the cabin by using the threat of violence, and (3) able to breach the cockpit door and enter the flight deck.

LONE-HIJACKER HIJACKING

On March 17, 1970, a McDonnell Douglas DC-9 aircraft (Eastern Airlines Flight 1320) was hijacked from Newark to Boston. Shortly after take-off, an individual armed with a .38 revolver stood up from their seat, quickly made their way to the forward area, and breached the cockpit door. Inside the cockpit, the hijacker struggled with the captain and co-pilot for control of the aircraft. During the fight, Captain Robert Wilbur Jr. was shot by the hijacker and bled profusely while his co-pilot, First Officer James Hartley, was able to shoot the hijacker three times before he himself was shot and mortally wounded by the hijacker. Captain Wilbur managed to relay a message to air traffic control, telling them that his co-pilot had been shot. Despite everything he had already done, the captain fought with the hijacker once again and was able to disarm the hijacker before lapsing into unconsciousness. Despite his grave wounds (and as the hijacker clawed at him once again), Captain Wilbur regained consciousness and landed the aircraft safely.

FIRST COORDINATED HIJACKINGS
OF MULTIPLE AIRCRAFT

On September 6, 1970, four jet aircraft (a Boeing 707, Douglas DC-8, Boeing 747, and Vickers VC10 aircraft) bound for John F. Kennedy International Airport were hijacked by members of a Palestinian group; an attempted hijacking had also been made on a fifth aircraft (an El Al Airlines, Boeing 707 aircraft), but that attempt was stopped. Although there was only one fatality and one injury reported on one of the five aircraft, the violent and extreme nature of these hijackings set into motion an expansion of inflight security programs in the United States and other countries. Three of the hijacked aircraft were brought to an airfield in Jordan (known as Dawson's Field), rigged with explosives and blown up, while another aircraft was flown to Cairo and blown up there.

The hijackers of these aircraft had many tactics in common: they all initiated their hijackings shortly after take-off and they all gained cabin compliance through the threat of violence, took control of the forward area, and breached the flight deck within two to three minutes. In the early morning of September 6, two hijackers attempted to board an El Al Airlines aircraft (El Al Flight 219) in Amsterdam, but Israeli security blocked them from boarding. The hijackers were escorted from the El Al terminal, but they went on to board a different aircraft in Amsterdam instead; the hijackers ultimately ended up boarding a Boeing 747 (Pan Am Flight 93). Two other hijackers, however, were able to board El Al Flight 219, and they attempted to hijack the aircraft shortly after take-off. A sky marshal shot one of the hijackers as they tried to gain control of the forward area and a passenger hit the other hijacker over the head with a liquor bottle; one of the hijackers later succumbed to their injury. The pilot also made a rapid pitch adjustment during the hijacking in order to throw the hijackers off balance and disorient the hijack team quickly enough for flight crew and inflight security personnel to respond.

The two hijackers in Amsterdam who had been denied boarding on El Al Flight 219 walked to another terminal with their hidden grenades and pistols and boarded Pan Am Flight 93. Pan Am had been warned about the two men by El Al security and, for this reason, the captain of Pan Am Flight 93 searched the hijackers; unfortunately, the captain failed to find the hijackers' concealed weapons. Approximately 20 minutes after take-off, the hijackers stood up from their seats while brandishing their grenades and pistols, threatened passengers and crew with violence, moved to the forward area, and breached the flight deck. In the cockpit, the hijackers threatened the pilots with violence and forced them to divert the aircraft to Beirut. During the hijacking, the hijackers moved up and down the aisles and continually threatened passengers in order to maintain cabin compliance. In Beirut, the hijackers picked up two other terrorists who brought more explosives and weapons on board. Although the Boeing 747 aircraft was too large to land at the small Jordanian air strip, the hijackers forced the pilots to fly it to Cairo instead. After the aircraft landed in Cairo, the hijackers ordered all of the passengers off, placed their explosives in and around the aircraft, and detonated the explosives as passengers sat nearby and watched.

HIJACKER TEAM HIJACKING

On May 8, 1972, four individuals armed with pistols, grenades, and explosives stood up shortly after take-off and hijacked a Boeing 707 aircraft (Sabena Flight 571) that was en route from Vienna to Tel Aviv. The hijackers quickly gained control of the cabin by threatening passengers and crew with the detonation of an explosive, gained control of the forward area, breached the flight deck, and made entry into the cockpit. Inside the cockpit, the hijackers threatened the pilots and forced them to divert the aircraft to Lod International Airport in Israel. On the ground at Lod Airport, the terrorists separated passengers into groups, Jewish and non-Jewish, and then forced the Jewish passengers to the rear of the aircraft. Israel was prepared to respond to a hijacking on the ground and a military counter-terrorism group in Lod began to rehearse to enter the aircraft when it arrived. The soldiers wore aircraft mechanic uniforms and claimed that the aircraft needed to be repaired; by using this deception, the soldiers gained entry into the cabin and killed two of the hijackers and took the other two prisoner. One of the two hijackers who survived (an 18-year-old named Theresa Halsa) later spoke of how they participated in six months of training to prepare for the hijacking. The hijacker was trained in Beirut and was taught how to use handguns, grenades, and explosive belts. Tactics to be used inside the cabin by the hijackers were also planned for extensively. The four hijackers (two female and two male) posed as husband and wife in order to avoid suspicion inside the aircraft.

ISRAEL AIRPORT ATTACK

On May 30, 1972, three Japanese Red Army terrorists posing as tourists flew to Israel and landed at Lod International Airport (they arrived on Air France Flight 132 from Rome). At baggage claim, the terrorists picked up their luggage which contained weapons, ammunition, and hand gre-nades; they then went into the terminal and opened fire, killing 24 people and injuring 75 others. Kozo Okamoto was the only terrorist to survive the attack. Through their interrogation of Okamoto, Israeli security learned that the Japanese Red Army had been hired by a Palestinian group to attack a target in Israel. In return for this cooperation, the Palestinian group would attack a target in Japan. At that time, Israeli security person-nel associated terrorist activities with Arab nationals and Arab ethnicity, not Japanese; therefore, a Japanese individual would raise less suspicion from Israeli security than an Arab individual. This example of cross-pollination between terrorist groups illustrates why racial profiling is a security vulnerability that cannot be overlooked. The Lod International Airport attack represents one of the first attacks carried out in an airport's non-sterile security area; although the weapons, ammunition, and explo-sives had passed through the sterile security process, they were retrieved by the terrorists at baggage claim and used in the non-sterile security area.

FIRST ATTEMPTED USE OF AN AIRCRAFT AS A WEAPON

On February 22, 1974, 44-year-old Samuel Byck drove to the Baltimore/Washington International Airport armed with a .22 caliber pistol and a canister filled with gasoline. Inside the airport, Byck shot and killed Maryland Aviation Police Officer George Ramsburg and then boarded a Douglas DC-9 aircraft (Delta Airlines Flight 523 to Atlanta). The cap-tain and the first officer were performing their pre-flight checks when the hijacker came on board, waving his pistol in the air. The hijacker entered the open cockpit door and ordered the pilots to take off, but the hijacker was told by the captain that the aircraft could not take off until the wheel blocks were removed. Angered by the captain's response, the hijacker shot both pilots, killing the first officer in the process. As the aircraft waited on the tarmac, local police officers shot at its tires, but their bullets would not penetrate the thick rubber; law enforcement had learned that the hijacker intended to fly the aircraft into the White House to kill President Nixon and they wanted to do everything they could to keep the aircraft on the ground. After shooting the pilots, the hijacker told a flight attendant to close the aircraft door to prevent law enforcement officers from coming on board, but the flight attendant refused. The police boarded the aircraft shortly thereafter and exchanged gunfire with the hijacker. Although the hijacker was wounded by police during the confrontation, he killed him-self before they could restrain him. This hijacking signaled a departure from previous hijackings and added the potential that an aircraft could be used by a hijacker as a weapon. In time, terrorist groups would eventually take notice of Byck's audacious plan and would implement its design into future hijack plots.

HIJACKER TEAM HIJACKING AND RESCUE MISSION

Between June 27, 1976, and July 4, 1976, the hijacking of an Airbus A300 aircraft (Air France Flight 139) was featured on television news channels around the world. The flight had originally departed from Tel Aviv, Israel, with 248 passengers and 12 crew members on board when, shortly after take-off, four armed individuals stood up from their seats and began threatening passengers. After controlling the cabin, two of the hijackers took control of the forward area while the other two patrolled the cabin and maintained cabin compliance. The hijackers in the forward area then breached the flight deck and ordered the pilots to fly to Benghazi, Libya. In Libya, the aircraft was refueled and a female passenger was released. The plane then departed Benghazi on June 28 and headed to Entebbe International Airport in Uganda.

The original four hijackers were joined by four others in Entebbe, with further support from pro-Palestinian forces on the ground. The hijackers then demanded the release of 40 Palestinian prisoners in Israel and 13 prisoners in Switzerland, France, Germany, and Kenya. The hijackers said that if their demands were not met by July 1, 1976, they would begin executing passengers. The hijackers then began separating passengers into two groups (Israelis and non-Israelis).

Passengers were held as hostages in the old terminal of Entebbe airport for the next week. Some of the hostages were released, but over one hundred of them remained as the hijackers continued to threaten to kill them if their demands were not met. Preparation for a rescue operation by Israeli Special Forces had already begun and on July 4, 1976, an Israeli rescue operation took place that involved 100 commandos of the Israeli Defense Force who flew over 2,500 miles to Entebbe airport to rescue the hostages of Air France Flight 139. In the 90-minute rescue mission, all of the hijackers and 45 Ugandan soldiers were killed; unfortunately, three passengers were also killed. The Air France Flight 139 hijacking signaled a new violent wave of hijackings and showed just how far terrorists were willing to go to carry out their plans.

HIJACKER TEAM HIJACKING

On October 13, 1977, a Boeing 737 aircraft (Lufthansa Flight 181) made an early morning departure from Palma de Mallorca, Spain. The flight was headed for Frankfurt, Germany, with a total of 86 passengers and crew on board. Shortly after take-off, four individuals armed with pistols stood up from their seats and began threatening passengers and crew to gain cabin compliance. One or two of the hijackers took control of the forward area and then breached the flight deck. Inside the cockpit, the hijackers threatened the pilots and ordered the captain to fly the aircraft to Larnaca, Cyprus; however, the aircraft did not have enough fuel for the long flight to Cyprus and the captain was allowed to fly the aircraft to Rome.

After the aircraft was refueled in Rome, the hijackers forced the pilots to fly to Bahrain, where there was a brief standoff between the hijackers and military forces. After the aircraft was allowed to depart the hijackers forced the pilots to fly to Dubai, where the hijackers were provided food, water, medicine, and newspapers as ground units tried to figure out how to end the hijacking without bloodshed. While the aircraft was in Dubai, the terrorists also demanded the release of prisoners held in Italy and Turkey. There was a tense standoff on the ground until October 18, at which time the aircraft was allowed to depart once again; this time, the hijackers demanded that the pilots fly the aircraft to Aden, Yemen. Although there had been an attempt to end the hijacking without military intervention in Dubai, a German counterterrorism group named GSG-9 had begun training in Dubai for a rescue mission; however, before a response could begin, the hijacked aircraft had been allowed to take off. Soldiers from GSG-9 followed Flight 181 in a borrowed aircraft and prepared to assault the aircraft on the ground wherever they landed. The hostage rescue team even watched as Flight 181 attempted to land at the airport in Aden but was blocked by airport vehicles, fire trucks, and ambulances. Luckily, the captain was able to put the aircraft down on an adjacent landing strip and prevent a disaster.

After the landing, the captain voiced his concern about the aircraft's landing gear to one of the hijackers. The hijackers allowed the captain to go outside to inspect the aircraft; however, as time passed by, the hijackers became angry and worried that the captain was coordinating with Yemeni authorities for a rescue mission. Shortly after the captain re-boarded the aircraft, he was shot and killed by one of the hijackers. The aircraft was then refueled and the hijackers forced the first officer to fly to Mogadishu, Somalia. By the time Lufthansa Flight 181 landed in Mogadishu on October 18, the aircraft had already flown over 6,000 miles. And as the aircraft sat on the ground, the German counterterrorism group GSG-9 burst through the aircraft doors: One passenger later recalled the rescue, saying, "I saw the door open and a man appear. His face was painted black and [he started] shouting in German 'We're here to rescue you, get down!' and then . . . started shooting." A counterterrorism response can be expected when a hijacked aircraft is on the ground. The example of Lufthansa Flight 181 highlights the possibility of a ground assault and the need to be prepared if one should occur. You will learn more about how to respond to a ground assault in a later section.

LONE-HIJACKER HIJACKING

Shortly after take-off from Kuala Lumpur airport on December 4, 1977, the captain of Malaysia Airlines Flight 653 (a Boeing 737) called air traffic control and reported that the aircraft had been hijacked by "an unidentified hijacker" and "We're now proceeding to Singapore." Although the case remains unsolved to this day, cockpit voice recordings and other evidence suggest an attempted hijacking. The Boeing 737 eventually crashed in Malaysia and one hundred passengers and crew were killed. The after-accident investigation indicated an autopilot disconnect or "possible pitch input by someone entering the cockpit to try to control the aircraft." Some investigators speculated that there was a deliberate attempt to crash the aircraft. This hypothesis was reached during the review of the cockpit voice recording in which noises heard in the cockpit were indicative of a struggle and reported as "[a] reasonable amount of screaming and cursing." The investigation suggests that a lone hijacker breached the flight deck and then struggled with the pilots for control of the aircraft, possibly in order to force a crash of the aircraft or to divert it to another location (e.g., Singapore).

FIRST TEENAGE-HIJACKER HIJACKING

On December 21, 1978, 17-year-old Robin Oswald stood up from her seat in the cabin of a McDonnell Douglas DC-9 aircraft (TWA Flight 541) and stated that she had "a bomb." The aircraft was en route to Kansas City, Kansas, from Louisville, Kentucky, when the teenager stated her intention of hijacking the aircraft. Witnesses later described what appeared to be an explosive device strapped to the teenager's chest. The hijacker demanded that a prisoner (imprisoned for air piracy) be released from federal custody. Oswald was eventually talked out of the plane on the ground by FBI negotiators, and the "bomb" that the teenager had been carrying was determined to be a fake. Luckily, no passengers or crew were harmed during the hijacking of TWA Flight 541, but it did prove that, with the right planning and determination, even a teenager could hijack an aircraft in the late 1970s.

HIJACKER TEAM HIJACKING

On May 24, 1981, a McDonnell Douglas DC-9 aircraft (Turkish Airlines) was hijacked by four individuals armed with handguns and explosives; the aircraft was on a domestic flight from Istanbul to Ankara. The hijackers stood up from their seats shortly after take-off, threatened passengers and crew, and moved to the forward area and breached the flight deck. After forcing the pilots to fly toward Burgas, Bulgaria, the hijackers asked passengers to hand over their passports and discovered five banking executives from the United States. After landing in Bulgaria, the hijackers demanded $500,000 and the release of 47 prisoners held in Turkish prisons. When two of the hijackers deplaned to negotiate on the ground, passengers attacked the two remaining hijackers on board. By successfully disarming the hijackers, passengers gave rescue forces time to board the aircraft and liberate the passengers.

TERRORIST BOMBING OF AN AIRCRAFT INFLIGHT

On August 11, 1982, an explosion on a Boeing 747 aircraft (Pan Am Flight 830) caused the pilots to make an emergency landing in Honolulu, Hawaii. Fifteen passengers were treated for injuries on the ground; it was also discovered that a 16-year-old Japanese citizen (seated near the blast) had been killed. The aircraft had been headed to Honolulu from Narita, Japan, at the time of the explosion. Evidence collected from the Pan Am Flight 830 investigation suggested that the explosive device which killed the Japanese citizen had been placed in the life-vest compartment directly below his seat. The bombs were called *under-the-seat-cushion bombs* due to the location of their placement; explosives experts were surprised at their ingenious engineering. A bomb maker named Husain Muhammad Al-Umari was later implicated in the attack and was connected to many more under-the-seat-cushion bombs found in other commercial aircraft in the future.

BOMB FOUND ON FLIGHT

On August 25, 1982, a suspicious item was found on a Boeing 747 (Pan Am Flight 440) aircraft by a cleaning crew in Rio de Janeiro; the aircraft had previously traveled from London and Miami. Upon inspection of the item (which looked like a wallet upon initial inspection), it was found to be a sophisticated explosive device. Upon further study of the device, explosives experts hypothesized that it was likely another under-the-seat-cushion bomb, similar to the one that detonated on Pan Am Flight 830 two weeks earlier. This was a lucky break for law enforcement officials since they now had an intact explosive device to study; they could use information about the device to implement new security measures to try to stop these bombs from being brought on future flights. Although the most common violent threat up until the early 1980s came from hijackings, it was becoming obvious during this time that the surreptitious placement of an explosive device inside an aircraft was a tactic that was beginning to be used on a more regular basis by terrorist extremist groups.

HIJACKER TEAM HIJACKING

On December 3, 1984, an Airbus A310 aircraft (Kuwait Airways Flight 221) was hijacked by four individuals shortly after take-off from Dubai; the aircraft was originally destined for Karachi, Pakistan. Armed with pistols, the hijackers stood up shortly after take-off and began threatening passengers and crew in the cabin; two of the hijackers moved to the forward area and breached the flight deck. In the cockpit, the hijackers demanded that the pilots fly the aircraft to Tehran. A flight attendant who had been on board during the hijacking reported that soon after take-off from Dubai, two men were seen talking in the business-class cabin and one of the men appeared to have a bloody nose. A flight attendant tried to offer a handkerchief to the man with the bloody nose, but he turned the flight attendant away. Minutes later, the flight attendant witnessed a struggle between these two men and a passenger. The flight attendant later recalled, "One of the men had a pistol in his hand and was waving it around. I was so frightened; I didn't know what to do. I was frozen stiff. I eventually had to be pulled away to the back of the aircraft by one of the senior flight attendants."

The flight attendant soon heard gunfire as the hijackers shot a security agent on board.

Kuwait Airways said that there were always two security agents, like air marshals on this particular route, since it was considered high-risk. I don't know what happened to the other security officer, but maybe they just figured there was nothing they could do and stayed in their seat like the other passengers.

Once the aircraft landed in Tehran, the hijackers gathered passports from passengers, searched for US citizens, and separated passengers into groups (US citizens, Kuwaiti citizens, and non-Western citizens) for interrogation. One of the passengers selected for interrogation was a US citizen named William Stanford. Mr. Stanford hid his occupation as an American diplomat, saying that he worked for an auditing firm instead. He likely withheld this information because he knew that he would be targeted as a government employee; by this time, the hijackers had been selecting US citizens at random to go to the front of the aircraft to be interrogated. The hijackers could be heard yelling, "Are you CIA? We know you are CIA!" The hijackers demanded the release of the Dawa 17, a group implicated in the US embassy bombing in Kuwait. The hijackers released all of the women and children on board as a show of goodwill during the negotiation in Tehran.

By the sixth day of the hijacking, the hijackers complained that their demands were not being met. Radio reports broadcast US President Reagan's refusal to negotiate with the hijackers. The hijackers began to torture the US and Kuwaiti passengers at this time, burning their hair with lighters. On December 8 and 9, the hijackers murdered two US citizens, Charles Hegna and William Stanford: in a sinister act, the terrorists told Hegna and Stanford that if they could run down the stairs away from the aircraft before the terrorists counted to ten, then they would live. Mrs. Hegna and Stanford did not make it, however; each man was shot in the back as they tried to escape.

On December 9, 1984, the Iranian government reported that commandos had boarded the aircraft and had brought the hijackers into custody. Some of the passengers' statements contradicted this, however, and it was widely reported that the hijackers had escaped with a cleaning crew. The tactics and operational planning used by the hijackers of Kuwait Airways Flight 221 showed that they would go to great lengths to carry out their plots. Unfortunately for civil aviation, attacks on commercial aircraft would only continue to get more sophisticated. The four hijackers of Kuwait Airways Flight 221 had arrived in Dubai from Beirut on Middle Eastern Airlines Flight 426. As part of their operational planning, they planned to use a dirty airport to gain armed access to the target aircraft. By using this security portal, the hijackers either came into Beirut armed or gained access to their weapons shortly after boarding the aircraft.

HIJACKER TEAM HIJACKING

On June 14, 1985, a Boeing 727 aircraft (TWA Flight 847) was hijacked shortly after take-off from Athens, Greece, by two German-speaking Lebanese passengers; the aircraft had a scheduled destination of London Heathrow airport. The hijackers were armed with 9-mm pistols and grenades and they quickly gained cabin compliance, controlled the forward area, and breached the flight deck door. The hijackers also used pepper spray to control passengers. During the hijacking, a US Navy diver Robert Stethem and several other Western citizens were selected for torture. Before landing in Beirut, some of the passengers suggested that they should attempt to subdue the hijackers to stop the hijacking, but flight attendants told them that this was not a good idea.

Shortly after arriving in Beirut, Robert Stethem was shot and killed and his body tossed onto the tarmac. A flight attendant on board attempted to hide the identification of many of the passengers from the United States, but they were discovered anyway. Several other hijackers (some witnesses estimate up to ten) boarded the aircraft in Beirut, significantly changing the dynamic for a future rescue mission. The hijacking eventually ended after a total of 17 days; many of the passengers were held hostage in Beirut while negotiations proceeded. Most of the hijackers' demands were met during negotiations: a dangerous prisoner was released by Greece, and over 700 prisoners were released by Israel.

COORDINATED TERRORIST-BOMBINGS
OF MULTIPLE AIRCRAFT

On the morning of June 23, 1985, an explosive detonated in the cargo hold of a Boeing 747 (Canadian Pacific Airlines Flight 003) as it quietly sat at an arrival gate at Narita International Airport, Japan; the flight was scheduled for a final destination of Vancouver, Canada. The detonation killed two baggage handlers and seriously wounded four others. If the flight had not been ten minutes behind schedule, the aircraft would have been blown up in the air (where 390 people were scheduled to be on board).

24

Fifty-five minutes later, a bomb exploded in the cargo hold of another Boeing 747 aircraft (Air India Flight 182) as it flew over Ireland. The explosion caused the fuselage to separate and pieces of the aircraft and bodies of the 329 passengers and crew on board to fall into the Atlantic Ocean. A Sikh extremist group was implicated in both attacks. Investigators determined that the group had been able to place an explosive device in a piece of checked luggage on both of the respective flights.

TEAM HIJACKING

On November 23, 1985, a Boeing 737 (Egypt Air Flight 648) was hijacked by three individuals approximately 20 minutes after take-off from Athens, Greece, with a scheduled destination of Cairo, Egypt. The hijackers were armed with handguns and grenades and they used the threat of violence to gain cabin compliance, to control the forward area, and to breach the flight deck. In the cockpit, the hijackers ordered the pilots to fly the aircraft to Malta. In Malta, the hijackers separated passengers into two groups (Western and non-Western). After rearranging the seating of passengers based on their citizenship, the hijackers selected two Israelis and a US citizen to be killed. The hijackers then made the three passengers walk down the aircraft stairway and shot them in the back. Egyptian commandos were sent to Malta to attempt a rescue mission; however, several of the commandos mistakenly shot and killed passengers in the confusion. In the end, 58 passengers and two of the three hijackers were killed.

ROME AND VIENNA AIRPORT ATTACKS

On December 27, 1985, seven terrorists walked up to the ticket counters of El Al Airlines and Trans World Airlines at the Leonardo Da Vinci-Fiumicino Airport (in Rome) and Vienna International Airport (in Vienna) and fired assault rifles and threw grenades at crowds of passengers. Security personnel and local police killed four of the terrorists and captured the other three; however, 16 people lost their lives and over 100 were injured in the coordinated attacks. Investigators determined that another terrorist cell had planned to attack the Frankfurt International Airport at the same time, but did not. Attacks carried out in the non-sterile area of an airport were easier for terrorists because access to these areas required no special security checks. The ease of exploiting security vulnerabilities in the non-sterile area of an airport is something that the terrorists would use advantageously in future attacks.

TERRORIST PLACEMENT OF AN EXPLOSIVE DEVICE INFLIGHT

On April 2, 1986, a woman with a ticket on a Boeing 727 aircraft (TWA Flight 841) en route to Rome from Cairo, traveling under the name May Elias Mansur, sat in seat 10-F and rigged an explosive to it during the flight. Passengers recalled that Mansur had listened to music during the flight and had her tray table extended over her lap for a majority of the time. The explosive was suspected to be similar to the under-the-seat cushion bombs, with a timer that would begin to count down when pressure was applied to it. Investigators hypothesized that, after pressure was applied to the device, a certain amount of time was pre-programmed to elapse before the explosive detonated; thus, if a passenger sat down (the timer starts) and then stood up again (the timer stops) the timer would start and stop counting-down to detonation until the passenger sat down again. After the aircraft arrived in Rome, Mansur programmed the explosive device, deplaned the aircraft, and boarded another aircraft for Beirut. The Boeing 727 was cleaned and a new flight crew prepared the aircraft and then boarded new passengers as TWA Flight 840 bound for Cairo (with brief layovers in Athens and Rome). Among the passengers and crew on board that day was a team of United States Federal Air Marshals; they had been providing security on flights across the Middle East and were on their way to New York via Athens. The team of Federal Air Marshals settled into their assigned seats, unaware that there was an explosive device in the cabin.

The passenger seated in seat 10-F reportedly got up from their seat repeatedly. Whenever the passenger stood up, they inadvertently stopped the explosive's timer; and whenever the passenger sat down, the timer started again. After landing in Athens, many passengers (including the Federal Air Marshals) deplaned, while others remained and new passengers boarded the aircraft. The unfortunate passenger seated in 10-F on the return flight to Rome remained seated for the entire trip, allowing the timing device attached to the explosive below the seat to finish counting down. Upon detonation, the passenger seated in 10-F was violently ejected from the aircraft, along with three other passengers who were seated near the blast. An important lesson taken from this event is that the passengers seated around the blast who were wearing their seat belts were spared from being sucked through the blast hole in the side of the fuselage. One passenger remembered the blast on board that day, saying, *"We heard a big bang outside the window, and then I saw the man sitting next to me disappear and I felt myself being pulled out."* Luckily for this survivor, they were wearing their seat belt. The Federal Air Marshals on TWA Flight 841 were so shocked by their near-death experience that they all resigned from their jobs when they got back home.

ATTEMPTED AIRCRAFT BOMBING

On April 17, 1986, a bomb was discovered on a passenger at London Heathrow airport; an Israeli security agent had conducted a profile search on a passenger during the pre-board security screening process for a Boeing 747 aircraft (El Al Airlines Flight 013; with a scheduled destination of Tel Aviv) and found them to be carrying a suitcase containing an explosive device. Deceived by a confidant, the passenger had unknowingly carried an explosive that was concealed in a specially designed compartment of the suitcase. The explosive had a sympathetic detonator concealed in a calculator that was wired with an electronic fuse. Although this particular bombing was stopped, it is likely that the plot would have succeeded if it had targeted an aircraft with relaxed (or nonexistent) pre-boarding security measures.

TEAM HIJACKING

On September 5, 1986, a Boeing 747 (Pan Am Flight 73) began boarding passengers in Karachi, Pakistan, when four individuals armed with assault rifles and explosives drove up to the aircraft in an airport security van, began firing into the air, and then entered the aircraft, ran upstairs, and entered the cockpit and ordered the pilots to fly to Cyprus. The pilots, however, had escaped the cockpit (using the inertial reels) and were already on the ground; this act took the initiative away from the hijackers and they executed a passenger and dumped the body onto the tarmac in response. The hijackers then began speaking to negotiators on the ground and continued to demand that they be flown to Cyprus. Negotiations for the release of the passengers lasted for nearly 17 hours and a ground power unit was brought to the aircraft to supply power for the lights and air conditioning. During this time, the hijackers prepared for a ground assault by herding passengers and crew into the center and rear of the aircraft. (This action exhibited knowledge of law enforcement and military tactics, suggesting that the hijackers were especially dangerous.) Eventually, the power unit ran out of gas and the lights inside the aircraft went out. The hijackers suspected a rescue operation had begun and started shooting and lobbing hand grenades into the group of passengers in the rear of the aircraft. Amidst the screams and commotion, 22 passengers were killed and 125 were injured during this attempted hijacking.

TEAM HIJACKING

On December 25, 1986, four passengers armed with pistols and hand grenades stood up inside the cabin of a Boeing 737 (Iraqi Airways Flight 163) that had just entered Saudi Arabian airspace; the aircraft was en route to Amman, Jordan, from Baghdad. The four hijackers attempted to gain cabin compliance by threatening passengers in the cabin; however, in a deviation from previous hijack tactics, the hijackers spread out around the aircraft, controlling the forward area, center, and rear of the cabin. An inflight security team from Iraq was on board and, after waiting for an opportunity to act, they attempted to stop the hijacking; unfortunately, one of the hijackers tossed a grenade into the center of the aircraft and another hijacker threw a grenade into the cockpit. A brief gun battle then ensued in the cabin and three of the hijackers exchanged gunfire with the six Iraqi security agents. Miraculously, the grenade that was tossed into the cockpit did not kill the pilots and they initiated an emergency descent. The pilots flew for another 20 minutes and landed at a small airstrip near Arar, Saudi Arabia. Upon landing, the aircraft struck the tarmac, broke into pieces, and caught fire; of the 106 on board, 63 passengers and crew were killed. The hijackers had entered Baghdad from Belgrade, Yugoslavia, where they used the relaxed security at the airport to their advantage so they could smuggle their weapons and explosives. The hijackers then managed to carry their weapons and explosives onto the aircraft by remaining in the secure area throughout the rest of their travel (removing the need for them to return through airport security screening); the hijackers had spent the night in a Baghdad transit lounge so they did not have to pass through the airport's security checkpoint the following morning.

LONE-HIJACKER HIJACKING

On July 24, 1987, a hijacker armed with a pistol and an explosive strapped to their body stood up inside the cabin of a McDonnell Douglas DC-10 aircraft (Air Afrique Flight 56; en route to Paris from the Republic of Congo) and began threatening passengers and crew with violence. After breaching the flight deck, the 21-year-old hijacker told the pilot to fly the aircraft to Beirut. On the flight to Beirut, the captain convinced the hijacker that the aircraft needed to refuel in Switzerland. On the ground in Switzerland, the hijacker shot and killed a French citizen and seriously wounded a flight attendant and was then overpowered by other flight crew members. Swiss forces stormed the aircraft shortly thereafter and arrested the hijacker.

INFLIGHT BOMBING

On November 29, 1987, a Boeing 707 (Korean Air Flight 858) boarded passengers in Abu Dhabi and then continued on its multi-layover flight toward Seoul (the aircraft had previously flown from Baghdad to Abu Dhabi).

The plan to bomb Korean Air Flight 858 began in 1984, when it was announced that Seoul, South Korea, would host the 1988 summer Olympics. Soon after this announcement, two North Korean intelligence agents (an elderly man and a young woman) began training to bomb a South Korean aircraft. On November 12, 1987, a flight left Pyongyang, North Korea, carrying two Japanese passport holders (father and daughter Hachiya Shinichi and Hachiya Mayumi). The pair had taken a trip to Europe two years earlier and had declared the same reason for travel on their customs forms: shopping and sightseeing. Instead of sightseeing, however, they met two other North Korean intelligence agents from whom they collected a sophisticated bomb. The explosive had been specifically designed for this mission and was developed under the direct order of Kim Jong Il, the self-pronounced Supreme Leader of North Korea. Kim's instructions were to blow up a South Korean passenger aircraft to discourage other nations from participating in the 1988 Seoul Olympics. By November 12, 1987, the two agents were well on their way to execute these orders. And by November 27, 1987, the two intelligence agents had already made it to Belgrade, Yugoslavia, with their explosive device and two sets of airline tickets (one pair of tickets was for a flight from Baghdad to Seoul; the other pair of tickets was for a flight from Abu Dhabi to Amman).

29

On November 29, 1987, the bombers approached a security checkpoint at Baghdad airport for their flight to Abu Dhabi (on Korean Air Flight 858). During the cursory security inspection, the elderly intelligence agent was questioned by an airport security officer; the security officer had a problem with the small clock radio the agent was carrying since the batteries in the radio were not permitted on board. This was standard practice for airport security at this time since by confiscating batteries in electronics airport security could remove the power source for a potential explosive device. The crafty intelligence agent quickly responded by turning the clock radio on to show that it worked. The intelligence agent pleaded with the airport security officer, telling the security officer that the flight was a long one and that the small radio was all the intelligence agent had to keep him occupied. The deception worked, and the radio was returned with the batteries inside.

During the flight from Baghdad to Abu Dhabi, the intelligence agents placed the bomb (concealed in a handbag) inside an overhead compartment, directly above seats 7B and 7C; the explosive consisted of a main charge of liquid explosive placed inside a whisky bottle, with a sympathetic detonator and digital watch delay fuse mechanism concealed inside the clock radio. In Abu Dhabi, the bombers deplaned and began to follow their escape plan, but they were caught and arrested by police for traveling on false passports. Korean Air Flight 858 boarded more passengers and continued toward Thailand on its way to Seoul. The bomb exploded as the aircraft was somewhere over the border between Thailand and Burma, killing all 115 passengers and crew on board.

HIJACKER-PILOT TEAM HIJACKING

On April 5, 1988, three individuals armed with pistols and grenades stood up from their seats in a Boeing 747 aircraft (Kuwait Airways Flight 422 from Bangkok to Kuwait), made their way to the forward area, shot an inflight security officer, and breached the flight deck; at the time, the aircraft was nearly four hours into its seven-hour flight. In the cockpit, the hijackers instructed the pilots to not touch anything. The hijackers then disengaged the auto-pilot control, changed course to a different heading, and re-engaged the auto-pilot. As part of a seven- to nine-person hijack team, the hijackers controlled the upper deck of the aircraft as other hijackers controlled the lower deck. (Western intelligence agencies are still not sure of the exact number of hijackers on board Kuwait Airways Flight

422; it is hypothesized that two or three of the hijackers remained in their seats during the hijacking to act as additional security if needed.)

The aircraft was then flown to Mashhad, Iran, under the supervision of one of the hijackers in the cockpit (most likely a trained flight engineer). Although a hijacker-pilot had been used during previous hijackings, this was the first hijacking where a hijacker-pilot physically controlled the aircraft's course heading. (Pilots were often the main obstacle to a successful hijacking, and it made tactical sense that hijackers would eventually use their own trained pilot to control the course of a hijacked aircraft.) In Mashhad, the hijackers demanded the release of prisoners in Kuwait. Negotiations stalled as the hijackers threatened to kill passengers; on the sixteenth day of the incident, the aircraft left Mashhad and flew to Larnaca, Cyprus (over 1,200 nautical miles away). In Larnaca, the hijackers' demands for fuel were initially denied; however, the aircraft was refueled soon after the hijackers killed a second passenger (another inflight security officer) and threatened to kill others. After the aircraft was refueled, the hijackers flew to Algiers, Algeria (over 1,400 nautical miles away). After the aircraft arrived at Hourari International Airport, Algeria, it was surrounded by local police and media. Police officers placed powerful floodlights around the aircraft to illuminate the fuselage; however, for some unknown reason, these exterior lights were turned off on the night of April 22. Seizing upon the opportunity to escape under cover of darkness, the hijackers climbed down the side of the aircraft and fled the scene.

The hijackers of Kuwait Airways Flight 422 exhibited behavior throughout the hijacking which suggested that they were tactically proficient and highly trained. For example, the hijackers (1) waited up to four hours after take-off to hijack the aircraft, (2) rapidly breached the flight deck and changed the aircraft's course after the hijacking was initiated, (3) controlled passengers on both decks in a systematic way, (4) separated passengers into groups for ease of cabin compliance and passenger/crew control, (5) questioned passengers about their citizenship and occupation to use them as leverage during negotiations, (6) searched among the passengers for inflight security officers, (7) closed window shades in the cabin in preparation for a ground assault, and (8) killed passengers to have their demands met. This hijacking is an important one for you, as a first responder in civil aviation, to understand because it will teach you to recognize the multitude of hijack tactics that are used during a hijacking (hijack tactics which have been repeated on numerous hijackings in the decades since). For these reasons, the tactics used during the hijacking of Kuwait Airways Flight 422 are used as an example throughout this book to teach you hijack countermeasures, to increase your awareness in the cabin, and to expand your ability to predict potential future threats to the aircraft, passengers, and crew.

INFLIGHT BOMBING

On December 5, 1988, the Federal Aviation Administration sent a security notice to US embassies and consulates around the world which said it had received information that a Pan Am flight from Frankfurt to the United States would be blown up in the next two weeks. The security notice was also sent to all US airlines. Sixteen days later, on December 21, 1988, a flight from Malta landed in Frankfurt and exchanged passengers and baggage to a Boeing 747 on its journey to London; one of the bags that was transferred to the aircraft contained an explosive hidden inside a cassette player. In London, the aircraft exchanged baggage and passengers; this time for its flight to New York as Pan Am Flight 103. Unfortunately, the bag with the explosive stayed inside the aircraft cargo hold. Shortly after take-off (as the aircraft continued to ascend) the explosive device detonated, causing the aircraft to break up over Lockerbie, Scotland. All 259 passengers on board were killed, along with another 11 people on the ground who were killed by falling debris. During the subsequent investigation into the incident, a Boeing 747 aircraft expert remarked that the Pan Am Flight 103 bombing "was a diabolically well-planned event, handled by experts in the knowledge of the aircraft, its structure, the flight plan, the works."

LONE-HIJACKER HIJACKING

On October 2, 1990, a passenger on a Boeing 737 aircraft (Xiamen Airlines Flight 8301) stood up from his seat and, with flowers in hand, approached the flight deck door; the passenger said they wanted to give the flowers to the captain for a Chinese celebration and was allowed inside the cockpit by a flight attendant. Once inside, the hijacker told the pilots to head to Taiwan. The captain refused, however, and headed for Hong Kong instead. As the aircraft was in its final approach to Hong Kong, the hijacker fought with the pilot and deliberately forced the aircraft into the ground. The hijacked aircraft then hit a Boeing 757 that was taxiing on the runway. Seven of the nine crew, and 75 of the 93 passengers on the hijacked aircraft were killed.

TERRORIST EXPLOSIVE DEVICE PLACEMENT AND INFLIGHT BOMBING

In 1994, a man named Khaled Sheikh Mohammed began testing airport security with his uncle and co-conspirator, Ramsi Yousef. The two men had previously booked separate flights in which they carried 14 bottles of contact lens solution containing nitroglycerin. (Civil aviation security did not have the technology or security protocols in place at this time to detect liquid explosives.) The flights had been rehearsals for the planning of a sinister aircraft bomb plot. As part of this plot, Yousef left a bomb inside a life jacket in an aircraft that landed in Cebu from Manila on December 11; Cebu was a stopover on the aircraft's next flight to Narita, Japan, as Philippine Airlines Flight 434. Youssef placed his bomb under seat 26K of the Boeing 747 aircraft. The explosive detonated inflight when the aircraft was en route to Japan, killing a Japanese businessman who was seated over the explosive, injuring 10 passengers who were seated within the immediate vicinity of the blast. The captain made an emergency landing in Okinawa.

FIRST SUICIDE TERRORIST HIJACK-TEAM HIJACKING

As an Airbus A300 aircraft (Air France Flight 8969) boarded passengers in Algeria for its flight to Paris, four individuals dressed in Algerian police uniforms came on board, brandished assault weapons, and asked passengers for their passports. As the four individuals reviewed passports, some of the crew began voicing suspicions that these were not real police. The individuals responded by removing grenades, dynamite, and detonation cord from their bags and told passengers and crew to sit down, to place their hands on top of the heads, and to interlace their fingers. These hijackers were part of a terrorist group from Algeria called the Armed Islamic Group, or GIA, and they had planned extensively for the hijacking. The group wished to destroy something in France as a way of expressing their hatred for the French government.

The hijackers demanded that members of a terrorist organization called the Islamic Salvation Front be released from prison. When the hijackers' demands were not met, they started to become violent with passengers. During the hijacker's review of passenger identification, they had come across an off-duty Algerian police officer. To get the Algerian government to agree to their demands, which included fuel for the aircraft and clearance to take off, they shot and killed the off-duty police officer. Shortly after the murder, another passenger, a commercial attaché for the Vietnam embassy, was also shot and killed.

The hijackers of Air France Flight 8969 appeared to be tactically aware of law enforcement capabilities and went to great lengths to disguise themselves, such as putting on crew member uniforms. The hijackers also forced the women on board to make veils for their heads with blankets. The French government found out through an informant that the true purpose of the hijacking was to crash the aircraft into the Eiffel Tower, and they ordered a French counterterrorism group in Paris to begin preparing for a rescue mission as Algerian police negotiated with the hijackers on the ground in Algeria. The plot to fly an aircraft into a target made this the first instance that a team of hijackers had threatened the use of an aircraft as a suicide missile as the main act of that plot. During negotiations, the hijackers released some passengers; however, by December 25, approximately 170 passengers still remained on board. As these negotiations continued, the hijackers threatened to execute one passenger every half-hour if the aircraft was not allowed to take off by a specific time on Christmas evening. When the specified time came and went, the hijackers executed a passenger. The aircraft was quickly given clearance to take off and headed toward Marseilles shortly thereafter.

As the hijacked aircraft headed to Marseilles, French commandos began training on an empty Airbus A-300 aircraft at the airport where the hijacked aircraft was to land. At 3:30 a.m. local time on December 26, the hijacked aircraft landed in Marseilles, and negotiations between the hijackers and law enforcement started and then continued for the next 12 hours. Sometime in the early afternoon, a hijacker shot at the airport control tower and sparked a rescue operation by the French commandos. The rescue operation had some initial problems because the French commandos had trained on an empty aircraft; Air France Flight 8969 was much heavier (because of the extra weight of the fuel, passengers, and luggage on board). Thus, when the rescue team went to enter the aircraft doors via a mobile platform, the rescue team was too high up. The French commandos were eventually able to gain entry into the cabin and a 20-minute gun battle ensued. All of the passengers survived the rescue operation, although all four of the hijackers were killed. The hijacking of Air France 8969 could have ended much worse: This was a brazen new type of terrorist-hijack plot where a terrorist planned to use its enemy's flagged air carrier by flying it like a suicide missile into a specific target.

And although the hijack team did not complete their mission, their plan would be used later as a model for the 9/11 hijackings.

PLOT TO BOMB MULTIPLE AIRCRAFT

During the first week in 1995, Ramsi Yousef and Khalid Sheikh Mohammed were ready to move into the attack phase of their sinister bomb plot during a rehearsal which had killed a Japanese businessman on Philippine Airlines Flight 434 during an attack rehearsal less than one month earlier. The plot involved the surreptitious placement of an explosive device on 12 United States-bound aircraft. These bombs, like the device placed on Philippine Airlines Flight 434, would be placed inside life jackets on United States-flagged aircraft. The plan was that terrorists (posing as passengers) would place their explosives on the first leg of the respective aircraft's flight. The aircraft would all originate in Asian countries, where the terrorists did not need a US travel visa to board the aircraft. The explosives were to be placed inside the target aircraft on January 21, 1995.

On January 7, 1995, a chemical fire erupted in an apartment in Manila that Ramsi Yousef and his team of terrorists had been using as a safe house for preparing explosives for their aircraft bomb plot. Several people were injured by the fire; however, both Ramsi Yousef and Khalid Sheikh Mohammed avoided capture. Documents and other evidence found in the apartment fire, along with the interrogation of a co-conspirator, uncovered their plot (later referred to as the Bojinka plot). The estimated death toll for this attack totaled 4,000.

HIJACKER TEAM HIJACKING FOR POLITICAL ASYLUM

On November 23, 1996, a Boeing 767 aircraft (European Airlines Flight 961) was hijacked by three inebriated individuals who ran toward the forward area from the back of the aircraft. The aircraft had originally been en route to Nairobi from Addis Ababa. In the forward area, the individuals breached the cockpit and armed themselves with a fire axe and fire extinguisher. The individuals told the pilots that they had a bomb and told the crew and passengers that there were up to 11 hijackers on board (this was a lie). They then ordered the pilots to fly the aircraft to Australia, where the hijackers wished to gain political asylum. Instead, the pilot flew the aircraft along the African coastline and steered it toward a small airstrip on the Comoro Islands; the hijackers began fighting the pilots inside the cockpit after discovering this plan. The captain was eventually forced to make an emergency landing approximately 500 meters off the coast of the northern end of Grande Comoro Island. The aircraft broke apart upon impact and a total of 125 passengers lost their lives; unfortunately, many of the passengers drowned after inflating their life vests prior to impact.

LONE-HIJACKER HIJACKING

On July 23, 1999, an individual who had just taken a very large dose of an anti-depressant and was armed with a large knife stood up from his seat on a Boeing 747 (All Nippon Airlines Flight 61; a domestic flight en route from Tokyo International Airport to New Chitose Airport, Chitose, Japan) and began threatening passengers in the cabin. The hijacker breached the flight deck and, once inside, told the pilots that he wished to fly the aircraft into the Rainbow Bridge in Tokyo. The hijacker threatened the pilots with violence and then stabbed the captain in the chest when the pilots refused to fly toward the intended target. The hijacker attempted to take control of the aircraft shortly after stabbing the captain, forcing it into a steep dive. Luckily, crew members were able to control the hijacker, after which the pilots made an emergency landing in Tokyo.

HIJACKER TEAM HIJACKING

On December 24, 1999, an Airbus A300 aircraft (India Air Flight 814; from Nepal to Delhi, India) was just entering Indian airspace when a bespectacled individual wearing a mask stood up, announced that they were hijacking the aircraft, showed passengers an explosive vest they were wearing, and told passengers: "There should be no movement. This is a bomb, to blow up the plane." Another four hijackers also stood up from their seats and began threatening passengers and crew in the cabin, controlled the forward area, and then breached the flight deck. In the cockpit, the hijackers ordered the captain to change course toward Pakistan. A Pakistan-based Islamic group had planned this hijacking in an attempt to negotiate the release of three militants being held in India, and they began making their demands known during the hijacking.

After the aircraft flew to Amritsar, India (narrowly missing a truck that was intended to block the aircraft from landing), Indian authorities stalled refueling the aircraft to give Indian military rescue forces time to arrive. This angered the hijackers and they began separating passengers into two groups based on their appearance ("male" and "female"). "Male" passengers were then brought to the front of the aircraft for torture; one of these passengers was stabbed multiple times in the chest and later died of his injuries.

The hijackers then forced the pilots to take off (even though the aircraft was desperately low on fuel) and ordered the pilots to fly to Lahore, Pakistan. In Pakistan, the aircraft was refueled rapidly and then forced by the Pakistani government to take off. The hijackers then had the pilots fly the aircraft to Dubai where they released 27 passengers and the body of the murdered passenger, refueled, and then departed for Kandahar, Afghanistan. In 1999, the Taliban was trying to show cooperation with other governments in order to try to gain recognition as the legitimate government of Afghanistan. In their attempt, the Taliban agreed to mediate between the hijackers and the Indian government. Instead of honoring their agreement, however, the Taliban surrounded the aircraft with its fighters in order to prevent the Indian military from attempting a rescue operation. Eventually, on December 31, 1999, all remaining passengers were released by the hijackers and flown back to India; in return, the five hijackers were taken across the Pakistan border by the Taliban and allowed to escape.

FIRST SUICIDE-HIJACKER TEAM
HIJACKING OF MULTIPLE AIRCRAFT

On the morning of September 11, 2001, four commercial passenger jet aircraft were hijacked by 19 individuals. Over two decades later, these coordinated attacks still serve as the most vivid example of the use of an aircraft by a hijacker pilot (and hijack team) as a suicide missile. The hijackers intentionally crashed two of the aircraft into the World Trade Center towers in New York City and one of the aircraft into the Pentagon in Arlington, Virginia. The hijackers intended to fly a fourth hijacked aircraft into either the White House or Capitol Building, but it crashed into a field in Pennsylvania soon after some of the passengers and crew attempted to retake control of the aircraft. In total, nearly 3,000 people died as a result of these four hijackings.

Flights were targeted by the hijackers based on the fact that they were all long-haul, transcontinental flights; the aircraft assigned to these flights held a considerable amount of fuel (they were essentially flying bombs). The hijackers had performed surveillance flights during the operational planning for these coordinated attacks, although they avoided detection and were successful in carrying out their intended attack. The total cost for the operational planning for these coordinated hijackings was reportedly between $400,000 and $500,000. The following is a brief description of these four coordinated hijackings, the tactics involved, and the aftermath:

A five-person suicide terrorist hijack team took part in the hijacking of American Airlines Flight 11 (a Boeing 767 aircraft). The aircraft departed out of Boston's Logan International Airport at eight o'clock in the morning with an intended destination of Los Angeles. The hijacking is believed to have started just shortly after take-off at approximately 8:14 AM. The hijackers claimed to have a bomb and then stabbed two flight attendants. In the first class cabin, ex-Israeli military officer Daniel Lewin was stabbed as well; investigators later hypothesized that Lewin, based on his seating assignment near some of the hijackers (and his specialized military training), had tried to stop the hijacker in front of him without realizing there was another hijacker positioned behind him. Much of the information from this hijacking came from two flight attendants in the cabin who contacted American Airlines via the interphone and relayed vital information that helped investigators piece together the events that took place on American Airlines Flight 11. The hijackers reportedly made their way to the forward area, breached the cockpit, and killed the two pilots. The hijackers then flew the aircraft by using their own trained pilot and changed its course heading toward New York City. The aircraft was then intentionally crashed into the North Tower of the World Trade Center.

United Airlines Flight 175 (a Boeing 767 aircraft) was scheduled to depart out of Boston and, like American Airlines Flight 11, was also bound for Los Angeles. United Airlines Flight 175 departed 14 minutes after American Airlines Flight 11. Thirty minutes into its flight the pilot called air traffic control and reported that they had heard a "suspicious transmission" broadcast from another aircraft (a transmission that had been sent by one of the hijackers in the cockpit of American Airlines Flight 11). This was the last radio transmission of United Airlines Flight 175, and it is believed that the flight was hijacked by a five-person suicide terrorist hijack team at approximately 8:45 AM.

The ensuing investigation of the United Airlines Flight 175 hijacking suggests that, shortly after take-off, the hijackers stood up from their seats, threatened to use a fake explosive device, stabbed flight attendants and passengers, breached the flight deck, and stabbed pilots in order to gain control of the aircraft. One or more of the hijackers might have remained in their seats during the first minutes of the hijacking in order to surprise any first responders who tried to counter the hijacking. After killing the pilots, the hijacker pilot turned the aircraft toward New York City; the aircraft was intentionally crashed into the South Tower of the World Trade Center at approximately 9:03 AM.

American Airlines Flight 77 (a Boeing 757 aircraft) departed Washington Dulles International Airport for Los Angeles at 8:20 AM (ten minutes after its scheduled time of departure). It is believed that the aircraft was hijacked by five individuals between 8:51 and 8:54 AM, shortly after making its last radio transmission. Evidence suggests that the hijackers of American Airlines Flight 77 used the same tactics as the other hijackings. Passengers made phone calls to the ground and reported that the terrorists had knives (or box cutters) and had breached the flight deck. Passengers also reported that the hijackers had moved all of the passengers to the rear of the plane (most likely done in order to facilitate their control of the cabin). There were also reports that the hijackers may have used pepper spray in the cabin. After murdering both pilots, the hijacker pilot turned the aircraft toward Washington, DC; the aircraft was intentionally crashed into the Pentagon at approximately 9:37 AM.

HIJACKING OF UNITED AIRLINES FLIGHT 93

A Boeing 757 aircraft (United Airlines Flight 93) departed from Newark Liberty International Airport in New Jersey, at 8:42 AM, more than 25 minutes after its scheduled departure time; the aircraft had a scheduled destination of San Francisco. Evidence suggests that at approximately 9:28 AM, four individuals stood up from their seats, claimed to have a bomb, and stabbed two people in the aircraft (most likely the pilots). A hijacker pilot reprogrammed the aircraft's auto-pilot and changed course for Washington, DC (the intended targets: the White House or the Capitol Building).

Passengers on board Flight 93 began planning an assault on the hijackers approximately 30 minutes after the hijacking started, at which time the passengers stormed the forward area (in an attempt to retake control of the aircraft from the hijackers). The passengers began their assault by 9:57 AM, but unfortunately, their attempt did not work and the aircraft crashed into a field in Pennsylvania approximately three minutes later. All five crew members and 37 passengers (including hijackers) perished in the crash. This brave attempt made by the passengers and crew on board United Airlines Flight 93 undoubtedly prevented an unknown number of casualties. The United Airlines Flight 93 hijacking and passengers and crew response provides two important lessons, however: (1) although passengers and first responders are willing to respond to stop a hijacking or bombing attempt, (2) they lack information and training on how and when to respond to a hijacking or bombing attempt. If the passengers and crew had previous knowledge on how to stop a hijacking, it is highly likely that all of the hijackings on September 11, 2001, would have ended with a more positive outcome. Unfortunately, inflight security training for first responders working in civil aviation today is still no better than it was on September 11, 2001.

ATTEMPTED INFLIGHT SUICIDE BOMBING

On December 22, 2001, a Boeing 767 aircraft (American Airlines Flight 63) was en route to Miami from Paris when an individual named Richard Reid tried to ignite a wire protruding from one of their shoes. Reid was confronted by a flight attendant but continued to try to detonate the improvised explosive by trying to ignite the fuse with a lighter. A quick-thinking passenger grabbed and held Reid's arms as others grabbed Reid's legs; a doctor who was a passenger on the aircraft sedated the would-be bomber; while yet another passenger grabbed a fire extinguisher to use as a weapon. The response by the passengers on board American Airlines Flight 63 was instrumental in protecting the integrity of the aircraft. It was determined during the subsequent investigation that Reid had performed surveillance on United States-flagged aircraft during the planning of the coordinated September 11 hijackings and that Reid's surveillance reports had helped in planning the attacks.

SUSPECTED HIJACKING REHEARSAL

On June 29, 2004, a suspected hijacking rehearsal was witnessed by two federal air marshals on board Northwest Airlines Flight 327 (a Boeing 757 aircraft; en route from Detroit to Los Angeles). During the flight, 12 Syrian citizens (posing as band members) and a Lebanese citizen (posing as a band promoter) ran down the aisles, went into the lavatories for extended periods, and (even though these individuals had acted like strangers prior to boarding) used hand signals to communicate. All of these individuals were found to have records in the National Crime Information Center (NCIC) database and all were traveling on expired visas. The Lebanese citizen had been previously investigated for suspicious activity on a separate flight and he was detained again three months later during a return trip to the United States from Istanbul. This example shows that surveillance and rehearsal flights are often being conducted, even though the final attack plan may not necessarily be executed. The terrorist planning cycle is explained in more detail in the next chapter.

COORDINATED SUICIDE TERRORIST INFLIGHT BOMBINGS

Late in the evening of August 24, 2004, two aircraft (a Tupolev Tu-134 and a Tu-154 that had departed the Domodedovo International Airport in Moscow) exploded in the air nearly simultaneously and then crashed. By August 29, investigators in Russia had found traces of explosives in the wreckage. Security services identified the explosive Hexogen. The bombing of both Volga Avia Express Airlines Flight 1353 and Siberia Airlines Flight 1047 was claimed to have been carried out by a little-known Chechen terrorist group. Further investigation by Russian intelligence found that the plot involved individuals who had been paid to be airport workers in order to smuggle explosives onto aircraft.

PLOT TO BOMB MULTIPLE AIRCRAFT

On August 9, 2006, 24 suspects were arrested in London on suspicion of a plot to use liquid explosives to blow up multiple aircraft over the Atlantic Ocean (almost an exact copy of the Bojinka plot over a decade earlier). The targeted flights (a mix of Boeing 777 and Airbus A330 aircraft) were as follows:

United Airlines Flight 931 to San Francisco
Air Canada Flight 849 to Toronto-Pearson
Air Canada Flight 865 to Montreal-Trudeau
United Airlines Flight 959 to Chicago-O'Hare

41

United Airlines Flight 925 to Washington Dulles
American Airlines Flight 131 to New York-JFK
American Airlines Flight 91 to Chicago-O'Hare

This plot would have major repercussions for aviation security; for example, new civil aviation security rules issued by the Transportation Security Administration prohibited any of more than three fluid ounces liquid from being carried in carry-on luggage. This rule also required that any liquids less than three fluid ounces needed to be separated by passengers prior to passing through security.

LONE-HIJACKER HIJACKING

On September 9, 2009, a Boeing 737 aircraft (Aero Mexico Flight 576; from Cancun to Mexico City) was hijacked shortly after take-off by a lone individual. The hijacker claimed to have an explosive and demanded to speak to Mexican President Felipe Calderon. Mexican federal police stormed the aircraft shortly after the aircraft touched down in Mexico City, removing the hijacker without firing a shot. Like many of the previous hijackings before this, where hijackers falsely claimed to have an explosive, the "explosive device" on Aero Mexico Flight 576 was also a fake. Interestingly, a July 22, 2004, Congressional report stated, "Hijackers should be given the benefit of the doubt [of having an explosive device] until circumstances prove otherwise." This old way of thinking, which teaches flight attendants to dissuade passengers from attempting to stop a hijacking and to remain docile and accommodating to the hijackers during a hijacking, is a sure recipe for disaster in light of the violence displayed by past hijackers.

ATTEMPTED INFLIGHT SUICIDE BOMBING

On November 19, 2009, a middle-aged man walked into the US embassy in Abuja, Nigeria, with information about his son. There, he spoke with two CIA officers regarding the extreme views his son had begun to demonstrate and said that his son was likely in Yemen. On December 25, 2009, v man's son, Umar Farouk Abdulmutallab, boarded an Airbus A330 aircraft (Northwest Airlines Flight 253) in Amsterdam, the Netherlands. He had been trained by the terrorist group Al-Qaeda in the Arabian

Peninsula (AQAP) in Yemen to carry out an attack against the United States using an explosive and he was wearing a bomb concealed in his underwear as he passed through the Amsterdam airport security checkpoint.

A man in his 50s was seen helping Abdulmutallab in Amsterdam at the Northwest Airlines ticket counter prior to boarding Northwest Airlines Flight 253. The two US citizens who witnessed the exchange also ended up boarding Northwest Airlines Flight 253, and the individual who was seen with Abdulmutallab was reported as being an "Indian looking man . . . smartly dressed" and "speaking in an American accent." The witness' account led to later speculation as to whether Abdulmutallab had a "handler" to encourage him go through with the suicide attack, or that this had been an undercover intelligence operation.

During the flight, Abdulmutallab was seen getting up to go to the bathroom shortly before the crew was to begin preparing for landing. He spent 20 minutes in the lavatory and then returned to his seat and draped a blanket over his body. Passengers jumped on him after hearing popping noises and smelling something burning on his body; other passengers witnessed a fire on Abdulmutallab's pants before they grabbed him. Abdulmutallab was taken to the front of the aircraft and questioned by a flight attendant about what he had in his pants. Abdulmutallab replied only that he had an "explosive device." Upon landing, Abdulmutallab was taken into custody by law enforcement. Abdulmutallab's underwear was found to contain a bomb made of the explosives PETN and TATP, enough of which could have caused significant damage to the integrity of the aircraft.

DOMODEDOVO AIRPORT BOMBING

On June 24, 2011, a 20-year-old Islamic terrorist entered Domodedovo International Airport and detonated an explosive device on his body in the airport's crowded baggage claim area. The blast killed 37 and injured 173. The vulnerability of the non-sterile area of an airport had long been known, and Domodedovo's non-sterile area was just as unsafe as nearly every other airport around the world. In response to the bombing, however, the Domodedovo airport passed new security rules that required passengers to be screened before entering the non-sterile area; unfortunately, although this is a significant upgrade to this particular airport's security, it is rare for an airport to implement these kinds of security measures.

ATTEMPTED HIJACKER TEAM HIJACKING

On January 29, 2012, six individuals armed with pipes stood up from their seats inside an Embraer ERJ-190 aircraft (Tianjin Airlines Flight 7554), threatened passengers and crew in the cabin, and then moved to the forward area. Several of the hijackers feigned injury when passing through airport security checkpoints earlier that day and smuggled their weapons inside of walking crutches; in the forward area, the hijackers used the crutches in an attempt to breach the locked cockpit door. Passengers and specials responded and fought the hijackers in the forward area in a coordinated effort to stop the hijacking. The pilots then made a safe landing at an airport in Hotan, China. Another hijacker was later found in the cabin hiding among passengers (the hijacker had stayed seated during the hijacking in case of need; a tactic seen during many previous hijackings). This hidden hijacker, or *sleeper*, is a security element for the main hijack team that remains seated until needed, but they failed to act in this particular hijacking because of the overwhelming force used by the passengers and specials who responded.

TERRORIST BOMBING OF AIRCRAFT

On October 1, 2015, Metro Jet Flight 9268 (an Airbus A321 aircraft) exploded and broke into pieces as it flew over the northern end of the Sinai Peninsula. The aircraft had originally been scheduled to fly into Saint Petersburg, Russia, from Sharm el-Sheikh. All 217 passengers and seven crew members on board were killed. A terrorist group named ISIS claimed responsibility for the attack. Evidence suggested that an explosive device that contained up to one kilogram of TNT brought down Metro Jet Flight 9268. Investigators hypothesized that the explosive device had been placed on board that aircraft by an airport employee, highlighting the vulnerability of the *insider threat*.

BRUSSELS AIRPORT BOMBING

On the morning of March 22, 2016, two coordinated suicide terrorist bombings were carried out at Brussels airport. Less than one hour later, another suicide terrorist bombing was carried out in the Brussels Maalbeek Metro Station. Dozens of people were killed in these attacks and the terrorist group ISIS again claimed responsibility. This serves as yet another example of the vulnerability of the non-sterile area. Unfortunately, these attacks are likely to continue to be an appetizing target for terrorists due to ease of access.

SUICIDE BOMBING OF AN AIRCRAFT INFLIGHT

On February 2, 2016, an Airbus A321 (Daallo Airlines Flight 159) en route to Djibouti from Mogadishu, Somalia, was damaged by an explosion in the cabin centered near seats 15-F and 16-F. A passenger seated in the immediate vicinity of the explosion was ejected from the aircraft and landed near Balad, Somalia. Airport security cameras captured video footage of the same passenger at Mogadishu airport being given a laptop computer by airport workers; evidence later suggested that this laptop was equipped with an explosive that was detonated by the passenger who was ejected from the aircraft during the explosion. Luckily for the other 80 passengers and crew on board, the explosive detonated while the aircraft was still ascending and the aircraft was only flying at approximately 10,000 feet above sea level. This bombing is yet another example of the vulnerability to civil aviation security posed by the insider threat.

LONE-HIJACKER HIJACKING

On March 29, 2016, an Airbus A320 aircraft (Egypt Air Flight 181) was hijacked while en route to Cairo from Alexandria, Egypt. The pilot of the aircraft was threatened by a lone hijacker shortly after take-off who told the pilot to fly the aircraft to Larnaca, Cyprus. The lone hijacker threatened passengers and crew on the aircraft with what appeared to be an explosive device strapped to the hijacker's body. The hijacker successfully diverted the aircraft to Larnaca, where they released the Egyptian citizens and kept all of the other passengers and crew on board. Interestingly, the hijacker's motive was to get a letter to their spouse (the hijacker had been having marital problems). The explosive that the hijacker used to threaten passengers and crew was later determined to be fake. This incident highlights the unfortunate fact that a hijacker (or hijack team) can hijack an aircraft as easily as they could on September 11, 2001, by simply threatening passengers and crew with the detonation of a fake explosive device inflight.

SUSPECTED INFLIGHT BOMBING

On May 19, 2016, an Airbus A320 (Egypt Air Flight 804; en route to Cairo from Paris) crashed into the Mediterranean Sea. Although the cause of the crash is still undetermined, it has many of the hallmarks of a bombing (it may also have been due to an inflight fire that originated in the cockpit). Although nobody has claimed responsibility for bombing the aircraft, that does not mean it was not the target of an attack; terrorist groups do not always claim responsibility for an attack. (Although most terrorist organizations do want to claim responsibility, they may forgo this in order to stall coordinated efforts among global intelligence agencies to stop their terrorist plots.) Even though Egypt Air Flight 804 departed from an airport that was considered to have robust security, over the past several decades, terrorists have continued to improvise new ways to circumvent the aviation security process and bring dangerous items into the secure area of airports.

Even though investigators may never know what caused the Egypt Air Flight 804 crash, the disaster serves as an exercise in critical thinking. Although it may not be possible to determine what brought down Egypt Air Flight 804, it provides an opportunity for you to think more critically about potential threats to aircraft and airports. Was the crash of Egypt Air Flight 804 caused by an inflight fire? Or was the aircraft brought down by a new explosive that cannot be detected by current detection technology? Is this the reason nobody claimed responsibility for the crash? By thinking critically, we freely consider these kinds of possibilities. When we fail to think critically, however, we fall prey to the complacency of the past by thinking in ways that lack foresight. The future of aviation security and the safety of passengers and crew inflight and in-transit begins and ends with first responders, like you. As you continue to read and expand your knowledge, keep these past incidents in the back of your mind. By doing this, you will be more effective at implementing the security protocols and upholding the tenets of inflight security that are prescribed later in this book, and you will be better equipped to predict future attacks inflight and in-transit.

PREDICTING FUTURE THREATS

Since 1931, there have been over 300 hijackings, attempted hijackings, bombings, and attempted bombings in aircraft and airports around the world. Although rare, these types of threats to civil aviation are likely to continue. By understanding these threats, first responders can learn to make safer security decisions in aircraft and airports when confronted by potentially dangerous situations which appear harmless at face value. To adapt to future threats in civil aviation, first responders must rely on these past examples to think critically about other things that individuals might do to jeopardize the safety of passengers inflight and in-transit. Thousands of people have died because of a failure to predict threats to civil aviation. Fortunately, this lack of foresight does not need to continue. Change *is* possible. And that change begins with critical-thinking first responders, like you.

3

Terrorist Attack Planning and Hijack Tactics

In the previous chapter, you learned that the most dangerous attacks against civil aviation have come from individuals who are willing to die in the process. This poses a serious threat to passengers inflight and in-transit. Therefore, the most dangerous threat to an aircraft inflight comes from an armed aggressor who is willing to indiscriminately kill passengers, crew, and first responders in order to divert an aircraft from its original flight path or intentionally crash it into a target. Likewise, the most dangerous threat to passengers in-transit at an airport is an armed aggressor who is able to enter the non-sterile area (or sterile area) undetected and unchallenged (and is willing to die) in order to indiscriminately kill as many passengers and first responders as possible.

Hijackers and bombers plan extensively for their attacks. And they assume (like most of you) that passengers today are much more likely to take action in order to stop a hijacking, bombing attempt, or airport mass shooting than they were before September 11, 2001. Frequent flyers are especially aware that an aircraft can be used as a guided missile. And many able-bodied passengers, when asked, readily voice their willingness to protect the aircraft if necessary. Therefore, it would make sense that, even though inflight security officers provide security on a very small number of flights, one could assume that passengers will always step in if needed during an inflight security incident. Unfortunately, you saw from the previous chapter that this is not true the most recent hijacking was carried out by an individual who controlled passengers in the cabin with a fake explosive.

DOI: 10.4324/9781003336457-4

Terrorist organizations have been planning attacks against civil aviation for decades, and there is no sign that they will stop anytime soon. Terrorist attacks against civil aviation come in waves, and it is likely only a matter of time before another wave comes. As stated earlier, the most serious danger against civil aviation is posed by suicide terrorists. But why do terrorist groups use suicide terrorism? And, how are suicide terrorists motivated to do what they do? How do terrorists plan their attacks? And, when is the best time to discover a terrorist plot?

To begin, suicide terrorism began in the first millennium BCE. In the 11th century, *assassins*, also known as *Hashashins* (a group that practiced a form of Shia Islam), reportedly smoked hashish when they received orders to assassinate people. Over the course of several hundred years, these assassins were responsible for the deaths of many political and religious leaders in Persia. After killing their targets, the suicide terrorists would wait to be captured or killed. Islamists, however, are not the only group that has used suicide operations; some other groups include the Liberation Tigers of Tamil Eelam, Japanese Kamikaze, Viet Minh Marxists, and Kurdistan Workers Party. Most recently, the Islamic State of Iraq and the Levant (ISIL, or ISIS) has carried out suicide attacks against military units in Iraq and Syria and may have plotted to attack aircraft.

A contemporary history of suicide terrorism would include the April 18 and October 23, 1983, bombings of the US embassy and Marine barracks in Beirut. It is reported that these attacks became the models for future suicide attacks. A *profile* for suicide terrorists began to form soon after these events and, as suicide terrorism continued, intelligence and law enforcement officials fine-tuned this suicide terrorist profile. During the early to mid-1980, the suicide terrorist profile was:

- 18–35 years of age
- Male
- Single
- Un-educated
- Poor
- Arab
- Islamist Extremist

On April 9, 1985, the first known female suicide bomber was used in an attack, turning the suicide terrorist profile on its head. On this day, a 16-year-old named Sana'a Youcef Mehaidli drove an explosive-laden vehicle into an Israeli convoy in Lebanon. Current statistical analysis of terrorist events suggests that 15–25 percent of suicide terrorist attacks are conducted by women. Unfortunately, terrorism research has grouped aggressors as a gender binary (Female/Male) and therefore, there is no available data on the number of attacks perpetrated against civil aviation by individuals who identify themselves as outside the gender binary. Other differences in attack patterns in recent decades have caused a revision of the suicide terrorist profile (e.g., education, ethnicity, socioeconomic status). Therefore, four decades of terrorism case study analysis contributes to the current suicide terrorist profile:

- 18–35 years of age (this could vary from 16 to 64 years of age)
- Single or married (with or without children)
- Male or female (individual could potentially be any gender)
- Un-educated or advanced degrees
- Poor to upper middle-class
- All racial and ethnic backgrounds.

Suicide terrorists are no longer seen as a bunch of poor, angry, uneducated Islamic men. So, what changed? Mohammed Atta (one of the American Airlines Flight 11 hijackers on September 11, 2001) was from an upper middle-class family in Egypt and had an advanced degree from Hamburg, Germany. Why would an educated person like Mohammed Atta be willing to die in order to kill others? The motivations of individuals who conduct suicide attacks may include political grievance, religious ideology, revenge, socioeconomic reward, and nationalism, among others; of course, we can never know the true motivations of a suicide terrorist because we cannot ask them after they commit their suicide act.

Suicide terrorism is popular with terrorist organizations for a number of reasons. To begin, suicide terrorism is inexpensive; the September 11 attack only costs between $400,000 and $500,000 to conduct (approximately $130–$170 per death). Suicide terrorism also increases mass casualties and causes extensive damage. For example, although the September 11, 2001, attacks cost less than half a million to conduct, the economic cost of the attacks is estimated at between $2 trillion and $3 trillion. And terrorist organizations don't have to worry that a suicide terrorist like Mohammed Atta will surrender important information after the attack since the terrorist's death is pre-planned and assumed. Further, suicide terrorism precipitates a fear and sense of helplessness and despair, and there is an immense impact on the public and the media; for example, the media reproduces terrorist images that have an impact on the psyche of citizens of the target country. And there are a significant number of recruits willing to commit suicide terrorism. Finally (and possibly most importantly), this sensational form of terrorism has the ability to effect political change (e.g., the Madrid train bombings). It is for all of these reasons that suicide terrorism will likely remain popular with terrorist organizations. Civil aviation will continue to remain a target of choice for suicide terrorism by terrorist organizations. Terrorists follow a kind-of protocol to plan their attacks, called the *terrorist planning cycle*. Because of its popularity among terrorist organizations, the terrorist planning cycle is particularly important for you to understand.

TERRORIST PLANNING CYCLE

Terrorist organizations typically plan their attacks in a cyclical way. An attack is planned, rehearsed, executed, and exploited before the cycle begins anew. There are seven phases to the terrorist planning cycle. The name *terrorist* planning cycle is somewhat of a misnomer because most criminals and criminal organizations also use a similar type of planning cycle. Therefore, criminals carry out many of the same planning processes and cycles of activity, and exhibit much of the same behavior, as terrorists do when they plan for (or carry out) an attack against civil aviation. Therefore, it is important for you to be able to understand the terrorist planning process so you will be more effective at recognizing criminal and terrorist behavior in aircraft and airports. The topic of criminal and terrorist behavioral recognition will be presented in a later chapter, however, understanding the terrorist planning cycle is an important step in understanding how to identify that behavior. The seven stages of the terrorist planning cycle are:

1. Broad Target Selection
2. Information Gathering and Surveillance
3. Specific Target Selection
4. Pre-Attack Surveillance and Planning
5. Rehearsal
6. Execution
7. Escape and Exploitation*

---

* Suicide terrorists do not need to follow this final step of *Escape and Exploitation*, since the object of their mission is to die during the *Execution* phase; instead of the individual terrorist, the terrorist *organization* is likely to be the one to attempt to later exploit the attack.

During the *Broad Target Selection* phase, terrorists select the industry sector they wish to attack (e.g., economics sector, transportation sector, energy sector). The organization typically performs broad target selection by collecting information on a large group of targets. After performing broad target selection and then deciding on civil aviation as a target in the 1990s, terrorist organizations infiltrated many of the major airports in the United States and used their trusted positions to conduct surveillance and gather information on civil aviation targets. Therefore, there is already a wealth of information available to terrorist organizations about how to attack aircraft and airports. Furthermore, information and terrorist resources are sometimes shared between terrorist groups (e.g., the Lod Airport Attack, 1972). An example of broad target selection is when the terrorist group Al Qaeda planned the September 11 attacks and chose the transportation sector as their target, further selecting civil aviation as the target within the transportation sector. The September 11 plot originally involved hijacking 10 aircraft on both coasts of the United States and, along with the Pentagon and World Trade Center, other targets included the George Bush Center for Intelligence in Langley, Virginia, and Federal Bureau of Investigation Headquarters in Washington, DC.

After a terrorist organization has chosen a target, they begin the *Information Gathering and Surveillance* phase. During this phase, they try to establish the easiest way to attack the target. The non-sterile area has become a particularly popular target for suicide terrorists in recent decades, and it is considered a *soft-target* because of the ease with which an armed individual can move unchallenged and undetected in this environment. The non-sterile area in an airport typically consists of parking lots, airline ticket counters, and restaurants. By planning an attack in the non-sterile area of an airport, a suicide terrorist plot is easier and cheaper to plan because there are fewer obstacles to hinder access to the target area. The Brussels airport and railway bombings are the most recent examples of an attack in the non-sterile area. An area that does not require pre-screening or security checkpoint processing of people will always be more vulnerable than areas that require these security processes.

On the other end of the vulnerability spectrum for the information gathering and surveillance phase of terrorist operations is the *hard target*, which is a target with few security vulnerabilities. An example of a hard target in civil aviation is the *sterile area* of an airport. Carrying out an attack in the sterile area would be a much harder task and would require much more planning, surveillance, intelligence, and money than would a soft target because an individual would need to pass through security

screening to enter the sterile area prior to their attack. A terrorist organization can often bypass many of a hard target's security by using an
insider, or someone who has access to the target environment because of
their job or other circumstances allow. During the second phase, or information gathering and surveillance phase, terrorists will try to determine
which targets are hard *or* soft. To help make this determination, the terrorist group will often perform a limited amount of surveillance on the target
from afar, such as researching the targets through internet searches.

After broad target selection has been made and the basic information
gathering and surveillance phase has concluded, terrorists move into the
Specific Target Selection phase. During this phase, the terrorists select the
specific target they want to attack. By selecting a specific target, the terrorist organization can seek to determine how to best attack that target.
Traditionally, planners of terrorist attacks have wanted the most media
attention they could get, because this brings more sympathetic awareness
to their cause. Thus, terrorist attack planners will also look at whether a
target provides a specific advantage for the organization and will weigh
the cost–benefits for conducting the operation. An example of activities
conducted during the specific target selection phase is the surveillance
flights that were conducted by Richard Reid for the September 11 attacks.
Reid performed numerous surveillance flights and then sent reports
back to Afghanistan one month prior to the attacks. These surveillance
reports assisted the planners in performing specific target selection and
further detailed where the hijackers should sit to put them as close to the
flight deck as possible (to be near the pilots) without arousing suspicion.
Another example of specific target selection is when domestic terrorist
Anthony McVeigh chose to attack the Murrah Federal Building. McVeigh
later described the building as an easy target; something he had determined during the specific target selection phase.

After a terrorist organization has selected the specific target, they
move into the *Pre-attack Surveillance and Planning* phase. This phase of the
terrorist planning cycle is one of the most important for you to understand. During this phase, terrorists must perform physical surveillance
of the target. A terrorist is especially vulnerable to being detected during
this phase because they must enter the target environment to gather information on the target. The pre-attack surveillance and planning phase is
the most probable time that a first responder like you can expect to catch
an individual in the act before the attack is executed. Although terrorists may attempt to use trained surveillance personnel during this phase,
they typically do not. Regardless of their level of training, however, the

behavioral signs for individuals conducting surveillance are well-known and can be easily spotted. You will become more familiar with these behavioral signs in Section II. By understanding the signs of surveillance and how the information from surveillance feeds into the terrorist planning cycle, you will be better prepared (and have a greater chance) of stopping a terrorist attack before one occurs.

An example of pre-attack surveillance and planning is the 1996 Khobar Towers attack in Saudi Arabia; Saudi Hezbollah terrorists had begun performing surveillance for this operation in 1993, showing the importance of this phase for the terrorist planning cycle and highlighting the length of time (three years in this particular example) that a first responder like you can potentially catch a terrorist prior to an attack. The information gathered during this phase is particularly useful for terrorists to better plan an operation and ensure its success. Although the surveillance phase was not detected during planning for the Khobar Towers attack, many people were able to escape the site of the blast thanks to the keen awareness of security personnel who were on-site prior to when the vehicle bomb exploded.

After a terrorist organization has conducted pre-attack surveillance on their chosen target, they will begin to plan how to execute the attack by moving into the *Rehearsal* phase, or *attack rehearsals*. Like the information gathering and surveillance phase, the rehearsal phase creates its own risks for being detected by first responders. Individuals performing attack rehearsals may exhibit strange behavior, making them vulnerable to detection. As mentioned in the previous chapter, the two federal air marshals on board Northwest Airlines Flight 327 (on June 29, 2004) observed a suspected hijacking rehearsal. The two inflight security officers watched as 12 Syrian citizens periodically ran down the aisles, went into the lavatories for extended periods, and used hand signals in the cabin to communicate. Another example of this phase is the series of rehearsals conducted prior to the July 7, 2005, bombings in London. Terrorists had performed multiple rehearsals one month prior to the attacks by riding around the trains and double-decker buses that would be their targets. Closed-circuit television recorded the attack rehearsals and allowed investigators to learn crucial facts about the planning that went into the attack. The terrorists exhibited bizarre behavior during the rehearsal phase, likely a reflection of their lack of training. For example, while performing a rehearsal to attack one of the trains, one of the terrorists purchased a ticket, walked to the boarding area (where they stood around and stared at the train platform), and then walked out of the metro station and onto the street. (The terrorist organization involved in planning this attack also used surveillance detection methods to maintain operational security during rehearsals.)

The next step in the terrorist planning cycle is the *Execution* phase. Execution of the attack is performed at a specific time, as determined by the attack planners and may be triggered by an *attack signal,* such as the use of a hand signal, an infrared strobe light, or some other special signal that is known in advance by the perpetrators. The use of an attack signal means that (1) rehearsals are being conducted or (2) an attack is imminent. An example of the execution phase is the June 14, 1985, hijacking of TWA Flight 847. The hijackers of TWA 847 had planned extensively for the hijacking and were methodical in their control of passengers on board. The hijackers sat in the rear of the aircraft (a good place for them to watch and assess the cabin) and initiated the hijacking when one of them stood from their seat and ran up the aisle toward the forward area. This is a common attack signals for hijackers because they all must make some attempt to make it to the forward area as quickly as possible so they can control this important position of advantage in the aircraft. The behaviors exhibited by the hijackers of TWA 847 suggest that the terrorist planning cycle, including pre-attack surveillance and rehearsals, was used by the planners of this attack. If you remain alert to behaviors in the cabin, it is possible for you to spot an attack signal prior to (or during) the execution of the attack.

The final step of the terrorist planning cycle is the *Escape and Exploitation* phase. Terrorists generally want to live to attack other targets in the future, however, as previously noted, suicide terrorists do not. The suicide terrorist does not expect to escape, nor exploit their attack. In this case, the terrorist organization that planned the attack will most likely (but not always) try to exploit the attack by claiming responsibility for the attack. By claiming responsibility for an attack, a terrorist organization is able to use media coverage of the event to further awareness to their ideology. An example of escape and exploitation is the 1999 Indian Air Flight 814 hijacking, during which Ahmed Sheikh (one of the hijackers on board) escaped to Pakistan. Ahmed Sheikh was later implicated in the death of journalist Daniel Pearl and was suspected of having ties to the September 11 attacks.

HIJACK TACTICS

Over the last few decades, hijackers have used the same strategies, or *hijack tactics,* to hijack aircraft. All of these hijack tactics have, for the most part, evolved from the tactics used by previous hijackers. Now that you understand threats to civil aviation and the terrorist cycle of planning, you can likely recognize some of the most common hijack tactics. As you will recall, hijack tactics of the past have included *control of the forward area, cabin compliance, spraying an aerosol in the cabin, breach of the flight deck, active violence, the threat of violence, deception, trained hijacker-pilots, ground assault, the threat of an explosive device, the surreptitious placement of an explosive device, placing an explosive device in checked-luggage, herding passengers and crew in the aircraft, separating passengers into groups, the use of a sleeper,* and *using aircraft as a suicide missile.* Likewise, common tactics that have been used against targets in civil aviation on the ground include *the use a dirty airport to bring weapons into the sterile area, cross-pollination between terrorist groups,* and *the use of mass-shootings in the non-sterile area.* Terrorists have used most of these tactics in the air during violent hijackings and bombings, or on the ground during mass shootings. Therefore, you should have a basic understanding of them so you can make more effective safety and security decisions as a first responder. This understanding will be helpful when you learn how to respond to attempted hijackings and bombings in aircraft, and mass shootings in airports, in a later section.

Each of these tactics will be explored more in detail here; however, it is important to understand that regardless of what tactic is used there is typically a brief period of *surprise* for passengers during which time passengers become aware of the hijacking as the hijacker communicates their intention of hijacking the aircraft. Communication of the hijacker's intention to hijack the aircraft could be made to everyone at one time, or to specific individuals, inside the aircraft (e.g., pilots, crew, passengers). Hijackers have announced their hijackings in the past by standing up and announcing the hijacking in the aisle, by announcing it on the public address (PA) system, by passing a note to a crew member or passenger, and by email and other forms of electronic message. For example, a hijacker may stand up in the aisle and announce their intent in the following way:

"Stay in your seats! If you move, we will kill you!"
"This is a bomb to blow up the plane!"
"This is a hijacking! Nobody move!"
"I'm the captain now!"

Understanding the language that an individual might use to communicate their intention to hijack an aircraft is important because this language is a type of attack signal which can help you to identify that an attack is imminent (or in progress). It is also important for you to have a thorough understanding of how an aggressor might behave in aircraft or airports as well because this will make you a more effective spotter of potential attacks. Therefore, to enhance your ability to detect threatening individuals in aircraft and airports and to help you better predict the movement of an aggressor in these environments, we now turn our attention to a more in-depth study of the tactics used by hijackers and bombers of aircraft and mass-shooters of airports.

CONTROL OF THE FORWARD AREA

During the execution phase of a hijacking, hijackers typically try to get to the forward area as quickly as possible, that is, within 3–5 seconds, once they have stood up from their seats. This is because the flight deck is located in front of the forward area. If a hijacker is going to hijack the aircraft, they must breach the cockpit door. Therefore, seizing access to the forward area is necessary for a hijacker because it gives that individual the ability to attempt a cockpit breach. The forward area is also the most tactically advantageous place in the cabin, reflected in its other name: *position of dominance*. This is because, when an aggressor positions themselves in the forward area, (1) it forces first responders in the cabin to come up the aisle(s) from one direction, and (2) it is the easiest place to keep watch in the cabin over passengers and crew. A hijacker may use food carts to block the forward area of the aircraft as a delay during an attempted cockpit breach.

Some hijackers choose to forgo positioning themselves in the forward area. These hijackers prefer to breach the flight deck as quickly as possible instead of lingering in the forward area. They do not spend time trying to control the forward area or gain cabin compliance. This type of tactic has historically been carried out by lone hijackers, however, it is possible that this tactic could also be used by a hijack team. Regardless of whether a hijacker plans to stay in the forward area for a long period of time or wants to transit through it quickly on their way to the flight deck, you should always remain vigilant and watchful of individuals who run toward the forward area.

CABIN COMPLIANCE

Cabin compliance is important for hijackers. It is common for a hijacker to try to get cabin compliance by forcing passengers and cabin crew members into a position of disadvantage. This makes passengers and cabin crew members easier to control. As noted previously, hijackers do this by telling passengers and crew to remain seated (or to sit down), to place their hands on top of their heads, to interlace their fingers, and to turn their bodies away from the nearest aisle. By having passengers and cabin crew members seated in a position of disadvantage, the hijacker(s) can (1) quickly spot movement in the cabin, and (2) have more freedom of movement in the aisle(s). In this way, a hijacker can control the cabin more easily, especially when they are able to simultaneously maintain a position in the forward area.

A hijacker might demand cabin compliance in many different ways. The hijacker may use the threat of violence to force a passenger's head between their legs as a model for other nearby passengers to follow, setting off a chain of compliance. A hijacker may demand cabin compliance in many other ways, such as by telling passengers:

"Place your hands on top of your head!"
"Interlace your fingers and turn away from the aisles!"
"Close your eyes and don't look at us!"

Hijackers also commonly shove, hit, slap, and punch passengers and crew members while they give cabin compliance commands. Violence is used by hijackers as a means of trying to get people in the cabin to comply with their demands and to discourage passengers and crew from resisting. Depending on the size of the aircraft, many passengers in a hijacked aircraft may not immediately know that the aircraft has been hijacked, nor realize that a hijacker (or hijack team) is making cabin compliance demands. In large aircraft, it is hard to hear someone speak two or three rows away; therefore, cabin compliance may be limited to a specific cabin, since hijacking a large aircraft requires a lot of hijackers and thus, their demands may not immediately be heard by passengers and crew in other cabins. For example, there were many passengers in the hijacked aircraft on September 11 who did not know their aircraft was hijacked until minutes before it crashed into its target.

The September 11 hijackers gained cabin compliance by telling passengers and cabins crew members near the front of the aircraft that they had an explosive device; by killing passengers and stabbing flight attendants; by spraying a self-defense aerosol in the cabin; and by clearing the first-class cabin to ensure a physical delay between themselves and first responders. All of these actions are a form of cabin compliance because the violence of these actions makes passengers and crew members reluctant to respond. Sadly, passengers and crew typically comply with hijacker demands by remaining seated and docile. Previously averted inflight hijacking and bombing attempts were stopped by passengers who refused to comply with hijacker demands and who applied critical thinking to ensure the integrity of the aircraft and the safety of the crew, passengers, and fellow first responders. A thorough understanding of hijacker tactics, like cabin compliance, can help you to think more critically about inflight security, too.

BREACH OF THE FLIGHT DECK

The ultimate goal of a hijacker is to breach the cockpit. A hijacker is not likely to be successful in diverting an aircraft without accessing the flight deck, because a pilot will not likely change the aircraft's course unless they receive a direct threat from a hijacker. Prior to the September 11 attacks, most cockpit doors in commercial could be breached by simply pulling on the door from the outside; the cockpit doors on some aircraft were even known to open by themselves during take-off. After the September 11 attacks, many commercial aircraft were equipped with hardened cockpit doors in order to prevent a breach of the flight deck. Unfortunately, the hardening of a cockpit door can delay a breach, but it cannot prevent one; a well-trained and minimally equipped hijacker can breach a hardened cockpit door within 90 seconds.

Hijack teams may place food carts in the aisles to prevent first responders from moving unencumbered in the aisles; they may pull out the steel cable security barriers to block off the forward area; they may prowl the aisle(s) and assault and berate passengers and crew; and they may stand just forward of the forward area to watch the cabin and ensure cabin compliance or issue commands to passengers. Although hijackers may do all of these things, they need to make entry into the flight deck in order to successfully hijack the aircraft. Entry into the flight deck is a major obstacle for any hijack plan and thus, a terrorist organization will devote a majority of their planning and resources to find a way to breach the flight deck as quickly as possible.

Although a hijacker may use brute force to breach the flight deck, they could also potentially intimidate a flight attendant to open the cockpit door for them. An attempt to coax the pilots to open the door from the inside is not outside the realm of possibility. A hijacker may also run up the aisle toward the cockpit when a pilot is preparing to re-enter the cockpit after using the lavatory, or when the pilot is returning from a scheduled rest break on a long-haul flight. By thinking of new ways a hijacker might breach the cockpit door, you will be more effective at spotting potential threats in the cabin and be able to respond to those threats in a way that considers the safest course of action for the aircraft, passengers, and crew.

ACTIVE VIOLENCE

Hijackers often use violence to control passengers in the cabin. This active violence may include shoving, punching, kicking, stabbing, and shooting. The attempted detonation (or actual detonation) of an explosive device is another form of inflight violence used during attacks against civil aviation; however, unlike other forms of hijacker violence, a suicide bomber uses this type of violence to destroy the aircraft, not to gain cabin compliance. Active violence is more dangerous than the threat of violence because active violence occurs in real time and therefore shows an aggressor's willingness to engage in violence. Hijackers will attack passengers, pilots, cabin crew members, and first responders in an attempt to maintain control of the aircraft or to give them leverage in negotiations to get fuel, permission to take off, food, money, release of political prisoners, or any number of other demands. Regardless of the type of violence used, all forms of active inflight violence have the potential to jeopardize the lives of everyone on board the aircraft.

Violence is used during the vast majority of hijackings which involve the use of armed hijackers. During the September 11 hijackings, for example, the hijackers (armed with box cutters) killed the pilots, stabbed flight attendants and passengers, and deliberately used the aircraft as a pilot-guided missile (another form of active violence). The immediate danger to one's life is compounded inside the aircraft during flight because there are no avenues of escape. Therefore, as a first responder, you should be prepared to act as quickly as possible to stop active violence inside the aircraft.

THREAT OF VIOLENCE

Hijackers usually threaten passengers and crew with violence. An *inferred threat* is a threat that is not directly stated, for example, a hijacker who says, "Sit down! I have a bomb!" In contrast, a *direct threat* is a threat that is stated directly, for example, a hijacker who says, "Remain seated or we will kill you." A hijacker could breach the cockpit, kill the pilots and announce a threat via the public announcement system, for example, saying, "Stay seated and no one will be hurt," or "If anyone tries anything, we will crash the aircraft." The threat of inflight violence must be taken seriously. First responders cannot assume that a hijacker will not act on a threat, because research suggests that hijackers who make threats during the course of a hijacking do eventually become violent.

A hijacking represents an extremely dangerous situation for an aircraft inflight. This is because a hijacker may have plans for the aircraft (like crashing it) that will result in the death of everyone on board and others on the ground. Therefore, you must consider an individual to be an immediate threat to everyone on board if they make a threat that has the potential to harm the integrity of the aircraft, for example, the threat of detonating an explosive device or of crashing the aircraft. First responders on board are in a unique position to stop a hijacking or inflight bombing attempt. There are few options to stop a hijacking from the ground, beyond shooting the aircraft out of sky. Only passengers and crew can stop the violence and regain control. First responders like you must be willing to act if an individual begins making threats in the cabin that, if acted upon, can negatively impact the integrity of the aircraft and the safety of passengers, crew, and other first responders. Certain strategies and tactical principles will be explored later in this book to make you a more effective decision maker when confronted with an inflight security threat.

DECEPTION

Deception has typically always been practiced in some form or another by criminals and terrorists who have attacked civil aviation. Hijackers have used disguises and false passports, smuggled weapons and explosives, faked injury, and lied to carry out their attack plans. The study and practice of spotting deceptive behavior is one of the easiest ways to strengthen aviation security on the ground and in the air because all criminals and terrorists use some form of deceptive behavior while surveilling a target and while carrying out an attack.

Watching for deceptive behavior is the primary duty of inflight security officers around the world today, highlighting the importance of its use by terrorists and criminals in the aviation domain. First responders have the ability to strengthen aviation security inflight and on the ground by learning the profiling and behavioral recognition techniques explained later in this book.

UNDERSTANDING OF SECURITY PROCEDURES

During the 1990s, over a dozen terrorist sympathizers secured jobs at major airports in the United States. These individuals used their positions to gather inside knowledge of security screening protocols, baggage handling procedures, and other sensitive security operations. This information was eventually shared between several terrorist organizations. Although many new security procedures and technologies have adapted over the years as modern threats have emerged, terrorists have a thorough understanding of the security protocols, procedures, and overall security posture at most international airports. Many terrorist groups only need to do a limited amount of pre-attack surveillance on a selected target in civil aviation in order to increase their chance of attack success. This makes commercial aviation a tempting target for terrorist organizations.

In the United States, *security checkpoint evaluations*, which measure the effectiveness of a security checkpoint at detecting prohibited items, have consistently shown a near 90% failure rate. This suggests that there are considerable vulnerabilities in today's high-tech, money-driven, aviation security processes. Since most countries model their aviation security programs on the same International Civil Aviation Organization (ICAO), Annex 17 security recommendations, most countries around the world have security procedures and security technology systems in place which are similar to those in the United States. In order to think more effectively and proactively in the aviation environment, you should take notice of the security procedures at airports whenever and wherever you travel. Over time, this growing awareness will help you (1) readily identify aviation security procedures in unfamiliar airports and (2) make more effective safety plans (discussed in a later section) when needed.

USE OF HIJACKER-PILOTS

Terrorists have used trained pilots during hijackings for over three decades. By using their own pilot, hijackers place themselves at a distinct advantage. Pilots typically pose the biggest obstacle to hijackers. For example, pilots sit in the cockpit in front of a locked door and, after a hijacking has begun, they will use any number of tactics to get the aircraft on the ground as quickly as possible. The pilots may say that the aircraft needs to land to refuel, or they may change course from the hijacker's intended destination. If a hijacker has no knowledge of air navigation or flight control, then they will not be able to understand when these kinds of tactics are being used. Pilots have also been known to physically resist a hijacking; pilots have wounded hijackers and have been killed while attempting to prevent a hijacker from obtaining control of the aircraft. The lone hijacker pilot who attempts to take control of the aircraft, or the hijack team that tries to inject their hijacker pilot into the flight deck, will likely use violence to accomplish their goal. In the past, hijackers have hit, stabbed, and shot flight attendants and pilots in order to get their own pilot in the captain's chair.

A hijacker must gain access to the cockpit as quickly as possible in order to remove the legitimate pilots and replace them with a pilot of their own. The advent of hardened and locked cockpit doors is another obstacle for hijackers. Hardened cockpit doors have forced hijackers to time their breach of the cockpit very carefully, for example, waiting until the pilots open the door for a bathroom break. Some airlines have added steel cable barriers so that cabin crew members can use them to help delay hijackers from reaching the forward area (and cockpit). These steel cables are supposed to be locked in place by flight attendants before the captain or co-pilot leaves the cockpit, for example, when they come out to stretch, to get refreshments, to sleep in designated rest areas on long-haul flights, or to use the lavatory. It is important for you to be especially aware of when a pilot leaves the cockpit during flight. The aircraft is especially vulnerable to a hijacking at this time. Therefore, whenever the cockpit door is opened, first responders should maintain a heightened state of awareness for an attempted hijacking.

GROUND ASSAULT

A ground assault has been used on several occasions as a tactic by hijackers in order for them to board an aircraft with their weapons. Armed hijackers have accomplished this by using vehicles to drive up to the aircraft while disguised as law enforcement officers, therefore you should always be aware of any armed uniformed security, military, or police officers on board the aircraft when you are traveling through countries that are known for internal strife. It is advantageous for first responders for an aircraft to be commandeered on the ground instead of hijacked in the air because the aircraft is not yet airborne. A first responder has options on the ground that are not available to them in the air. For example, an emergency exit can be opened on the ground to prevent the aircraft from taking off. Being on the ground also gives law enforcement officers more options to rescue passengers and crew. These options are lost when an aircraft becomes airborne. Therefore, every attempt should be made to keep the aircraft on the ground. A ground assault can be dangerous, however, when first responders like you think critically and follow the response protocols explained throughout this book, it can provide an opportunity to keep the aircraft on the ground.

USE OF HIJACKER SLEEPER AGENTS

Hijack teams have used sleepers during many past hijackings. For example, during the hijacking of Kuwait Airways Flight 422, a sleeper team on board waited until the initial hijacking had taken place and then joined the others. A *sleeper* is a member of the hijack team who does not immediately join the initial execution phase of the hijacking. The sleeper may stay in their seat for several minutes or up to one hour (or longer) before acting. A sleeper may also hide in another part of the aircraft (like a lavatory) prior to the execution of the hijacking. Sleepers may (1) provide security and surveillance detection for the main hijacker team, (2) serve as a second hijack team that will act if the main team is unsuccessful, or (3) be a highly specialized member of the hijack team. For example, a sleeper could be a trained pilot who waits for the other members of the hijack team to obtain cabin compliance, control the forward area, breach the flight deck, and kill the pilots until they run into the cockpit to control the aircraft. In contrast, a suicide bomber may employ sleeper agents for surveillance detection and personal security.

To help you identify sleeper behavior, you should be on the lookout for individuals in the cabin who are especially watchful during a hijacking or bombing attempt. Also, always look behind you before getting up from your seat before acting to stop an active threat in the cabin; a sleeper agent could be seated behind you. The threat from a sleeper is something that is taken into account when, in a later section, we discuss the specific actions and techniques which you can take to stop a hijacker, hijack team, or attempted bomber inflight.

65

THREAT OF AN EXPLOSIVE DEVICE

Hijackers have threatened to detonate an explosive device during the course of many past hijackings. Interestingly, the historical record reflects that the majority of explosives used by the individuals who made these threats were fake. If a passenger can bring a knife or firearm through airport security, however, there is a much higher probability that they can successfully smuggle an explosive through security as well. Likewise, if a hijacker is unarmed inside the aircraft (and making threats with an explosive), there is a higher probability that the explosive device is fake. Regardless of whether a hijacker is armed or unarmed, if an individual threatens to use an explosive device inflight, you should try to gather as much information about the explosive as possible. Does the explosive look real? Is it visible? What type of material is it? By gathering information that is readily observable, you will be in a better position to make a decision that accounts for the totality of the circumstances.

Although a hijacker who threatens passengers with an explosive device inflight is not actively detonating the device, they are still a suicidal threat. A suicide bomber plans to die during the course of their attack, and by threatening to detonate an explosive device that is either strapped to their body (or within the vicinity of their body), they should be considered an immediate and active threat to the integrity of the aircraft and the safety of the passengers, crew, and other first responders on board. Protocols on how to react to an inflight bomb threat are explained in detail in a later section.

SURREPTITIOUS PLACEMENT OF AN EXPLOSIVE DEVICE

Terrorist bombers may employ a number of different tactics when trying to place an explosive device inside an aircraft. Although the *under-the-seat-cushion bombs* of the 1980s have not been used for a long time, there are still many places in an aircraft where a bomb could be placed prior to the aircraft's next flight. Passengers should be especially aware of the lavatories located over the aircraft's wings and those sharing a bulkhead with the flight deck. Lavatories have numerous doors and compartments where paper towels and toilet paper are held and where essential plumbing for toilet and sink functions are routed. These doors can be opened easily, without detection, and an artfully designed explosive device could be placed in these compartments in a way that it could pass a cursory visual inspection. Special care should be taken to inspect the security tags and seals around these compartments and to take notice of any obvious tampering. Although many of these compartments often have their security tags tampered with (and have not been replaced by the respective airline), these compartments can be opened and inspected quickly to rule out any explosive devices hidden in these areas.

In the desire to keep aircraft in the air as often as possible, they may or may not be given a thorough search on the ground after a flight lands and before boarding new passengers. This was a security vulnerability during the reign of bombings in the 1980s, and terrorists exploited this by placing bombs in places on the aircraft that were not typically inspected by cleaning crews. This continues to be a considerable vulnerability to aircraft. The economic benefits of keeping aircraft in the air would be offset if cleaning crews spent more time checking under seats, inside of hidden compartments, and replacing broken security tags; however, these checks are often overlooked due to complacency. Therefore, it is up to first responders like you to be especially aware of anything out of the ordinary in areas of the cabin that are close to the fuselage, or near the front of the aircraft. The forward area lavatories are especially vulnerable because of the large amount of cabling and other vital electrical wirings that spread out from the flight deck and course through the entire aircraft where they help control essential aircraft functions. During the Egypt Air Flight 804 crash investigation, it was discovered that there had been a signal from the lavatory smoke detector in one of the forward lavatories which indicated that there was smoke in the cabin or an inflight fire. Although this crash is still under investigation, it serves as a good example for exercising critical thinking skills. Do terrorist groups still want to attack targets in civil aviation? Did someone start a fire in the forward area lavatory? Did a terrorist group decide not to claim responsibility for this attack because they found a secret new way to bring down an aircraft? There are many unanswered questions about the crash of Egypt Air Flight 804. The more you continue to learn about the behavior patterns of aircraft hijackers and suicide bombers, the more effective you will be at making decisions as a first responder which consider the integrity of the aircraft and the safety of the passengers, crew, and other first responders.

DETONATION OF AN EXPLOSIVE DEVICE INFLIGHT

The bombings and attempted bombings of aircraft over the last decade highlight the danger of the detonation of an explosive device in flight. Unlike hijackings, suicide bombers have no desire to control the aircraft or to divert it to another country; instead, the suicide bomber wants to destroy the aircraft and kill everyone on board. An explosive, however, needs to be powerful enough to damage a section of fuselage that is at least three meters in diameter in order to bring about its total destruction. A small explosive device could also be used, but it would need to be placed in an area of the aircraft where it could cause the most destruction, such as (1) near the cockpit, (2) above the center-wing fuel tanks, or (3) against the fuselage. You should be especially aware of these vulnerable areas. It is also important to remain vigilant of passengers who go into the lavatories near the cockpit or above-the-wing section of the cabin for extended periods. A suicide bomber will have a specific location inside the aircraft where they will plan to detonate their explosive device, but they will likely have a specific time and geographic location as well. For example, a suicide bomber may wish to detonate their explosive when the aircraft is flying over a particularly deep section of the ocean because this would make recovery efforts and air accident investigation problematic.

Suicide terrorists typically want privacy to assemble and detonate their explosive devices. This gives the bomber time to steady their shaky hands and privacy for their illegal activities. A suicide bomber will likely be under a significant amount of stress. Privacy may be a psychological requirement for suicide terrorists, providing them a safe space to calm them enough to allow them to continue on with their suicide mission. It is for this reason that you should be especially aware of passengers who have been in an aircraft lavatory for an extended period of time. An explosion near the cockpit or above the fuel tanks would seriously threaten the integrity of the aircraft and thus the bathrooms in these areas should be carefully watched.

PLACING AN EXPLOSIVE DEVICE IN CHECKED LUGGAGE

Individuals have, on numerous occasions, placed explosives into the checked luggage of aircraft. Many aviation security experts proclaim that the advent and implementation of new detection technologies over the past decade at airports in the United States and around the world have made commercial air travel much safer; however, many security vulnerabilities still remain. Passenger security screening has a reported 90% failure rate at detecting weapons and explosives during security audits. This suggests that it is relatively easy for an individual to bring a weapon or explosive onto an aircraft. This is a security vulnerability that hijackers and suicide bombers can easily exploit. Airports that lack body-imaging technology are most vulnerable to individuals who want to bring weapons or explosives into the secure area. The use of trial and error through rehearsals, or the use of an individual who has access to the secure area, that is, an *insider,* are two examples of avenues that individuals could use to bring weapons or explosives into the secure area of an airport. Exercising your critical thinking skills will help you identify other potential ways that people could bring dangerous prohibited items into the secure area.

USE OF A DIRTY AIRPORT

Airports with poor security procedures, or *dirty airports,* have been used numerous times in the past by individuals to smuggle weapons and explosives onto aircraft. It is easy to assume that the type of airport that is most likely to be used by this type of devious individual would be an airport that has had aviation security issues in the past. But there are many modern airports around the world that are often labeled "safe" by aviation security experts when this is not true. For example, Schiphol airport in Amsterdam was used by Umar Farouk Abdulmutallab in 2009 to board a Northwest Airlines flight to Detroit in the attempted bombing of the aircraft. The ability for a passenger to get on an aircraft with a weapon or explosive in one country, fly to another country, and then board an aircraft destined for yet another country was a huge security vulnerability in the past. What makes this particular incident so disturbing is that, although this vulnerability had long been known by executives at Schiphol airport and they had issued a mandatory security policy to fix it, the vulnerability had not been fixed when Abdulmutallab landed in Amsterdam with his bomb.

You do not need to look far to find examples of other airports with security vulnerabilities. The airport in Mogadishu, Somalia was used in 2016 to gain access to a special laptop explosive device prior to the bombing of Daallo Airlines Flight 159. Terrorist organizations that are planning suicide attacks also sometimes use dirty airports to test their explosives prior to using them in major attacks. In the early 1990s, Ramzi Yousef used a dirty airport in Asia to bring an explosive on board an aircraft. Yousef then left the explosive on board the aircraft prior to disembarking so its destructive capabilities could be tested on the connecting flight. Unfortunately for current commercial air travelers, security screening technology is relied upon in the vast majority of airports around the world to detect weapons and explosives before they enter the secure area. Terrorist organizations that plan attacks in civil aviation within the secure area (inside the airport or in the aircraft) will attempt to make explosives that are made from materials or disguised in such a way that they can avoid detection. Unfortunately, the majority of airports do not take the kind of proactive approach to aviation security (for lack of budget or management constraints) that would most benefit the aviation domain, relying instead on a technology-based security approach. This reliance on technology and reduction on human detection often leads to complacency which can be exploited by terrorists during the terrorist planning cycle. Although all commercial airports around the world use technology to help detect prohibited items before they enter the secure area, Israel is the only country that also uses proactive profiling and investigative techniques during the aviation security screening process. The aviation security screening process will be discussed in further detail later in this book.

Terrorists have been getting progressively more sophisticated over the years to combat law enforcement investigations. For example, terrorist organizations now choose suicide bombers who have no criminal record. The use of *clean* individuals is especially alarming to intelligence agencies dedicated to hunting terrorist groups because these people can more easily bypass aviation security and enter the sterile area with weapons and explosives. These evolving terrorist strategies make the job of investigators much harder and expands the number of dirty airports around the world by stifling global law enforcement, intelligence, and aviation security capabilities.

SEPARATING PASSENGERS INTO GROUPS

Separating passengers into different groups during a hijacking is a popular hijacker tactic, most often used by hijacker teams with three or more hijackers. This tactic helps the hijack team because it places passengers (and often cabin crew members) in a smaller area where they can be more easily controlled. Hijackers often also place individuals in the back of the cabin in order to create a delay for any counter-hijack response. This tactic is also used by hijackers to help them search passenger identification to identify Western citizens; citizens from Western nations are often used as leverage during later negotiations. Violence is statistically more likely to occur during a hijacking where passengers and cabin crew members are separated into different groups; therefore, the separation of passengers into groups, or the herding of passengers into a particular area, of the aircraft is a good predictor of violence during a hijacking.

The September 11 hijackers herded passengers into the rear of their respective aircraft. This caused passengers to be oblivious to what the hijackers were doing in the front of the aircraft; many passengers called people on the ground from the back of the hijacked aircraft and reported that they were unsure whether or not the legitimate pilots were in control. In order to retain control of the cabin, hijackers rely on passengers and cabin crew members to not resist. Because of the violent danger that is precipitated by not resisting, you should always avoid being herded into the rear of the aircraft or separated into different groups during a hijacking.

CROSS-POLLINATION BETWEEN TERRORIST GROUPS

Terrorist organizations often share information with one another; however, they also sometimes attack targets for the benefit of the other. The airport attack in Lod Israel on May 30, 1972, is a good example of terrorist organizations from opposite ends of the world that shared information and cooperated to attack a target. During the planning of the Lod Airport Massacre, the terrorist group Popular Liberation Of Palestine, or PLO, contracted with the Japanese Red Army to hit a target in Israel, for which the PLO would then hit a target in Japan. With the crackdown on terrorists by global intelligence and law enforcement agencies, it is likely that terrorist organizations will attempt to share resources and information in the future to avoid detection.

NON-STERILE AREA ATTACKS

The *non-sterile area*, or *non-secure area*, represents the most vulnerable area of an airport to terrorist attack. Terrorists have repeatedly targeted the non-sterile area for ease of access, cost-benefit, and potential for mass casualty. The non-sterile area is a major place of congregation for people transiting through the civil aviation environment; however, it is easy to bring firearms and explosives into the non-sterile areas of airports around the world. Thankfully, some airports (like Domodedovo International Airport), have learned from previous attacks and have improved security in the non-secure area. Small improvements for the external perimeter of an airport can turn the non-secure area of an airport into a *semi-secure* one, by establishing dedicated security screening channels for passengers entering the traditional non-secure area, or by re-allocating security assets in the non-secure area to bolster deterrence.

4

Inflight Jurisdiction, Inflight Awareness, and Layers of Aviation Security

Inflight legal considerations are important for first responders like you to understand. This will you an idea of the various crimes that can occur on board an aircraft and the laws which govern inflight security. For armed law enforcement officers who may need to respond in the absence of inflight security, a thorough understanding of the legal considerations and civil aviation security guidelines will better help you rationalize any response you might make inflight. One of the first things worth considering is *racial profiling*. Basically, law enforcement officers are told that racial profiling is bad; specifics can be found in the Department of Justice Publication *Guidance Regarding the Use of Race by Federal Law Enforcement Officers, 2003*. This guidance more or less states that, when evaluating threats in civil aviation, first responders should focus on behaviors, not race. For example, if you were trying to determine if an individual in an aircraft had a weapon concealed on their body, you would look for bulges in the suspect's clothing, but you would not base your determination on their race. Prior to the September 11 attacks, inflight security officers were not sworn federal law enforcement officers and thus, they did not follow such guidance. Instead, they had agreements with the countries where they flew and only had law enforcement status when the aircraft was inflight. An aircraft is considered *inflight* when all external doors are

DOI: 10.4324/9781003336457-5

closed and until which time one of the external doors is opened to allow passengers to disembark.

INFLIGHT SECURITY OFFICER LEGAL AUTHORITY & JURISDICTION

In the United States, inflight security officers gained federal law enforcement authority when President George W. Bush signed the Aviation Transportation Security Act (ATSA) in 2001. ATSA also established the Transportation Security Administration (TSA) and greatly expanded the Federal Air Marshal Program of the Federal Aviation Administration (FAA). The Aviation Transportation Security Act has had a major impact on inflight security programs around the world and has generally been adopted as the model by which most of the world's aviation security programs operate.

INFLIGHT SECURITY OFFICER JURISDICTION

There are different types of jurisdictions in civil aviation. These include special aircraft jurisdiction, which involves specific jurisdiction inside the aircraft inflight; *exclusive jurisdiction,* which is found in the sterile area of the airport or inside the aircraft at the boarding gate; or *shared jurisdiction* in the non-sterile area where other federal or local law enforcement entities have a presence. In the United States, special aircraft jurisdiction is found under Title 49 of the United States federal code (USC), section 46501.

TITLE 49 OF THE UNITED STATES FEDERAL CODE (49 USC)

Title 49 of the United States federal code (49 USC) specifically covers transportation and aviation security programs. It says, when inflight security officers are on board an aircraft, they have *exclusive responsibility* for directing all law enforcement activity to ensure passenger safety on that aircraft. This is extremely important for first responders like you to understand. If an inflight security team is on board and responds to an onboard threat, you should stay seated and follow their instructions. Law enforcement officers in the United States who are authorized to carry a loaded firearm inside the cabin of a commercial aircraft are already familiar with this requirement; the TSA's *Flying Armed* teaches them this and a few other basic principles of inflight security. Everyone should follow instructions from inflight security officers and if you are an armed law enforcement officer, you should never take out your firearm unless you are instructed to do so. An inflight security officer can be readily identified by the gold-colored badge that will hang from a chain around their neck; they will also identify themselves as "police" by communicating this message in the cabin.

Although an inflight security officer will identify themselves as a law enforcement officer, it may be difficult for you to tell the difference between them and a hijacker. The tactics used by inflight security officers are often the same as a hijacker's. For example, when an inflight security officer responds to certain inflight security threats (each of which will be explained in detail in a later section), their primary objective is to control the forward area (a common hijacker tactic). Ever since the September 11 attacks, passengers' willingness to try to stop a hijacking in progress has become increasingly more vocalized. The willingness of passengers to act during a hijacking is often referred to in the federal air marshal service as *Let's Roll syndrome*. Let's Roll syndrome is often viewed negatively by most inflight security officers, because of the possibility that first responders may confuse inflight security officers with actual hijackers during a hijacking and mistakenly attack them in the process.

Another important consideration is 49 USC 114, which gives inflight security officers in the United States their federal law enforcement officer status outside of the special aircraft jurisdiction. This law enforcement status was not in effect outside the aircraft for most inflight security officers around the world until after the September 11 attacks and its implementation now allows inflight security officers to enforce laws not only inside aircraft but in airports as well. This law enforcement authority is important because it widens the scope of inflight security officer duties and allows them to proactively patrol both the non-secure and secure areas of an airport, along with enforcing laws within the special aircraft jurisdiction.

CRIMES AND INFRACTIONS

Aside from the crime of air piracy, there are a number of crimes that are often committed in airports and aircraft. The majority of these crimes are covered under Title 18 of the United States federal code (18 USC). Some of the more common crimes committed on board aircraft and inside airports are larceny, groping and pickpocketing, interfering with a flight crew, and carrying unauthorized weapons. Some of the crimes that may occur on board within the special aircraft jurisdiction of the United States and that you should be aware of are:

1. Assault—18 USC, section 113
2. Maiming—18 USC, section 114
3. Theft/Larceny—18 USC, section 661
4. Receiving stolen property—18 USC, section 113
5. Murder/Manslaughter/Attempted Murder—18 USC, section 1111
6. Sexual Abuse—109A of the District of Columbia Code
7. Assault on Federal Officer—18 USC, section 111
8. False Information/Hoaxes—18 USC, section 1038.

In the United States, the code of federal regulations (CFR) parallels the structure of the United States federal code. These are administrative laws. For example, smoking in the lavatory inflight is not a crime but an administrative violation under the code of federal regulations. Therefore, a passenger is not likely to go to jail for smoking in the lavatory, but they could be fined by the airline.

Periodically, cabin crew members must accommodate federal air marshals in first-class seats that are already occupied. This can be a hassle because the people who are already sitting in these seats must be either relocated to other seats in the cabin or bumped from the flight. Many cabin crew members often wonder why this is. After the September 11 attacks, there were many US federal codes and codes of federal regulations that were written to specifically deal with the deployment of federal air marshals. One of these federal codes was 49 USC 44917, which authorized the deployment of federal air marshals and requires all United States-flagged air carriers to give a seat to an air marshal upon request. This federal code applies to all airlines, and it does not matter whether a passenger booked their seats months in advance. According to 49 CFR 1544.223, an inflight security officer in the United States must have their weapon accessible at all times and airlines must assign seats to an air marshal team if requested. Another code of federal regulation, 49 CFR 1544.219, gives federal air marshals their authority to carry weapons on aircraft.

AIRPORT SECURITY DIRECTORS AND JURISDICTIONAL AGREEMENTS

In US airports, a federal security director (FSD) is assigned to oversee all security-related activities. The federal security director is a Transportation Security Administration senior management official. There is also an assistant federal security director (AFSD) at airports who assists the federal security director with security-related duties and liaisons with other local, state, and federal law enforcement personnel. In the United States, the Federal Bureau of Investigation (FBI) has jurisdiction over air piracy under Title 28 USC, section 538. This also gives the FBI investigative jurisdiction over certain other crimes on board an aircraft inflight, such as Interference with a flight crew, or 49 USC 46504. Title 28 USC, section 538 further states that the FBI "shall investigate any violations" which include "entering [the] aircraft or airport area in violation of security requirements."

For inflight security officers in the United States, the federal bureau of investigation's jurisdiction does not supersede federal air marshal exclusive aircraft jurisdiction. A memorandum of understanding from 1997 between the federal bureau of investigation and the federal aviation administration states that the federal aviation administration administrator has the authority to direct all federal law enforcement activity during a hijacking or commandeering. The transportation security administration officially took over all security-related duties from the federal aviation administration in late 2001; however, although it is assumed that this memorandum of understanding would be honored if there was ever another hijacking or commandeering on a United States-flagged aircraft, this has not yet been tested. Only time will tell if the transportation security administration will be able to assert control over the federal bureau of investigation for law enforcement activities during such high-profile events.

AVIATION SECURITY CONVENTIONS

Although this book mainly discusses the jurisdiction involving inflight crimes on board United States-flagged aircraft and the authority of United States inflight security programs, there are many other countries with their own inflight security officers and jurisdictional concerns. Most of the countries that have adopted an inflight security program have modeled it after that of the United States. They have received their legal authority in a similar manner. Other countries with inflight security programs include Australia, Austria, Canada, Jordan, Israel, China, and Poland. All of these inflight security programs follow various protocols and procedures that mimic each other. Along with the United States, these countries receive their authority as signatories of the various treaties, or *aviation security conventions*. These conventions, ratified by the United States and many other countries, have the legal force of federal law. There are four aviation security conventions that govern or relate inflight security; these are the *1944 Chicago Convention*, the *1963 Tokyo Convention*, the *1970 Hague Convention*, and the *1971 Montreal Convention*. The Chicago Convention of 1944 was a convention on international civil aviation that specifically preserved a country's sovereignty of airspace above its territory, and gave the country its authority to regulate civil aviation operations in its airspace. The Tokyo Convention of 1963 was a convention that met to discuss the criminal offenses committed on board aircraft, much like the special aircraft jurisdiction. This convention also defined the captain, or *pilot-in-command*, as the ultimate authority for making safety and security decisions on board an aircraft inflight. The Tokyo Convention also set out the *state registry* of an aircraft as exercising jurisdiction over offenses committed on board an aircraft and when that aircraft is inflight, over the surface of the high seas, or in and around other territories. The state registry is much like an aircraft's *citizenship* or *venue*. Contracting states (countries), or *signatories*, of the Tokyo Convention must also take all appropriate measures to restore control of the aircraft to the pilot-in-command during an air piracy event and is obligated to secure the release of the aircraft, crew, and passengers.

The Hague Convention of 1970 discussed and enacted law that made the seizure of an aircraft punishable by severe domestic penalties. This law made it a crime for an individual to attempt to hijack an aircraft. The Hague convention also laid out a four-part jurisdiction test which included (1) the country of the aircraft's registry, (2) the country of the aircraft operator, (3) the country in which the aircraft lands with the offender still on board; and any country where the offender may be found. On September 11, 1970, United States President Nixon ordered the creation of the *sky marshal program* because of a rash of hijackings. The Montreal Convention of 1971 applies to certain acts of violence against persons or air navigation facilities. The Montreal Convention also makes it an offense to be an accomplice in ground-based attacks against civil aviation. Although the laws that were passed through these conventions may seem to you like common sense, many of these laws were not written until the threats against civil aviation presented themselves over time.

SPECIAL LEGAL CONSIDERATIONS FOR LAW ENFORCEMENT OFFICERS

Law enforcement officers should be aware of special inflight legal considerations, such as the arrest of a juvenile, a non-United States citizen, or a diplomat. These types of interactions bring special consideration for law enforcement officers. For example, juveniles must have Miranda rights read to them and their names must not be released to the media. Law enforcement officers must also carefully guard any personal data, such as photos or any fingerprints that they may take. Parental notification must be made. Non-United States citizens must have a representative from their government notified about their arrest. Diplomats must be handled in their own special way. For example, diplomats cannot be arrested; they can only be detained until which time that verification of their diplomatic status can be made. In the United States, the Department of State can be contacted for diplomatic status verification purposes, or for further guidance, whenever you encounter a diplomat on board that has been involved in an inflight crime. (Diplomats are required to carry identification cards that indicate their status and degree of immunity.) Congressional representatives are another group of people who require special considerations. For example, members of Congress can only be arrested for a felony, treason, or breach of peace both during, and when coming and going from, sessions of Congress.

Although inflight security officers have exclusive authority over law enforcement actions on board an aircraft inflight, the captain of the aircraft is the ultimate authority. The captain is ultimately responsible, as the *inflight security coordinator*, for protecting the passengers and crew and for ensuring the integrity of the aircraft. Some pilots participate as volunteers in the *federal flight deck officer program*. These federal flight deck officers are pilots who are authorized to carry firearms to protect the cockpit from criminal violence. These pilots are deputized by the transportation security administration for five years and have law enforcement jurisdiction inside the cockpit.

UNITED STATES AIR CARRIER COMMON STRATEGY

Title 14 of the code of federal regulations covers *federal aviation regulations* or FARs. Crew member emergency training is explained and regulated under Title 14 of the code of federal regulations, under 14 CFR 121.417 and 14 CFR 135.223; this emergency training gives the crew a common strategy, also known as air carrier common strategy, for dealing with threats inside the aircraft. This system also gives airlines in the United States a way of distinguishing the different threat levels inside the aircraft, of which there are four. *Threat Level I,* or *disruptive behavior,* is behavior that is disruptive to passengers and crew members; *Threat Level II,* or *physical abusive behavior,* includes striking, slapping, hitting, punching, pushing, or other similar types of physically aggressive and abusive behavior; *Threat Level III*, or *life threatening behavior*, is when the actions of an individual threaten the life of another person, or if an individual infers that they have a weapon or explosive; and *Threat Level IV*, or the *attempted* or *actual breach of the flight deck*.

The most common security threat on an aircraft inflight is disruptive behavior from an intoxicated passenger. Flight attendants are accustomed to dealing with these passengers and have the training on how to de-escalate situations involving intoxicated passengers. Disruptive behavior can be a useful tactic for hijackers to help them expose security or law enforcement officers on board. This deception is well known by inflight security officers and is one of the main reasons that inflight security officers avoid responding to intoxicated passengers. A hijacker can also use disruptive behavior to create a diversion somewhere in the aircraft (like in the back of the cabin) so other hijackers can perform actions elsewhere in the cabin, like moving to the forward area and breaching the flight deck.

In the hierarchy of inflight security threats, physically abusive behavior is considered a more serious threat than disruptive behavior. A physically abusive person might start out being disruptive and then later exhibit physically abusive behavior; for example, an abusive passenger who punches another passenger or cabin crew member after arguing with them. Repeated punches to a person's head can be considered a life-threatening act. Depending on the circumstances, for example, size of the suspect compared to that of the victim, the use for the force needed to stop physically abusive behavior may include deadly force if that abusive behavior threatens the life of passengers on board.

As noted in the last example, life-threatening behavior may begin to surface with physically abusive behavior. Obviously, the threatening of a crew member or passenger with a weapon (actual or inferred) is a serious threat. Such activity requires a carefully considered deployment strategy to preserve the life of those on board and to protect the integrity of the aircraft. As a first responder in civil aviation, you should consider responding if you witness any life-threatening behavior on board.

An attempted, or actual breach of the flight deck is considered the most dangerous inflight security threat. Breaching the flight deck is a tactic used by most hijackers to gain control of the aircraft. The forward area acts as the portal through which the hijacker enters to approach the flight deck; thus, the forward area is a highly sensitive security area that should be monitored carefully during flight.

If an inflight security threat occurs, cabin crew members will (1) provide a physical and psychological barrier of the flight deck and (2) make threat notification to the pilot-in-command. A cabin crew member may even restrain an aggressive passenger so they cannot harm themselves or others. Upon notification, the pilot-in-command will then make a decision as to what course of action to take in order to maintain the safety of the aircraft, passengers, and crew. In the event of a hijacking, the pilot will broadcast an emergency distress signal by squawking 7500 to alert emergency coordinators and flight control personnel on the ground.

LAYERS OF SECURITY

There are many different layers to aviation security. The strength of security in aircraft and airports depends on how these layers of security interact. The layers of aviation security at airports often include the use of *plainclothes surveillance agents* in and around ticket counters to monitor passenger activity; *customs agents* at international border crossings (in the customs arrival area) to verify the identification of arriving air travelers; *terrorism task force personnel* to investigate terrorist threats to civil aviation; a *no-fly list* to identify problem passengers; *behavioral detection personnel* in the sterile and non-sterile area who attempt to detect deceptive behavior; *transportation security personnel* at security checkpoints who attempt to detect and prevent prohibited items from entering the sterile area; *armed inflight security officers* who attempt to thwart inflight bombing and hijacking attempts; *local law enforcement officers* who provide local law enforcement support; *background investigations* for flight and cabin crew members in an attempt to avoid internal security risks; *explosives detection canines* to help detect explosives at the airport and inside air cargo; *travel document checkers* to verify the identity of air travelers; *baggage screeners* who attempt to prevent dangerous and prohibited items from being introduced onto aircraft; *self-defense training* to teach cabin crew members how to protect themselves during flight; *federal flight deck officers* who are trained to protect the flight deck during an unauthorized cockpit breach; and *armed security officers* who perform inflight security duties on select flights. Depending on an airport's investment in its security personnel, technology, and protocols, the layers of security utilized at a particular airport may contribute to a less, equal, or more robust security posture than those which are recommended by International Civil Aviation Organization guidelines. Layering security enhances the overall security

81

for a given domain; therefore, security in civil aviation is bolstered when more layers of security are added to the civil aviation environment. For those of you who wish to further your knowledge on the layers of aviation security (or if there are policy makers reading this who are in need of a strong example), Israel has the most robust aviation security and the most successful implementation of its layers of aviation security.

Section II

Behavioral Detection and Adversary Recognition

It is important to be able to recognize an individual who may be a threat as early as possible, while their behavior is still able to be controlled. Adversary recognition is also important because, if we cannot determine who our adversary is or what the threat may be, we will not be able to act to stop it. Learning more about our adversary will allow us to think like them. The study of adversarial recognition also includes recognizing certain passenger profiles, an understanding of proactive profiling techniques, and the examination of surveillance detection methods specific to the aviation environment. You can use this information as a first responder in civil aviation to 1) help you identify individuals who may pose a risk to you and others around you and 2) to detect pre-attack surveillance. The study of this section and the melding of its knowledge with the previous section is one of the most important things that you can do to keep yourself safe in the aviation environment. If nothing else is taken away from this book, you should understand and apply the information in this section whenever you are working in the civil aviation environment. The application of information in this section will not only help you better protect the traveling passenger: the information contained within this section has the power to strengthen civil aviation as a whole. A thorough understanding of this section will help you better distinguish between baseline and deceptive behavior and allow you to articulate your observations to the appropriate law enforcement personnel.

DOI: 10.4324/9781003336457-6

5

Passenger Profiles

There are many types of passengers who fly on commercial aircraft. There are certain commonalities between the different passenger profiles that you should be aware of when traveling in the aviation environment. Passenger profiles can help you select a person in the cabin who may help you in an emergency, or it can help you identify passengers who might be a potential problem during flight. Awareness of the various passenger profiles will also help you better understand what behavioral indicators to look for in order to detect criminal activity on board. By spotting passengers who are more likely to cause problems in the aircraft environment, you can make the civil aviation a safer place for all air travelers. Common passenger profiles of those often encountered inside the aircraft with whom you should be aware include the *able-bodied passenger*, the *aisle hog*, the *asshole*, the *child*, the *drunk*, the *fat person*, the *sleeper*, and the *watcher*.

An *able-bodied passenger* is a passenger who appears physically and psychologically stable enough to help during an emergency or violent confrontation. The able-bodied person you select may be chosen because they are young, physically fit, or because they appear to be a military veteran. The able-bodied passenger can be any one of these types of passengers, however, above all things, they must be someone who you believe you can trust. The able-bodied passenger can be an extremely important part of any counter-hijack response because to stop a hijacking or inflight bombing attempt you must have help from other passengers. You cannot do it alone. You will need help. Although you may be the first to take action to stop a hijacking, you will want to recruit the help of able-bodied passengers and first responders as quickly as possible. Able-bodied

DOI: 10.4324/9781003336457-7

passengers can assist with restraining hijackers, blocking aisles, or providing security and overwatch of the cabin while first responders attend to other emergencies. As a first responder, you should try to identify able-bodied passengers during the boarding process. Able-bodied passengers who are identified prior to departure can be recalled much faster during an inflight emergency.

The *aisle hog* is important to be aware of because they may present an impediment (knowingly or unknowingly) during a hijacking or bombing attempt. An aisle hog can be easily identified because they will typically get out of their seats repeatedly during the flight to loiter in the aisles. First responders should remain aware of aisle hogs who are active during their flight. The aisle hog may be seen stretching, talking to other passengers, or simply standing in the aisle. Aisle hogs can be a nuisance because their movement in the cabin draws the eye of first responders like you who are on the lookout for suspicion indicators. An aisle hog's loitering can also inadvertently block the forward area and lavatories. Inflight security threat protocols (which will be covered in detail in a dedicated section of this book) require that the forward area be accessed quickly (within 3–5 seconds) and that all lavatories in the forward area be checked for passengers, weapons, and explosives. Because these two sensitive security areas (the forward area and forward lavatories) need to be quickly accessed during an inflight security threat, the aisle hog can inadvertently hinder the movement of first responders like you when there is a critical need for you to move unimpeded. It cannot be emphasized enough that the security of the forward area is vital to the security of the aircraft. Therefore, certain emergency situations may require you to physically remove an aisle hog from this sensitive security area.

The *asshole* is a particularly interesting passenger profile. The asshole's behavior can often times be entertaining to individuals in the cabin when it is not profane, but the danger with the asshole is that their behavior is often fueled by alcohol and frequently becomes a safety or security concern to passengers and cabin crew members. An asshole who, prior to takeoff, complains about their seat, argues with cabin crew members or passengers about their overhead bin space, or who verbalizes their dislike with their leg room, with other passengers, or with the airline, is a passenger who is likely to become a security concern in the air. The drunk asshole is a particularly worrisome security concern because their behavior is often unpredictable and aggressive. The asshole who is of most concern in the aviation environment is one who is extreme in their actions; for example, the unprovoked violent asshole who unexpectedly begins to hit other passengers in the cabin. Alcohol is usually associated with the violent asshole profile; however, the bizarre, drunken behavior of a violent asshole may be used as a diversion tactic by hijackers during the execution phase of a hijacking. For this reason, you should always maintain the security of the forward area whenever an asshole has been identified in the cabin.

The *child* is someone who could pose a distraction to you during an emergency response to an inflight security threat. The stress of an inflight security incident would be compounded by a screaming child. First responders who are accustomed to working and training in a stressful environment may not be distracted by a screaming child, however, a child can also exhibit unpredictable behavior which can draw the eye of first responders like you away from the threat. You may not have this type of experience or training, and a screaming child could be a major distraction to you during a hijacking or bombing attempt. You should be aware of any children on board within your seating area (or within your area of responsibility in the aircraft) and make a mental note of their location(s). You should expect screaming from passengers and children in the cabin during a hijacking or bombing attempt and should think critically by accounting for children in the cabin if you are required to react to a threat that threatens the integrity of the aircraft and/or the safety of the passengers, crew members, or fellow first responders.

The *fat person* is another important passenger profile for you to consider as a first responder. These oversized passengers can be used to block aisles or lavatories during a counter-hijack response. The fat person is easy to spot. They can typically be found leaning into the aisle, crowding neighboring passengers, and partially blocking the aisle while wearing a seat belt extender (a useful weapon for a first responder) to safely fasten their seat belts. The neighboring passengers of a fat person typically allow the obese passenger to sit in the aisle seat because it relieves pressure on those passengers with whom the fat person shares a neighboring seat. Thus, the fat person may be easier to use during an emergency because of their close proximity to the aisle. The fat person who is seated in the aisle, nearest to the forward area, can be thought of as an *able-bodied fat person*. Blocking techniques and the use of the able-bodied fat person will be discussed in detail in a later section. Oversized passengers can be used in many different ways during a counter-hijack response. One example would be using the able-bodied fat person as a makeshift ballistic shield in the event that a firearm is used in the cabin.

The *sleeper* is an important profile for you to be aware of because hijackers have used this passenger profile numerous times in the past.

A sleeper is most often used to provide security for the main hijack team. Quiet passengers who are not particularly interested (or concerned) with any of the activity around them inside the cabin (particularly during the initial execution phase of a hijacking) exhibit behavior that makes them good candidates for being considered a sleeper and should therefore be watched closely. As previously discussed, terrorist sleeper agents may remain in their seats long after a hijacking has begun. They may stay in this docile state in order to provide security for the hijackers, or to watch and warn of a response by passengers, inflight security officers, or other first responders like you. Interestingly enough, the sleeper profile exhibits many of the same behavioral signs as an inflight security officer. The sleeper will have a keen awareness of passenger and crew activity on board during times of stress, such as during a hijacking or bombing attempt, and may display hypersensitivity toward violence: although a sleeper may attempt to feign interest in the activity around them during a hijacking, they will exhibit a hypersensitivity and awareness that contradicts their relaxed pose. The sleeper is likely to have some form of religious, philosophical, or other bonds with members of the hijack team. Like the bond between law enforcement officers, it will cause a sleeper to act in predictable ways. For example, the sleeper may appear to make mutual eye contact (with mutual awareness) with other members of the hijack team, or may be especially interested in hijacker activities on board.

Sleeper behavior can be expected by law enforcement officers or military veterans on board, untrained in inflight security, during a violent hijacking. These people are accustomed to running toward danger, not away from it. Because of their combat mindset and lack of inflight security training, the behavior of those previously mentioned will closely mimic that of a sleeper. Like the sleeper, these able-bodied passengers may show aggressive behavioral indicators (e.g., clenching fists, narrowing eyes) or more subtle behavior which suggests they wish to get up from their seat to counter the hijacking. First responder should be aware of these able-bodied passengers and channel their energy, if needed, in a useful way. This type of passenger can be thought of as an *able-bodied sleeper*.

Daniel Lewin is an example of an able-bodied sleeper. Mr. Lewin, a passenger on American Airlines flight 11 on September 11, 2001, was a former counter-terrorism expert and combat veteran. He was accustomed to keeping a low profile. Because of his training and experience, it is believed that Mr. Lewin observed the hijacker activities on board and planned to make an attempt to stop it during the initial execution phase. After witnessing the murder of a flight attendant or both pilots, it is assumed that Mr. Lewin's training led him to attack the hijacker in front of him. Although Mr. Lewin's actions were noble, he failed to realize that a sleeper was seated behind him. The sleeper who was seated behind Mr. Lewin was most likely waiting for the initial hijack team to finish gaining control of the cabin before joining them. Although the exact circumstances that led to the death of Mr. Lewin will likely never be known, inflight security officers use his death as a teaching point on tactics. When seated in the cabin while reacting to a security threat, you should always look behind you before standing up from your seat (known colloquially as a *six-check*).

The *watcher* is the final passenger profile we will discuss. The watcher is one of the most important passenger profiles for you to be aware of as a first responder because these passengers are especially aware of inflight security procedures and protocols. The watcher is a passenger who is observant of activity around them and hypersensitive to the movements of flight and cabin crew members during flight. These passengers can often be spotted watching the interactions of flight attendants with other passengers in the aircraft and the movement of other able-bodied passengers in the cabin. The watcher will be keen to observe flight crew members as they prepare to enter or exit the cockpit door and they may stare intently at the interactions between the flight crew and cabin crew members during this time. A passenger who fits this profile may exhibit behavior that suggests pre-attack surveillance is being conducted or that the preparation for the execution phase of a hijacking is underway. The watcher can be detected by their behavioral indicators, such as displaying an extra heightened awareness of their surroundings when compared with the baseline awareness of other passengers who are seated around them. Military veterans, law enforcement officers, air marshals, and other passengers with security experience will likely display these same behavioral indicators. Depending on your role in the aircraft as a first responder, critical thinking can be used to allow you to maintain a low profile in the cabin. It is important to maintain a low profile in the aircraft environment for certain first responders (e.g., air marshals) in order for them to better leverage their training during an inflight security threat. By maintaining low-profile, first responders like you can use the act of surprise when you are called upon to react to threats to the integrity of the aircraft or the safety of passengers, crew members, or fellow first responders.

After applying the principles in this book, you may begin to show some of the same behavioral traits that you seek to detect. Thus, it is important that you remain conscious of this and attempt to maintain a low profile while you assume a proactive security posture. By practicing proactive security in a low-profile manner, you can place yourself in an advantageous position for leveraging control during a hijacking or inflight bombing attempt.

6

Proactive Profiling

In this chapter, we turn our focus on how to spot criminal and terrorist behavior in the aviation environment. *Behavioral detection* is taught to inflight security officers around the world to help them detect criminal or terrorist activity during their daily duties. This includes those methods that are used in an attempt to detect terrorist behavior prior to an attack, usually during the pre-attack surveillance, or rehearsal phase. It should be noted that behavioral detection methods rely on signs of stress and behavioral indicators that could also be exhibited by a passenger who is simply under distress. Therefore, behavioral detection methods are more likely to cause first responders to rely on personal bias and racial indicators than on *suspicion indicators* and reasonable suspicion.

Because of these limitations, we combine the behavioral detection method with the Israeli method of *predictive profiling*. Predictive profiling focuses on suspicion indicators as they relate to known and predicted methods of terrorist attack planning in the civil aviation domain. Therefore, predictive profiling is less susceptible to personal bias than behavioral detection. By combining the two methods, we create a powerful tool for detecting deceptive activity. The combination of these two methods is known as *proactive profiling*. For our purposes, proactive profiling is defined as the search for and observation and analysis of suspicion indicators.

Proactive profiling cannot be performed with any success unless you can recognize baseline behavior in your immediate environment. Baseline behavior is that which is considered normal and which flows with a rhythm of commonality, following and closing matching local customs and societal norms. Therefore, baseline behavior can change depending on the environment where it is observed. A recognition of

DOI: 10.4324/9781003336457-8

baseline behavior can only be accomplished by going into the specific aviation environment within which you will work and actively observing passenger behavior.

If an inflight security officer tried to explain what behavior detection is, they would probably mention something about *profiling*. Many books have been written on the subject of detecting deceptive behavior in the controlled and structured environment of an interview room. Unfortunately, not much has been written on spotting behavioral signs of deception in the chaotic environment of an airport or aircraft. Although behavioral patterns and nonverbal indicators are important to be aware of, we do not want to simply profile people, situations, and objects. Rather, we want to profile the *method of operation* of the adversary as it applies to a person, situation, or object.

THE PROACTIVE PROFILING METHOD

An *adversary method of operation*, or AMO, is important for you to understand because it will allow you to profile the *protected environment*, or the specific environment where you wish to deny the threat of an adversary. The adversary method of operation is the method by which an adversary will carry out an attack in your specifically designated, protected environment. Some examples of behavior associated with the adversary method of operation are, an individual who establishes a commercial company for terrorist cover; an individual who recruits an employee from within the aviation environment to help with a terrorist attack; an individual who uses an unsuspecting individual to deliver a bomb into the aviation environment; an individual who uses an emergency vehicle for transportation during the ground assault of an aircraft.

As a first responder in civil aviation, it is important for you to think outside of the box and for you to realize that your determination of the adversary method of operation should not be based solely on what terrorists and criminals did in the past; your decision should account for past attacks against civil aviation and should also take into account what terrorist might be able to do to attack civil aviation in the future. If we only account for AMOs of the past and fail to predict AMOs of the future, we narrow our perspective and resort to a way of thinking that helped contribute to the security failures of September 11, 2001. This is one of the reasons why you should try to think like a terrorist when practicing proactive profiling because it will help you to think of new ways an adversary could attack the protected environment.

For every adversary method of operation, there are *suspicion indicators*. A suspicion indicator is defined as an indication based on known or predicted terrorist or criminal methods of operation and/or the deviation from a typical profile that would lead a reasonable person to believe that an observed situation, person, or object has the potential for harming the protected environment. By merely deviating from a typical passenger profile, a passenger cannot necessarily be called suspicious; however, terrorists and criminals who engage in hostile activity and use cover stories to hide their true identities will ultimately deviate from a typical passenger profile or from the profile which they initially portray during, and prior to, boarding the aircraft.

Consider the difference between *suspicious* and *odd*. The difference is that, in order to call someone suspicious, the indication, behavior, attire, or position must also correlate with an adversary method of operation. Odd is anything that is abnormal. Therefore, the *proactive security process* involves detecting suspicion, determining the threat, and identifying the adversary method of operation. Once we know the AMO, we can deploy against it. The proactive security process is essentially, (1) detect suspicion, (2) determine the threat, and (3) deploy against the threat after identifying the adversary method of operation.

DETECTING SUSPICION

To detect suspicion, we must identify suspicion indicators and attempt to refute them based on our environment and the context of the situation. This proactive security process is human-based because the ability to determine the method of operation, refute suspicion indicators, and deploy counter-measures against a threat can only be done safely and effectively by humans. The layout of this book is such that the first few sections teach you how to determine the method of operation and refute suspicion indicators, while the last few sections teach you how to deploy against a threat.

To refute suspicion indicators, we must focus on refuting the suspicion instead of the indicator. An example of this would be an individual who has extensive metal piercings on their body. This person may go through a magnetometer numerous times, but we can expect that they will continue to set off the alarm. A security officer who attempts to refute the *indicator* instead of the suspicion will continue to have the person remove their jewelry and pass through the magnetometer until the alarm stops.

A security officer who attempts to refute the *suspicion* instead of the indicator would do so by identifying whether or not the piercings could be used as part of a weapon or bomb and by determining if there is a plausible reason for the passenger to wear the piercings. By refuting the suspicion of this adversary method of operation (i.e., bringing an explosive into the sterile area of an airport), or disproving that the piercings could be used as pieces in a bomb or weapon, then the security officer can rule out the use of these ear piercings as a dangerous item. Always refute the suspicion, not the indicator.

Airport security officers, transportation security officers, and checkpoint security screeners too often attempt to refute the indicator instead of the suspicion. This type of security leaves security checkpoints (the gateway into the sterile area) extremely vulnerable. Refuting the indicator is considered a lazy approach to security. Refuting the indication, however, can often be a long and tedious security process. Some indications simply cannot be refuted, such as a person who has an artificial hip implant. This example requires refuting the suspicion, as opposed to the indication. This could be accomplished by questioning the individuals about their hip to find out if the backstory for the alarm (suspicion) is legitimate. These kinds of investigative methods are used by security personnel in Israel to refute suspicions instead of relying too heavily on the unreliability of indicators.

Detection technology is often considered an alternative to giving security officers better training in proactive profiling techniques. As we now know, the proactive security process is human-based, because determining the adversary method of operation, refuting suspicion indicators, and performing countermeasures can only be done by humans. A proactive security process that uses well-trained humans is better than a technology-based system because a human-based system is more unpredictable and harder to operationally defeat. An example of this is the fact that the majority of suicide bombers are first identified by suspicion indicators related to their behavior, attire, or identity, not because the bomb was detected by technology. *Find the bomber, then the bomb* is the analogy we can apply here. By using this analogy, you can remind yourself of the importance of behavioral detection and the need to refute suspicion indicators during the proactive security process.

Although detection technology can be helpful to the security process, it is really only useful in helping people detect suspicious objects. Technology cannot be relied on to find criminals or terrorists. An example of a major failure of technology to detect suspicious objects that is worthy of examination for critical thinking purposes occurred on September 11, 2001, when airport security officers failed to find box-cutters on two of the American Airlines Flight 77 hijackers who were both searched with a handheld metal detector. One of the hijacker's bags was even subject to secondary screening that used explosives trace detection technology; however, because the hijackers carried no explosives and were using a low-tech method of operation, the box-cutters they carried as part of their hijack toolkit were never discovered by technological means. Regardless of the security detection methods and procedures on September 11, box-cutters were not considered a viable threat at the time and would have been allowed through the security checkpoint even if they had been detected.

Suspicion indicators are important because they help us distinguish criminal and terrorist passenger behavior from baseline behavior that would be expected from normal passengers. Examples of suspicion indicators include, a person facing the wrong way in a crowd; an individual who is unusually dressed compared to others around them; someone wearing professional business attire while carrying a plastic bag for their personal items; a passenger who gets in and out of their seat continuously for no apparent reason. Certain passengers (like the aisle hog who stands in the aisle for long periods of time) may arouse your suspicion or warrant extra scrutiny during flight or in the airport. For example, passengers who seem to know each other in the airport and later ignore each other on the aircraft are presenting suspicion indicators that have been identified in previous hijackings. Suspicion indicators may include someone pushing a luggage cart through the airport but never taking their hands from the handles, as was the case with the terrorist suicide bombers who attacked the Brussels international airport in 2016. Therefore, when you search for suspicion indicators, you are not doing it without methodology; you refute the suspicion based on a past or predicted method of criminal or terrorist operation. After reading this book, your ability to think more critically about aviation security will expand exponentially and will allow you to predict other methods of operation; these predictions can be used by you to detect suspicion indicators in the aviation environment and to justify and articulate your actions as a first responder.

For each of the previous examples, you would need to have a potential method of operation to refute before you can say whether or not what you are seeing is a threat. A person who is facing the opposite way as others in a crowd may be signaling to their partner for the execution phase of an attack, or they may simply be a passenger searching for a loved one. To raise our suspicion, the environment needs to be one worth attacking. A large crowd is an attractive target to a terrorist, therefore, you should remain especially aware for suspicion indicators in dense groups of people. By taking into account your environment type and predicted method of operation, you can then refute the suspicion by either (1) directly investigating it or (2) notifying law enforcement officers or security personnel about your suspicions. Inflight security is especially precarious for first responders like you because these two options are not always readily available in the cabin during flight.

A good example of suspicion indicators during a terrorist operation would be the pre-attack surveillance conducted for the London Underground bombings which was captured via closed-circuit television. The terrorists who conducted surveillance for the bomb plot displayed suspicious behavior that could have potentially been detected before the attacks. These surveillance operatives did suspicious things. For example, they bought tickets and then walked down to the train platform and loitered around (presumably to observe passenger activity), and then turned around and walked through the rolling gates and out of the metro station. This behavior is suspicious because normal baseline behavior involves a predictable sequence of events: passengers normally buy a ticket, walk to their desired platform, and board a train.

DETERMINING THE THREAT

Security is typically approached with a risk-oriented mindset. Although this perspective can be useful in many security situations, it is not as effective for civil aviation security applications. Consequently, to determine a threat in civil aviation, you must be *threat-oriented*. The easiest way to distinguish the two is that a risk-oriented approach is when people use statistics to predict future risk, whereas a threat-oriented approach is when people accept that they will be attacked regardless of statistics. You may recognize hostile intent from an aggressor, identify vulnerabilities, or may have some prior experience that peaks your awareness to a particular threat. Therefore, when you refute suspicion indicators, you should remain threat-oriented in your security approach. The potential catastrophe that comes from high-consequence events, such as aircraft hijackings, bombings, and airport attacks requires a critical thinking approach that is made possible by adopting a threat-oriented mindset.

There are many benefits to being a threat-oriented first responder. One of the main benefits is that it will force you to actively search for suspicion indicators; this is in contrast to the risk-oriented approach where individuals discount the possibility of an attack and assume that some obvious signs of a terrorist attack will alert them to impending danger. By adopting a threat-oriented approach, you can significantly increase your chances of catching a terrorist during the terrorist planning cycle.

The consequences of an aircraft being hijacked and used as a weapon of mass destruction, or of a terrorist detonating a suicide bomb on board, are so high that first responders like you do not have the luxury of waiting patiently for this kind of violence to be committed. Instead, you must be proactive in your approach to prevent violent crimes in civil aviation from occurring. This is referred to as *proactive security*, the combined use of behavioral detection and predictive profiling. An environment where suspicion indicators are being scrutinized by first responders would be very uncomfortable for a terrorist operative, making those suspicion indicators all the easier to spot.

Terrorists and criminals are especially vigilant and suspicious of being detected. This state of heightened awareness and paranoia is sometimes used by law enforcement officers in order to probe individuals who are displaying suspicion indicators. This is done by staring at the suspect to make them feel uncomfortable; by standing directly over, or next to them; or by directly questioning the suspicious individual. Law enforcement officers typically make either *official or non-official* contact with a suspicious individual, distinguished by whether or not the law enforcement officer identified their official status during questioning. By asking a suspicious individual questions or placing them in a position of stress, you can also use probing to provoke a response that may lead to more suspicion indicators.

THREAT-ORIENTED VERSUS RISK-ORIENTED APPROACH

Risk-oriented people tend to think that, because nothing happened yesterday, last week, nor the past year, then nothing should happen today. Whereas a risk-oriented person would think "terrorists would never attack this airport, nor this aircraft," a threat-oriented person would think "attacks in aircraft and airports have happened before and are bound to happen again." Most people, unfortunately, use more of a *risk*-oriented approach to security when they are in public places or at work. In fact, the very system by which the TSA determines which aircraft inflight security officers should perform security for is done by using a risk-based approach. Take a moment to stop and think about this: What kind of security perspective (risk-oriented *or* threat-oriented) do you take when protecting the things that matter most to you? It may take you a few minutes to think about this, but that is okay. Take your time and give it some real thought. Most people tend to take more of threat-oriented approach when it comes to protecting the people they love and the important things they own. When we use a threat-oriented security approach, we are more aware of people, things, and situations.

THREAT ASSESSMENT

To perform a threat assessment, you should assess the potential methods of operation. This is done by following the previously discussed concepts; however, you must remain *threat-orientated*. An example of threat orientation would be if you came home from work early one day and found that your partner was not at home as usual. You call their cellphone and leave several messages but they do not answer. Your partner then comes home an hour later with messy hair and looks surprised that you are home early. You smell an odor of perfume on your partner that you do not recognize. Given this example, you may think that the method of operation was that your partner is cheating. This happens because you are being threat-oriented with your partner. If you were risk-oriented, you may think to yourself "My partner has never cheated on me, so why would they cheat on me now." There is no discernible difference with the process by which we detect potential infidelity and the process by which we detect criminal or terrorist activity. The only difference is your attitude and your orientation toward the threat and risk-based thinking.

Another thing for you to consider as you become accustomed to a threat-oriented security approach is that we should acknowledge something as either a *threat* or a *non-threat*. There is no in-between. There are also no ratings for our threat orientation, such as severe, elevated, high, low, red, green, orange, etcetera. Either there is a threat, or there is not a threat. By thinking in this manner, we are taking a more proactive approach to the civil aviation security process. Take a moment and imagine yourself sitting inside the cabin of an aircraft inflight. Is there a threat of the aircraft being hijacked? Yes, there is a definite threat of the aircraft being hijacked. Is there a threat to the aircraft being destroyed by a suicide bomber? No doubt about it, yes there is. By asking yourself questions like these and by thinking more critically about your protected environment, you will be a more effective first responder and bolster civil aviation security in the process.

DEPLOYING AGAINST THE ADVERSARY

In order to *deploy* against an adversary, we must identify the method of operation. (Deployment strategies can be thought of as a kind of playbook for how to react to a given threat or immediate danger to the integrity of the aircraft, or the safety of the passengers, crew members, or fellow first responders.) To identify the method of operation, we will use some of the previous examples of hijackings and bombings that we studied in the previous chapter to predict other attack methods that have not yet been used. On September 11, 2001, there was a failure to determine the method of operation, that is, a terrorist hijacking. Although the suicide hijacker-pilot plot had been tried before outside of the United States, nobody foresaw this tactic as being used to attack a commercial or government building in the continental United States (especially not the coordinated hijacking of multiple aircraft). Because of this failure to identify the method of operation on September 11, the deployment procedures of passengers and first responders on board the hijacked aircraft were inadequate by the time suspicion indicators had been identified. The adversary method of operation is important because it determines how and when you should take action to stop a threat. For example, a passenger in the cabin who is physically assaulting other passengers may have a method of operation in that they are drunk and frustrated and directing their aggression at passengers. An unlikely and unhelpful deployment strategy, therefore, would be to stand up and break the aggressor's neck. If you were flying on an aircraft and a passenger sitting next to you tried to light a fuse coming out of their shoe, however, breaking the suspect's neck may be a deployment strategy that you would consider. This is because the potential method of operation in the latter example is that, the passenger is a suicide terrorist attempting to detonate an explosive concealed in their shoe.

Law enforcement officers who perform security in civil aviation study subjects like *use of force* that teaches them to determine how much physical force should be applied (or what actions can lawfully be taken) in order to restrain or stop a threatening individual from harming others. Particularly inside the aircraft, the important thing for you to remember as a first responder inflight in particular, is that the aircraft environment is an especially unique security environment from which there is no viable escape during an emergency. You should always remain cognizant of this fact when inside the aircraft. Always exercise your critical thinking skills, training, education, and the totality of the circumstances before deciding what deployment strategy is warranted in a given situation. Most deployment strategies take only fractions of a second to put into action; however, a given situation may warrant a slow, more cautious approach. Regardless of the situation, if time allows, you should always carefully consider and weigh your various deployment options (explained in detail in a later section). Proactive security focuses on *prevention*. And as a practitioner of proactive security, your goal should be to prevent the adversary from approaching, entering, and operating within the protected environment. As a first responder in civil aviation, reasonable suspicion that is based on your knowledge, training and experience will guide your preventative security approach.

REASONABLE SUSPICION

Law enforcement officers must have reasonable suspicion that a crime has taken place, *or* is taking place, in order for them to make an arrest, detain an individual, or otherwise take some kind of law enforcement action. Reasonable suspicion is typically based on an officer's training and experience and is examined in court through the lens of what another "reasonable" officer, with similar training and experience, would do in a similar circumstance. It is difficult, however, for a law enforcement officer to find reasonable suspicion in an unfamiliar environment (like the inside of an aircraft cabin during flight). This includes a failure for law enforcement officers to realize how certain aspects of their environment may give them more, or less, leeway in assigning reasonable suspicion. This book can serve to expand the training and education of law enforcement officers who read it because its informational content is consistent with current US inflight security standards. The information in this book, used in combination with your specific experience and training as a first responder, can easily be used to justify and articulate reasonable suspicion in an aircraft or airport. You cannot reasonably justify restraining or physically attacking an individual because of your intuition. Instead, you must be able to intelligently articulate the reasons for your actions, and these actions must be considered reasonable by other first responders such as other cabin crew members, or law enforcement/inflight security officers. By thoroughly understanding the aircraft (or airport) environment and considering all aspects of how that environment affects your decision making process, you will be able to more critically evaluate threats to the integrity of the aircraft and the safety of passengers, flight crew members and fellow first responders, and will be better prepared to justify your actions during a hijacking or bombing attempt.

From a tactical perspective, the inflight environment is unique. The aircraft cabin is essentially a long, hollow tube. If there is a dangerous situation in the cabin during flight, there is no viable escape for a passenger without the use of a parachute. Reasonable suspicion should take this into account and should rely heavily on the use of suspicion indicators and the method of operation based on your training, knowledge, and experience.

BEHAVIORAL DETECTION

Many airports around the world have behavioral detection officers who look for suspicious activity. But what do these security officers do? Behavioral detection officers all have one thing in common: they focus on nonverbal indicators of criminal or terrorist behavior. Studies suggest that more than two-thirds of human communication is nonverbal. By closely observing nonverbal indicators, you can increase your chances of detecting deception.

Many of the methods used in behavioral detection come from case studies of past terrorist and criminal attacks. As a whole, terrorists exhibit many of the same behavioral indicators when they are preparing for an attack as does a pickpocket who is looking for their next target. Terrorists and criminals, therefore, not only follow the same planning cycle, they also exhibit the same signs of stress. Airports and aircraft have particular areas where criminals or terrorists are most likely to find themselves under stress and therefore, more vulnerable to observation; these *areas of stress* will be explained in detail later in this chapter. Behavioral detection officers are taught to look for indicators of stress like fidgeting; staring intently at a person or potential target; pacing; praying aloud; and other behavior that is out of context for the environment. Unfortunately, there is no single sign of stress that can tell you whether or not an individual is a danger to your protected environment. When you embrace proactive security and apply critical thinking to the proactive security process, however, it is possible for you to recognize the behavioral indicators and increase the confidence of your decisions.

Behavioral indicators for a terrorist hijacker who is preparing to hijack an aircraft might include intently watching cabin crew activities, and an interest in cabin and flight crew location, and of cockpit door procedures. In contrast, a pickpocket on a subway might stare intently at a particular passenger (e.g., someone who is not particularly aware of their surroundings) and will likely exhibit a keen awareness of their surroundings, nearby passengers and train exits. Although a terrorist hijacker and a criminal pickpocket will exhibit signs of stress in different ways, the common factor is that they both must surveil their target prior to initiating their attack. Surveillance of the target is necessary for the terrorist attack planner, and this is the best time for you to detect them.

Although a hijack team may perform dozens of surveillance flights during the planning phase, things can change on the day of the attack. Flight attendants may be more vigilant with aircraft security; pilots may be more conscious about flight deck security; some of the passengers may fit the profile of an inflight security officer; or there may be some other obstacle to the hijacking observed by the hijacker(s). This is an example of some of the information that a hijacker (or hijack team) would want to assess through surveillance prior to executing an attack. There are many suspicion indicators for the previous examples that would allow you to justify your actions if you chose to respond. These suspicion indicators most often include paying an abnormal amount of attention to flight crew duties and security procedures inside the aircraft during flight. The adversary method of operation could indicate that surveillance is being performed for a hijacking or that a hijacking is in progress (in the execution phase).

When passengers are situationally aware, it forces a would-be hijacker or bomber to change tactics, because they are not accustomed to having their activities readily observed or known. You can improve your ability to predict future attacks and to observe suspicion indicators in civil aviation by allowing yourself to think like a terrorist hijacker (or bomber). In fact, there is nobody better than you, to predict future attacks in civil aviation. This is because you work in the aviation environment on a constant basis. You understand things about aircraft and airports that the traditional passenger does not. You can use this understanding to predict future attacks and make civil aviation safer for everyone. Remaining situationally aware of your environment will enhance these abilities.

What does it mean to be *situationally aware?* Most people are so busy with their lives that they fail to notice their surroundings as they walk through an airport. Passengers may pay slightly more attention to an aircraft than they do to their surroundings in an airport, but this is only because everyone is forced into a smaller area. Unfortunately for civil aviation security, modern distractions make it fairly easy for terrorists and criminals to surveil targets in the public domain without being noticed. Having situational awareness means having an awareness of the behavior of those around you, even when you are carrying out daily tasks. For example, while working in the aircraft galley to prepare the aircraft for take-off, you become aware of a person boarding the aircraft who is wearing a heavy coat on a warm summer day. Perhaps this individual is concealing something? The passenger exhibits suspicion indicators, sweating heavily and avoiding eye contact with a law enforcement officer who is standing in the jetway. This behavior might suggest that the passenger is a potential threat to the protected environment and may warrant further investigation or notification of nearby security or law enforcement personnel. Remaining situational aware is one of the most helpful things you can do to make airports and aircraft safer. By remaining aware and maintaining a proactive security posture, you will be better able to recognize deceptive behavior.

As you continue to expand your critical thinking skills as a first responder in civil aviation, you may find yourself questioning the security of your protected environment on a more regular basis. Those of you who work in the aircraft might ask yourself: How could a terrorist breach the flight deck door? Does our flight crew have robust security procedures? Are there any major vulnerabilities on our flight? Those of you who work in airports may ask yourselves: Does our airport have behavioral detection officers? Are there particular areas of my airport that are especially vulnerable to attack? How can these areas be identified? Terrorists think about these things and, as a first responder in civil aviation, so should you. Some other questions you might ask yourself are: How could someone smuggle weapons and explosives past the security checkpoint at my airport? How might a hijacker react to a first responder like me who tries to interfere with their plans? Where might a terrorist place an explosive device on the aircraft (or inside the airport) without being caught? When we embrace a proactive security mindset, we think one step ahead of the prospective terrorist hijacker and bomber. In this way, it is possible for us to spot deceptive behavior in others.

Environment, context, and *location* are important factors for you to consider when trying to determine a method of operation and refute suspicion indicators. It is also important to understand that not all aircraft or airports will have the same expected baseline behavioral norms. Depending on what country's airport you are in (or which aircraft you are flying on), there may be a slight difference in baseline passenger behavior that you would typically find at your home airport. Also, depending on the particular location of the suspect, they may (or may not) be in a position to hurt themselves or others and therefore, they may not be an immediate threat. For example, a person who is avoiding eye contact with law enforcement officers and is also pushing an overloaded luggage cart near a concrete column may be in a position to execute an attack. In this particular example, the adversary method of operation would be: a terrorist placing a bomb near a load-bearing column of the airport. The suspect's location next to a large structural column would place the bag in a position that would cause maximum structural damage if there was an explosion. Therefore, the suspicion in this particular case would need to be refuted that this is not a terrorist attack. If during questioning, the suspect says that the bag is not theirs (even after the individual was observed walking in the airport with the bag), then the suspicion cannot be refuted and the bag must be considered a threat. The deployment against this threat would need to be considered carefully and would depend on whether the first responder who observed this behavior was an unarmed passenger, armed law enforcement officer, or security professional. A typical law enforcement response to this particular situation would be to evacuate the immediate area around the bag and to avoid using any radio or other device which transmits an electrical signal (because this may inadvertently cause the device to detonate). It is important that you always consider your immediate environment and the totality of circumstances of a situation before you consider something (or someone) a threat. And by concentrating on suspicion indicators and attempting to refute them, you will place yourself in the best possible position to determine if an adversary method of operation is an immediate threat to your protected environment.

SPOTTING BEHAVIORAL INDICATORS

When trying to spot behavioral indicators, you should try to answer the *Five Ws: who, what, when, where,* and *why*. We use the Five W's when we are comparing the suspect's behavior with the baseline behavior in the suspect's immediate environment. When someone draws your attention in the airport or aircraft, you may ask yourself: *Who* is this person? *What* is the possibility that this person may carry out an attack? *When* could an attack occur? *Where* might an attack occur? *Why* would this person want to carry out an attack?

We should also ask *How will the individual attack?* because it is of utmost importance to know what the mechanism of attack or adversary method of operation is, especially if we are going to develop a successful deployment strategy to counter the threat. In aircraft, there are two potential avenues of attack: hijackings and bombings. In airports, the two avenues of attack are bombings and mass shootings.

Your environment can offer clues to a particular adversary method of operation. Suicide bombers have been known to wear heavy coats to conceal their explosive devices. If a person is seen sweating in a heavy coat while transiting a hot airport, this could be considered a suspicion indicator. Why doesn't the person take off the coat if they are sweating? This is a good question, but it also depends upon other factors as well. For example, there was a fashion trend for many years in the United States where young men would wear heavy coats, even while it was hot outside. If this behavior was observed in the United States (during a particular epoch), then this choice of attire might not automatically suggest a potential suicide bomber.

A proactive approach to the previous example would be to determine the adversary method of operation and to try to refute the suspicion. Depending on the circumstances and your training, experience, and physical abilities and hindrances, you may or may not want to attempt to use physical force against an individual for whom a suspicion cannot be refuted, or against an individual who is observed as an immediate threat to your protected environment. By considering the totality of the circumstances and your education, experience, and physical abilities, you will be better prepared to offer an intelligent response to violent situations on board.

TRAPS OF BEHAVIORAL DETECTION

Inflight security officers who have little international travel experience before they begin flying missions have a tendency to use more of a racial profiling approach to detect deceptive behavior. These individuals are trapped by their own bias and therefore, they cannot truly apply proactive profiling techniques as their training prescribes. Focusing solely on a person's race, culture, and language will not help you detect deceptive behavior. When selecting suicide hijackers and bombers for attack preparation, terrorist organizations often select people who will blend in with locals and who have no documented contact with law enforcement or intelligence officials, and no known links to terrorists. Terrorists who have no previous law enforcement record are considered *clean*. A terrorist operative who is clean will not raise unwanted attention or scrutiny from law enforcement or intelligence agencies. Instead of basing our observations on racial cues, we want to concentrate on observing passengers who do not fit in with their immediate environment and who exhibit signs of stress in certain areas of that environment. To look for suspicion indicators and how they may relate to an adversary method of operation, we must ignore our bias and concentrate on the potential threats to our protected environment. As a proactive security practitioner, you should avoid the trap of using race as a means of detecting deceptive or criminal behavior because this will only cloud your ability to spot suspicion indicators.

AREAS OF STRESS

There are particular areas inside the airport and aircraft (and there are certain official persons who are commonly encountered in the aviation environment) that will cause stress reactions in deceptive passengers. To clarify, the deceptive passenger who you should be most concerned about is the passenger who is attempting to carry a bomb or weapon into a protected environment. These are the deceptive passengers on whom you should focus your attention when trying to determine what areas of the aviation environment will cause them the most stress. For example, some of the authority figures and physical areas inside an aircraft or airport that could invoke a stress response in a deceptive individual would be *baggage handlers and screeners; security officers at checkpoints; captain* and *first-officer; flight attendants* or other *flight crew members; uniformed law enforcement officers; airline gate agents; police canine units;* the *forward area of the aircraft; near aircraft lavatories;* and the *above-the-wing seating section.*

Deceptive passengers who are a danger to civil aviation security will be trying to perform some kind of violent action in an airport or aircraft. During operational planning (or just prior to attack execution), this individual will seek to determine when the best time to execute their attack will be. The individual will display signs of stress in areas that are vital to the success of the terrorist plot, such as the forward area, lavatories, or when the adversary is in close proximity to flight attendants and pilots who the individual may plan on killing or controlling during the hijacking. Since the physiological and autonomic responses of the body under stress cannot be controlled, the individual can be expected to show certain signs of stress. These signs may surface in the adversary for many reasons. For example, a hijacker who intends to kill a flight attendant in the cabin may exhibit signs of stress because they are thinking about whether or not the flight attendant knows their true intentions, or they may be visualizing the act of killing the flight attendant. The close physical proximity of a criminal to their target is likely to provoke a response. Some of the signs of stress that an adversary may display include a *nervous twitch*

or habit; avoiding or retreating from the area of stress; micro-expressions inconsistent with environment or context; sweating profusely; carotid artery pulsation;
and *performing known pre-attack rituals.*

SIGNS OF STRESS

A *nervous twitch or habit* can come in many forms. A twitch could come on as
an uncontrollable muscle spasm (or physical tic), while a nervous habit could
be a behavioral pattern that could probably be controlled with awareness and
conscious thought (such as placing and removing hands from one's pockets).
The flight or fight response is strong, causing a physical response that can be
observed by a situationally aware proactive security practitioner.

Avoiding or retreating from an area of stress includes a passenger who
approaches a security checkpoint and then quickly turns around and
leaves the area. This could happen in any of the previously described
areas of stress in airports and on the aircraft, or it could happen in the
presence of an authority figure. This is a flight response and a physical
reaction to the heightened psychological stress that a terrorist or criminal
succumbs to when they are close to the target area or within close proximity to a symbol of authority. This stress response is often provoked by
law enforcement using probing techniques. *Probing* is a proactive security
tactic, the goal of which is to provoke a stress response in a suspect individual. Undercover law enforcement officers may use probing in the airport by watching a suspect individual's response when plain-clothed law
enforcement officers walk within close proximity to them. Does the suspect show signs of stress? Does the suspect individual appear to retreat,
or avoid eye contact? Signs like these could be subtle. For example, a suspect may merely point their feet toward the nearest exit. Signs of stress
might also be more obvious; for example, a suspect could begin to walk,
or run away. Regardless of type, signs of stress indicate that the suspect
warrants further observation. Past suicide bombers have been known to
retreat prior to an attack and later be coaxed back to the target by other
members of the terrorist organization.

Micro-expressions inconsistent with environment or context means those
expressions that an individual displays within microseconds and which
are inconsistent with those expressions we would expect to see within the
context of a given situation. These micro-expressions are best spotted during direct questioning, such as during interrogation of the suspect; however, they can also be observed when you are having a casual conversation
with the suspect. The seven basic human facial expressions are anger, fear,

disgust, surprise, sadness, happiness, and contempt. Deceptive behavior can be spotted by observing these micro-expressions which do not fit the context of a conversation (or event) and by determining why these particular micro-expressions might be displayed. The method involved in using micro-expressions is somewhat subjective, and it may not be the perfect tool to use during a life-or-death situation. It is hard to determine what a person is thinking and why an individual's micro-expressions may be suspicious. Therefore, it is important to realize that any attempt you make at determining threats in the aviation environment using micro-expressions should be used in combination with other proactive security practices (e.g., refuting suspicion indicators). Although the art of reading micro-expressions is something that takes practice and expertise to be able to use with any reliability, it is important to have a good foundational understanding of micro-expressions. The following seven emotions and their hallmark features are explained here to assist you in your future observations and security awareness.

ANGER

With the anger expression, the person appears to glare. Eyebrows are pulled down together. Often confused with disgust, with anger, the eyebrows are pulled down much farther. Lips are typically pressed tightly together. The eyes also glare more with anger than with disgust.

DISGUST

The only trademark sign of expression for disgust is the square-shaped upper lip. Often confused with anger, all of the action of disgust is in the center of the face. There are two different versions of the disgust expression. The upper lip is raised in both versions; however, the brow is pulled down more in one version than the other. There is more of a scrunching of the nose when the brows are pulled down.

FEAR

Fear is often confused with surprise. Lips are often pulled back in the expression. Eyebrows are raised and straightened.

SURPRISE

Surprise is often confused with fear. Lips are often relaxed in the expression. Eyebrows are raised and curved.

CONTEMPT

The only unilateral face movement. All action occurs on one side of the face.

HAPPINESS

Easiest expression to recognize even when slight. The lips are pulled up in both expressions, which are distinguished as being more, or less, intense. For the more intensely felt smile there is a slight lowering of the skin between the eyebrows and the upper eye lid.

SADNESS

Upper eyelid often droops and the lip corners are pulled down slightly.
     The inner corners of the eyebrows are raised in the center of the forehead.

These micro-expressions happen quickly, in microseconds. The study of micro-expressions is a worthwhile one for those who wish to have a truly diverse proactive profiling approach. This subject was pioneered by psychologist Paul Eckman, PhD. Although there is a definite place for using micro-expression recognition in spotting deceptive behavior in the aviation environment, it should only be applied if the practitioner is well-versed in micro-expression detection methods. Further study on the subject can be found in the book *Telling Lies: Clues to Deceit in the Marketplace, Politics, and Marriage* by Paul Eckman.
     A passenger may also begin *sweating profusely* when they come under a significant amount of stress. As one of our previous examples pointed out, a passenger who is wearing a huge jacket in a warm environment and then begins to sweat profusely but does not remove their jacket could warrant concern and further observation. This person may have some mental,

behavioral, or other physical disorder that leads to this behavior. If this behavior is found in combination with other signs (e.g., if the passenger begins to perform known terrorist pre-attack rituals, such as praying or chanting loudly), however, then this may change our deployment strategy.

A passenger may also begin to have noticeable *carotid artery pulsation* when they are under a significant amount of stress. The carotid artery is located on each side of the neck. This major artery carries blood from the heart to the brain. An increase in carotid artery pulsation is caused by an increase in heart rate and blood pressure. This response can be brought on by stress; for example, when a terrorist or criminal is in a position where they may be caught, or when they are in close proximity to an area of high stress. This increase in heart rate and blood pressure often leads to a visible pulse that can be observed coming from the carotid artery on either side of the neck. An example would be a terrorist bomber who is preparing to detonate an explosive hidden in their aircraft seat. This passenger may have been observed exhibiting other signs of stress (or could even be unusually calm) before coming to the point in the attack where they will take their own life. The amount of stress that a suicide terrorist would be under at this point can only be imagined. This stress may then be displayed by a sudden increase in heart rate which could lead to a noticeable pulse in the carotid artery.

A suicide terrorist may *perform known pre-attack rituals* prior to an attack. As many case studies suggest, this is especially true for Islamist suicide terrorists. On the morning of an attack, suicide terrorists have been known to shave and apply a large amount of cologne. Islamist suicide terrorists believe they will go to heaven after their act of martyrdom and they perform these pre-attack rituals to prepare themselves for Heaven. Although these rituals do not arise directly from stress, these rituals and other signs may indicate a potential attack. Because the blast of suicide-vests projects outward and upward (and because of the Islamist suicide terrorists' divine beliefs), the severed heads of many Islamist suicide terrorists are found intact after this type of attack. Nearly all of them are smiling.

PUTTING METHODS INTO PRACTICE

Spotting terrorist and criminal behavior is not particularly hard once you begin putting proactive profiling methods into practice. With this newfound power of observation, it may surprise you the first time you witness criminal activity. You may currently rarely think about the possibility of theft or other common crimes occurring in the aircraft, but these crimes are quite common. Pickpockets and other petty criminals have been known to prey on passengers as they relax their situational awareness and attempt to navigate the labyrinth of ticket counters, baggage checkers, security screening officers, boarding gates, gate agents, jetways, and overhead bins as they try to make it to their aircraft and then stow their belongings. Merely finding their assigned seat can confuse many airline passengers, and it is these individuals who criminals often target for theft and other petty crime. The easiest way for you to stop criminal and terrorist activity is to understand the baseline behavior for your environment and have enough situational awareness of peoples' behavior in your immediate surroundings that you can detect suspicion indicators. Proactive profiling is an *active* process. As long as you maintain a heightened level of security awareness, your ability to profile will become better with repeated exposure to the aviation environment.

LOW-PROFILE SECURITY APPROACH

Although you should maintain a heightened state of awareness as you apply the principles of proactive profiling, it is also important for you to assume a low-profile security posture. At a heightened level of security awareness, it is possible that you may display some of the same suspicion indicators you are looking for. This can make your behavior suspicious and noticeable to deceptive individuals (and to other first responders). Deceptive persons are particularly sensitive to this awareness because they are at their most guarded when they perform their deceptive acts. This paradox needs to be taken into account when you use proactive profiling. By maintaining security awareness in a low-profile manner, you can better blend into the baseline environment to observe suspicion indicators in a more discrete way. Although you will be actively looking for suspicion indicators in an attempt to stop attacks before they occur, you will usually always be in a position where you are reacting to a threat. By keeping a low profile, you can place yourself in a more tactically advantageous position by using the act of surprise. This advantage can only occur if you make yourself appear non-threatening and unassuming. Always maintain a low profile. This may only give you a small advantage, but it could provide you with all the leverage you need to regain safe control of your protected environment. The ability to maintain a low profile will depend a lot on your specific job duties in civil aviation; however, everyone has the ability to watch for suspicion indicators in a discrete way. By watching for suspicion indicators in a low-profile way, you will significantly increase your chances of detecting deception.

If you do intend to maintain a low profile in civil aviation, it is important when you first enter a new environment that you are accepted by people in that environment as an unassuming, mellow person. Depending on where you work in civil aviation, the people around you may change on a constant basis (e.g., if you work near a boarding gate), or they may remain constant (e.g., if you work inside the aircraft cabin). Regardless of where you work, whenever you first enter a new group you should try to be unassuming and try not to draw too much attention to yourself. This will put you in the most advantageous position possible for you to observe those around you without arousing suspicion. People around you will continually profile you based on your observed behavior, most of which will be broadcast by your nonverbal communication. Remember that your behavior is on display just as much as the behavior of those around you. If you are subtle with your proactive security practices, you will put those around you more at ease. This will cause deceptive persons around you to be more relaxed and therefore, the suspicion indicators of these deceptive persons will be easier for you to identify. As you profile those around you, you may ask yourself questions like: Who is this person I'm looking at? What is their profession? Is this person married? Is that a gang tattoo on their arm? Is that a biker jacket resting on their lap? In contrast, when a terrorist hijacker profiles those around them, they might ask themselves questions like: Does that passenger appear especially aware of their environment for any particular reason? Are they a police officer? Are they an inflight security officer? Is that passenger likely to be a threat to me? Are they a military veteran, or mixed martial arts fighter? Is there anyone in this cabin who might resist a hijacking?

Although we would like to actively scrutinize our new environment for suspicion indicators, we will also be assessed by those around us when we initially enter a new environment. Most first responders who are (or were) law enforcement officers have previous habits that are hard to break and which make them vulnerable to detection (or suspicion) as having a security role (or as being a threat) in the aircraft or airport to individuals like terrorist hijackers who will be looking for people who may cause them problems during attack execution. If you are a first responder who is also a sworn law enforcement officer (with security duties in civil aviation) you should take time to reflect on habits that you might unconsciously display which could help someone identify you as a law enforcement officer. For example, when a law enforcement officer enters a new environment, they will normally scan their surroundings in order to evaluate it for potential threats. Years on the street have given many law enforcement officers a keen ability to detect criminal behavior and a heightened awareness of threats. They instinctively go into *cop-mode* during their daily lives in order to retain a feeling of control. Although these individuals are not typically aware of this behavior in themselves, it can usually be pointed out by people close to them. People have strong stereotypes about law enforcement and security personnel (e.g., stereotypes like police officers are always serious; cops never smile; police officers are confrontational). For those of you who are law enforcement officers, simply smiling at people when you walk into a room can disarm people and assist you to lower you profile and help to present you as a non-threatening individual to those in your environment. Once you are accepted into an environment as a non-threatening person, you can begin to covertly observe those around you for suspicion indicators.

SIGNS OF SURVEILLANCE

Some of the signs of surveillance have already been mentioned. Surveillance agents may display unusual behavior in the airport or aircraft environment that is outside the baseline, even for those behaviors that would be expected to be displayed by an extra observant person. The majority of passengers in the aviation environment are so caught up in their lives (e.g., checking their cellphones; talking to their friends on board; having a snack in the boarding area) that they usually fail to recognize suspicion indicators. The typical person is not consciously aware with how the behavior of those around them may affect their protected environment.

For you to imagine what surveillance might look like in civil aviation, it will help you to visualize typical interactions in the aviation environment and how these interactions might differ from the behavior of deceptive individuals who perform pre-attack surveillance against civil aviation targets. Imagine two friends who are traveling together. These individuals walk into the middle of the boarding area and sit down next to one another as they wait for their departing flight. The two individuals talk and discuss random topics about their lives, or the lives of their friends and family. If you close your eyes, you can almost see them sitting there, talking, and interacting. They look like two normal passengers. Now, imagine seeing two middle-aged individuals who are dressed similarly to one another and who are sitting against a wall that faces a moving walkway that stretches the length of the terminal hall. The two individuals make random comments to one another, and they even exhibit genuine expressions of happiness and friendship at times, but they seem more interested in observing people in the terminal and the nearby gate than they do with carrying on a meaningful conversation. So, who are these two groups of people?

The first group of people exhibit behavior that most frequent flyers would recognize as genuine friendship among traveling companions. Their behavior is consistent with people who know each other; not with people who are fulfilling a security role. The second example is of two people who are not necessarily friends. These two individuals likely know one another more professionally than they do personally. Their behavior is consistent with suspicion indicators of active surveillance, and they are most likely two inflight security officers who are performing surveillance in the terminal area as they wait to board their next flight. Terrorists who are chosen to perform surveillance are not likely to know each other. These individuals are usually only used for conducting pre-attack surveillance on limited occasions, and they are not typically very well trained for the occasion. This makes it that much more important for you to proactively search for suspicion indicators of surveillance because these untrained individuals will be that much easier to spot during the pre-attack surveillance phase.

7

Surveillance Detection

One of the main tasks of an inflight security officer is to perform surveillance detection in airports and aircraft. This skill is equally important for first responders in civil aviation to understand and implement. Surveillance detection involves looking for suspicion indicators of surveillance in airports and aircraft in order to detect pre-attack surveillance and pre-attack execution indicators. Because the pre-attack surveillance and rehearsal phases of the terrorist planning cycle are so important for a successful attack, terrorist operatives devote a good amount of resources and time in order to carry out successful pre-attack surveillance on their target. The mere act of approaching the target area will make a terrorist more vulnerable to detection than normal because their stress levels will be more heightened. In their book *Left of Bang*, authors Jason Riley and Patrick Van Horne note that, like soldiers, security professionals should attempt to stay "Left of bang"; in other words, they should learn to recognize an attack before it occurs. This can only be accomplished in civil aviation by a collective, proactive search for surveillance. Much like your use of proactive profiling, surveillance detection should be intertwined with your proactive security approach. You must be capable of employing surveillance detection methods as you perform your routine activities in the airport and aircraft. By practicing surveillance detection, you can learn to recognize surveillance operative behavior before an attack occurs and you can use your observations to notify the appropriate authorities when possible, or to justify your actions.

So, what is surveillance detection? In a nutshell, surveillance detection is the attempt to spot a surveillance operative in the act of surveilling a potential terrorist target of interest. We know that terrorists want

DOI: 10.4324/9781003336457-9

to attack airports and aircraft; by thinking about the potential adversary method of operation, we can predict future terrorist attacks in civil aviation and identify areas in aircraft and airports where it is most plausible for terrorists to use surveillance to study their target. With this information in mind, we can perform proactive surveillance detection in these high-consequence areas to increase our chances of detecting individuals who are conducting surveillance.

The signs of surveillance should be readily recognized before you put them into practice in the aviation environment. You should have a firm understanding of how to refute suspicion and the various signs of surveillance that an individual might display. A terrorist target of interest in civil aviation that might be worthy of surveillance may be a particular type of aircraft; a specific airline ticket counter; any confined area where crowds are known to gather, such as airport bus stations and hotel shuttle areas; and countless others. The following two examples are meant to help you visualize areas where surveillance can occur.

On July 4, 2002, a federal air marshal was sitting to have lunch at an upper-level food court at the Tom Bradley terminal of Los Angeles international airport. The security officer pulled out a small portable video player, placed it on top of the table in front of them, and began to watch a movie. The officer was unaware that an armed terrorist was performing pre-attack surveillance nearby, watching the ticket counters on the ground floor. Minutes later, the officer heard shots fired in the terminal below. Although the officer did not know it at that time, the shots had come from the El Al ticket counter. The officer quickly took cover behind a concrete column. The shooting did not last long, however, and the inflight security officer soon began to escort people away from the building as a bomb threat began to circulate. The shooter turned out to be a 41-year-old Egyptian national. The shooter had initially approached the ticket counter, pulled out two pistols, and began shooting at the more than 90 nearby passengers, killing two and wounding several others. An El Al security agent responded and shot and killed the aggressor. Intelligence officials later noted that a "Limited amount of pre-attack surveillance was performed by the shooter prior to the attack," serving as one of many examples of how surveillance detection might have prevented violence from occurring.

On September 11, 2001, two of the four hijacked aircraft departed from Boston Logan international airport. Both flights were scheduled flights to fly to the West coast of the United States. Closed-circuit television footage from that day shows the hijackers of American Airlines Flight 11 calmly passing through the main security checkpoint. The terrorists were relaxed because they knew they had nothing to worry about; this was not the first time these soon-to-be hijackers had been through that particular security checkpoint. Proactive profiling methods could have detected these deceptive individuals if the security measures were being applied, but they were not. The American Airlines Flight 11 hijackers were prepared. They had done their homework. And on the day of the attack, they knew they had nothing to worry about; making the signs of deception and pre-attack surveillance much harder to detect. There were opportunities to catch these individuals before they were successful with their attack; for example, suspicion indicators were observed and reported to appropriate security officials. If only someone had listened and more first responders were watching, thousands of lives might have been saved.

"THESE TWO 'CLOWNS' ARE UP TO SOMETHING"

On May 11, 2001, an American Airlines technician named Stephen Wallace noticed two individuals taking video and snapping photos of a security checkpoint at Boston Logan international airport. After approximately 45 minutes of observation, Mr. Wallace became so concerned that he walked up to the two individuals and asked them what they were doing. He also asked the suspicious people if they had any prohibited items in their carry-on bags. Instead of answering Mr. Wallace's questions, the two individuals cursed at Mr. Wallace in Arabic and walked off toward a departure gate for Washington DC. Wallace relayed this information to law enforcement authorities at the airport, reporting "These two clowns are up to something. They've been taking videos and pictures down at the main checkpoint."

Authorities never followed up on the report, nor did they follow up on the two other eyewitness statements they received about these suspicious individuals. The individuals were the terrorist hijacker-pilot Mohammed Atta and one of his coconspirators. The two men would later board a flight to Washington DC and then disappear from intelligence and law enforcement radar. Stephen Wallace had witnessed pre-attack surveillance for the September 11 attacks. Unfortunately, most reports that are made about surveillance (like that of Stephen Wallace) are never investigated; at least, this was the unfortunate case with Mr. Wallace's disclosure. The two terrorists were eventually able to smuggle weapons through the same American Airlines security checkpoint at Boston Logan International Airport on September 11, 2001. The undetected weapons allowed the hijackers to hijack American Airlines Flight 11 and then crash the Boeing

767 aircraft into the North Tower of the World Trade Center in New York City. It was not a failure of detection.

When the hijackers were planning the September 11 attacks, what specifically were they looking for during their pre-attack surveillance? The previous example suggests that Mohammed Atta and his coconspirator were interested in the security procedures at the American Airlines security checkpoint at Boston Logan. As was mentioned in a previous section, terrorists who are planning attacks in the aviation sector will want to have a thorough understanding of security procedures. It is easier for a surveillance operative to videotape or photograph an area of interest than it is for them to sketch it on a piece of paper. A videotape is also more helpful to the terrorist during the operational planning phase. Since using video and still cameras during surveillance is a known method for surveillance operatives, any videotaping or picture-taking near sensitive areas is a suspicion indicator of surveillance. Like other signs of surveillance in the aviation environment, this type of activity should be relayed to the nearest law enforcement or security official as soon as possible.

Other information a surveillance operative would want to gather to prepare for the September 11 hijackings would be *cockpit door procedures; flight attendant and pilot security awareness; the number of passengers flying on surveilled flight routes;* and *aircraft cabin configurations.* If your goal is to learn how to successfully stop an aircraft hijacking or bombing, it is important for you to think about the *most likely areas for surveillance to occur* whenever you are in the aviation environment. After some thought on the subject, it will be easy for you to understand how a surveillance operative might go about determining *where people congregate in an airport; what a particular airport's security posture is; where security checkpoints are located in the airport; where to sit inside the aircraft for a hijacking; what security procedures flight attendants implement; if the aircraft is small enough for the hijack team to successfully control all of the passengers;* and *if there are enough hijackers for the operation.* There are many, many other considerations for hijackers to take into account when planning a hijacking like those that occurred on September 11, 2001. Although this is not a complete list of every possible area of an aircraft or airport that a surveillance operative may want to consider for his particular attack, it should give you a good foundation for future consideration. By using the previous examples as a guide, you can determine where the most likely areas of surveillance will be by thinking like a terrorist and understanding what they might be interested in surveilling in your protected environment.

Based on some of the previous examples, a surveillance operative in the airport would likely spend a lot of time sitting within view of areas where people congregate in the airport and where they can observe police and other security activity at security checkpoints and departure gates. A surveillance operative might be observed sketching in a notebook, to make note of security checkpoints, avenues of attack, and other important areas which could assist in the planning of a terrorist attack. For example, a terrorist organization that wishes to carry out an attack inside an airport using firearms and grenades would want to look for areas which have ease of access for the terrorist and little escape for the intended victims. The terrorist would also be interested in finding locations that have a smaller law enforcement presence (like baggage claim in the non-sterile area) than other more highly-patroled areas. A terrorist will also cluster their surveillance activity around areas that will give the terrorist the easiest access to their target, offer the least resistance to the attack, and cause the most death. Once you are able to determine the optimal locations for terrorist attacks, you will be better able to use surveillance detection and your knowledge of the aviation environment to detect terrorist surveillance activities.

Surveillance operatives may use any of the following four surveillance methods: *technical, static, mobile,* or *mixed.* Although it is important to have a basic understanding of all of these methods, technical surveillance is not a major concern for you as a first responder in civil aviation. *Technical surveillance* involves the use of special equipment which monitors a target's use of technology, such as internet search history and phone and credit card use. The surveillance detection we are focused on involves detecting surveillance operatives who are planning attacks on airports, aircraft, and other physical symbols inside the aviation environment, so technical surveillance would not traditionally be applied inside this environment or against these types of targets. Technical surveillance is traditionally used when a terrorist is targeting a *person*, not an aircraft or airport.

Static surveillance involves an operative's use of a static position from which to gather information on the target. There may only be one static position used during a surveillance operation, or there may be many. Static observation posts can be found by finding *line-of-sight areas* where it would be possible for a surveillance operative to view a potential aviation target. This could be a seat on the aircraft, a coffee shop or restaurant in the airport, or any other area with an unobstructed view of the target area. Areas near security checkpoints that allow an individual to observe security procedures, or any location which lends itself to a wide

119

view of the target area would serve as a good location for a surveillance operative to position themselves. Signs of static surveillance could include *fixating on the target or target area; writing/typing notes or drawing diagrams while fixating on the target; using a camera to film or photograph the target area; avoiding eye contact with law enforcement officers or other uniformed persons near the target area; nervous tics or habits when in close proximity to the target;* and *jugular neck vein pulsation while near target;* among others. Finally, if the same individual is seen in many different areas of an airport where an adversary method of operation suspected and suspicion indicators are present, the likelihood of active surveillance increases substantially. This kind of activity should raise your suspicion and warrant reporting your suspicions to the closest law enforcement or security official.

A *cover story* is often used by surveillance operatives (especially by those who are occupying a static position) in order to protect them from detection. A cover story is a pre-planned story that a surveillance operative will tell an inquisitive person to provide them with a plausible reason for being in the target area. In the event that they are caught, a surveillance operative's story should explain why they are watching the target area. Imagine an individual sitting in an airport restaurant in Perth, Australia, all the while watching a nearby security checkpoint with interest. The person's cover story might be that they are waiting for their designated flight to arrive; however, if the individual's cover is expected to stand up to scrutiny, they should at least have a ticket on a departing flight, and they should have a legitimate reason for going there. Cover stories are important for people who practice operational security as part of their proactive security process, like federal air marshals. Depending on your job in civil aviation, you may or may not have a reason to have a cover story. If you encounter a suspicious individual, you should always ask yourself if the person has a plausible reason for being in the environment.

Mobile surveillance is surveillance performed on foot or by vehicle. Although surveillance in the aviation environment could involve vehicle-based mobile surveillance, it is more likely to be encountered as foot surveillance. A terrorist is likely to plan an attack on civil aviation in areas where vehicles have no access. Therefore, aside from static surveillance, foot surveillance is the most likely form of surveillance to be encountered in civil aviation. An example of foot surveillance is a person who walks by a target on multiple occasions, with no plausible reason for being in the area. The signs of foot surveillance might include a person pacing off distances between checkpoints and terminal building exits; using mirrors or the reflection in windows for a discrete view of a potential target; mirroring those around them while in the target area; and dividing their time between normal baseline activities and surveillance-related activities.

Mixed surveillance is a mix of technical, mobile, and static surveillance. You do not need to worry about technical surveillance in the aviation environment as a first responder (unless you work for the intelligence community), therefore you should focus your surveillance detection efforts on detecting a mix of mobile and static surveillance. Terrorist organizations commonly use one or two people to conduct surveillance operations; although this small number helps maintain operational security (by limiting the number of people who know the intended target), it makes the surveillance easier to detect. These individuals are typically not very well trained, further increasing the chances that they make a mistake which gets them caught. Many off-duty law enforcement officers exhibit behavior that draws attention to them and alerts others that they might have a security or surveillance role. This often includes behavior like walking around while they are on their cellphone in an attempt to avoid others from overhearing their call. This behavior draws attention from others and could be mistaken for an individual who is playing some kind of security or surveillance role. Color, contrast, and movement are something that all people with a heightened security awareness are on the lookout for when they search for threats in their environment. You will naturally do this, too. The individual pacing around on the phone in the previous example will draw attention to themselves because *color, contrast, and movement* attract the eye. Mixed surveillance is typically easier to spot than other forms of surveillance. This is because a surveillance operative will be making more physical movements that will draw attention to them. Inflight security parlance refers to this as *whack-a-mole*, serving to remind inflight security officers that a hijacker will try to "whack," or *stop* anyone who draws attention to themselves in an attempt to thwart the hijacker's actions. Therefore, it is often more prudent to maintain a low-profile security posture and remain seated when a hijacking is in the initial execution phase than it is to pop up in the cabin without a pre-planned response. By maintaining a low profile as a first responder in civil aviation and patiently observing threatening behavior in the cabin, you give yourself time to plan your response.

Law enforcement officers are often the first to act when there is a threatening situation. They put themselves in harm's way. They run towards the emergency. Their selfless actions are awe-inspiring. Unfortunately, this spirited behavior can lead to dangerous mistakes in the aircraft cabin. Although you are already aware, most law enforcement officers do not understand that there is a drastic difference between the inflight environment and those found on the ground. Mistakes are bound to happen when a first responder responds to a threatening situation; however, mistakes in the air are far less permissible than they are on the ground. This is why the information in this book is so important for first responders in civil aviation like you to understand: because it teaches you to view the inflight environment from a security perspective and gives you insight that was not previously available to you in other first responder training (unless you are a federal air marshal). Whether you are inside the airport or aircraft, you will benefit from choosing the most opportune time to respond to a threatening individual. This will make the threatening individual react to you, instead of making you react to the threat. This is a more advantageous position for you to be in to leverage control of your protected environment. A low-profile security posture will reduce the chances that your movements are detected and deterred. In the event that you respond to a threatening individual inside the aircraft or airport, color, contrast, and movement will make you more vulnerable to detection; plan your timing and response to inflight (and ground-based) security threats accordingly.

The acronym TEDD can help you detect surveillance. TEDD stands for *time, environment, distance,* and *demeanor*. Like all environments, the civil aviation environment has its own particular considerations when using TEDD to detect surveillance. *Time* refers to the time between sightings of a suspected surveillance operative. *Environment* refers to the specific environment where we spot suspicion indicators of surveillance. *Distance* refers to the distance between our last sightings of suspected surveillance operative. Finally, *demeanor* refers to the observed disposition of the individual of the suspected surveillance agent. By following TEDD and looking for likely areas where the suspicion indicators of surveillance might be, we can apply surveillance detection methods in a way that can help us spot pre-attack surveillance indicators and prevent hijackings and bombings before they occur.

When passengers become more aware of their environment while transiting airports and aircraft during their travel, they will inherently become better at spotting surveillance indicators. For example, I once flew from Los Angeles to San Francisco in first class and found myself sitting next to Elon Musk of *Tesla Motors*. Although I tried to have a low-profile security posture, I sensed that Mr. Musk knew I was working in a security role. I was a federal air marshal at the time and I was on my flight home. I was tired by the time I boarded my final flight. My exhausted mental state made the surveillance I was conducting especially prone to detection. Mr. Musk began to make small talk with me and asked me what I did for a living. I used my normal cover story and told him that I was working as a medical researcher at Stanford University, but I made a mistake by confusing my final destination and told him I was looking forward to seeing my family when we landed in Los Angeles. He caught my mistake. I knew he did not believe my story. Instead of continuing the charade, he made small talk with me for the duration of the one-hour-long flight. I assumed that Mr. Musk likely knew I was working in some kind of security role in the aircraft. Because he was accustomed to air traveling, he most likely saw how I was being treated by the flight attendants and concluded I was an air marshal. As a first responder in civil aviation who is especially accustomed to the aviation environment, you have the unique ability to hone your detection skills to a degree that is not possible for others who work outside the aviation sector. You can use this experience to help you think more critically about aviation security.

It is normal for first responders in civil aviation to see the same passenger on numerous occasions in different airports and aircraft around the country. This often occurs with frequent flyers as well. If the same individual is spotted exhibiting suspicion indicators of surveillance in multiple areas of an airport or aircraft where an adversary method of operation is also present, you may want to report your suspicions to a security or law enforcement officer. In our previous example, Elon Musk noticed my suspicion indicators. He likely thought that I was a federal air marshal, however, he was probably just being nice to me after he noticed my interaction with the flight crew and decided not to challenge my cover story. Mr. Musk had observed enough indicators to report my suspicious behavior to the flight crew, but he chose not to do so. He was threat-oriented in his approach, but he also likely accounted for the totality of the circumstances (e.g., my demeanor, my interaction with the flight crew, my security posture) and made an educated guess as to my role in the aircraft. In contrast, a risk-oriented passenger would not even have bothered to interact with me and would be so engrossed in their own activities that they would have failed to recognize the suspicion indicators. Follow the lead of Elon. Maintain your threat-oriented proactive security approach and actively search for suspicion indicators in the aircraft and airport. This will help you to heighten your detection and adversary method of operation prediction capabilities.

Section III

Safety and Security Considerations

"The good we secure for ourselves is precarious and uncertain until it is secured for all of us . . ."

—Jane Addams, *A New Impulse to an Old Gospel*

In this section, we will switch gears from previous lessons. As we accelerate our learning and begin to form a new tactical understanding over the next five chapters, we will move toward strategies that will teach you how to deal with a hijacker or suicide bomber and ultimately regain control of the aircraft. In this section, you will learn about special inflight considerations that can help you ensure the safety and security of yourself, the aircraft, the passengers, and the crew. This understanding will form as you learn the tactical mission statement and the hierarchy of security responsibilities inside the aircraft. This section will serve as an introduction to aircraft-specific tactics. A teamwork approach is essential to stop attempted hijackings and bombings. This section will help you to think more critically about civil aviation security and will prepare you to formulate your own counter-hijack response.

DOI: 10.4324/9781003336457-10

8

Flight Deck Door Procedures and Awareness

Breaching the flight deck door is one of the most important tactical goals for a hijacker. This means that the security of the flight deck door is one of the main safety priorities for a first responder during flight. The suicide bomber might not care to breach the flight deck door, but the hijacker will undoubtedly attempt it whenever tactically feasible. The aircraft cannot be controlled unless they can remove the physical and psychological barrier of the flight deck door between themselves and the pilots. The flight deck must be protected from a breach at all times. Fortunately, with the advent of hardened cockpit doors, breach of the flight deck has become harder and more sophisticated for less technically proficient hijackers. A well-trained hijacker can breach a hardened cockpit door within 90 seconds, however; therefore, this is the adversarial threat from which we need to protect the cockpit. A hardened cockpit door is nothing more than a delay for a highly trained and determined hijacker. Awareness of flight deck door procedures will indicate the most likely time a hijacker will try to breach the flight deck door. It is especially important for you to remain aware of flight deck door procedures whenever you travel in the aircraft environment. By remaining situationally aware and actively searching for suspicion indicators in the aircraft, you will be ready to respond to an attempted cockpit breach if one occurs.

DOI: 10.4324/9781003336457-11

TACTICAL MISSION STATEMENT

The tactical mission statement is a prioritization of inflight security priorities for first responders, which is to *ensure the security of the flight deck, the integrity of the aircraft, and the safety of passengers, crew, and fellow first responders.* This statement is something that has been mentioned numerous times throughout this book and should already be familiar to you. This statement highlights the importance of the flight deck in the hierarchy of inflight security responsibilities. It is of utmost importance for you to maintain security awareness of the flight deck at all times, and you should make a mental note of any lapses in flight deck door security procedures that may make it vulnerable to attack.

TACTICAL MISSION STATEMENT

Ensure the security of the flight deck, the integrity of the aircraft, and the safety of the crew, passengers, and fellow team members

AWARENESS

When you think like the adversary and are aware of adversary tactics you will be better at detecting terrorist and criminal behavior in the aircraft environment. You already know from your review of terrorist hijack tactics that most adversaries want to breach the flight deck door as quickly as possible in order to issue commands to the pilot. A hijack team may also want to get their own pilot in the cockpit. You should remain aware of flight deck door procedures during every flight and you should try to think like the adversary by asking yourself questions, like: How would I breach the flight deck if I were a hijacker? What are the weakest or most vulnerable points of attack? What security-related actions does a flight attendant take when a pilot enters or exits the cockpit during flight? Are there any lapses in security coverage? Are the flight attendants creating a physical barrier to the forward area when they open the cockpit door? Maintaining security of the flight deck is so important for you as a first responder that its protection warrants further attention and discussion.

FLIGHT DECK DOOR PROCEDURES

An understanding of flight deck door procedures is important for first responders like you to understand because these procedures will be one of the main points of surveillance for a would-be hijacker. Flight deck door procedures are the security procedures that restrict access to the cockpit to individuals who require access. These flight deck door procedures are carried out by flight attendants and pilots during the normal course of their duties. These procedures can either add or subtract from the security vulnerability of the aircraft. The flight deck door is the main portal to a successful hijacking and you should use all of the tools at your disposal to deny its breach.

Common air carrier strategy teaches flight attendants to use their bodies and voices to put a physical and psychological barrier between themselves and the flight deck during a security situation. This serves to protect the flight deck from a breach by adding further delay to an attack on the cockpit. These procedures are performed anytime the cockpit door is opened and whenever there is a threatening situation inside the aircraft cabin. Unfortunately, common air carrier strategy protocols are often not implemented. Flight attendants who follow common air carrier strategy help enhance inflight security by deterring hijacker attacks.

Flight deck door security procedures of the common air carrier strategy include (1) always secure the forward area during altercations in the cabin or when a pilot opens the flight deck door, (2) use food carts to block the aisle(s) to the forward area, (3) extend and lock the secondary steel cable barrier gate in place on aircraft that are equipped with them, (4) use the public announcement system to issue commands to passengers when needed, and (5) use your body as a physical and psychological barrier to the forward area. Unfortunately, the risk-oriented approach toward aviation security that is currently practiced in the United States has caused many airlines there to discontinue orders for secondary barriers on future aircraft. This cost-cutting arises from a risk-based approach toward civil aviation security that is often passed down from policymakers and airlines to the employees on the front lines (e.g., pilots and flight attendants). This infectious attitude can hamper the efforts of airlines to bolster security by causing flight attendants to assume a lackadaisical security mindset. This is a dangerous attitude to have toward civil aviation security. It is also another reason why you must always remain vigilant and maintain awareness of flight deck door security procedures and to implement the correct security procedures if it is your job as a first responder to do so.

A would-be hijacker or bomber is much more likely to carry out an attack inside an aircraft with a cabin crew that is less situationally aware. They will time their attack when they find themselves on an aircraft with a crew that they know can be controlled. If you can spot a flight crew's security vulnerabilities, so can a hijacker. You should watch the actions of flight attendants closely for this precise reason: First responders who wish to practice proactive security should consider actions that complement inflight security procedures carried out by flight attendants inside the aircraft. *Overlapping security coverage* is an important concept in protective security and refers to the arcs of security coverage around a protected environment. How this applies to the aircraft environment may not make sense to you immediately; however, it will be easier for you to understand if you think of each passenger on board an aircraft as having their own arc of security coverage, or *area of responsibility* inside the aircraft cabin. If something happens in a particular passenger's arc of security coverage, they will surely communicate this to nearby passengers and first responders if it is physically possible. They may alert others to a threat in the cabin by saying things like "They have a bomb!" or "Fire!" First responders like you will have your own arc of coverage inside aircraft and airports. This coverage will fluctuate depending on where in the aircraft cabin or airport you are working. For example, flight attendants move around inside the aircraft, but they often concentrate their activities in a specific section of the cabin. Therefore, because of their arcs of security coverage inside the aircraft, a flight attendant will be a better resource for security information in the respective cabin within which they are working than they will for other areas inside the aircraft. By remaining situationally aware, you can augment the security of other first responders in the aircraft (or airports) by looking for threats others may not see. This can be done in the aircraft by watching flight attendant activity.

Observing the activity of flight attendants will make you aware of the areas in the cabin that they cannot see so you can watch for suspicion indicators in those areas for them. In the airport, you can observe a whole host of first responders (e.g., law enforcement officers, gate agents, transportation security officers, baggage handlers) to help you understand the security posture of your protected environment; in turn, this will show you what arcs of security coverage need to be watched within your respective work area. In the aircraft, augmenting arcs of security coverage for flight attendants is a great way to bolster security inflight. In the airport, augmenting the arcs of first responders like police officers and gate agents is a great way to bolster security on the ground.

It is also important that you are aware of blind spots in the aircraft. Obviously, some areas in the cabin will be easier for you to view than others. It is important that, upon entering the aircraft and acquiring your seat (or work area), you acknowledge which areas can be seen by direct observation and which areas may need to be monitored by other means. Other means of observation involve monitoring the behavior of passengers and flight attendants on board. Flight attendants may signal an event in another part of the cabin that you cannot see. By watching flight attendant actions, understanding overlapping security coverage, and realizing what areas inside the aircraft are difficult to observe, you can improve your chances of detecting suspicion indicators.

WATCH THE FLIGHT ATTENDANT

A first responder in civil aviation like you should spend a lot of time watching the activities of flight attendants. A flight attendant can be considered an *inflight mirror*, or reflection of what is occurring in the cabin. For example, while sitting in the first class section you may *observe* every person who comes on board the aircraft, but flight attendants have an *interaction* with every passenger on board. They have a better understanding of what is happening inside the cabin than anyone else in the aircraft. Communication is fast between flight attendants if there is an onboard threat. If there is an issue with a passenger inside the cabin, flight attendants will pass the word to each other quickly. A flight attendant's actions will reflect the environment and alert you to danger in the cabin. It is for these reasons that a flight attendant should be used as a mirror when assessing the security of the protected inflight environment.

Observing flight attendant activity can warn you about a cockpit door breach; someone running up the aisle; passengers being stabbed in the rear of the aircraft; and many other threats that you may not immediately see through direct observation. Flight attendants will react to a threat on board the aircraft by attempting to intervene, by retreating in horror; by showing some facial expression of fear or surprise; or by taking action to protect themselves, the aircraft, passengers, and fellow first responders. If this type of behavior is displayed by a flight attendant on your flight, it should immediately alarm you to a potentially dangerous situation that may require your immediate attention.

"A MAN IN THE BACK JUMPED ON A PASSENGER"

On a long flight from San Francisco to Frankfurt in December 2008, I learned how flight attendants could be used as an inflight mirror. Luckily for me, the aircraft that day was a Boeing 747 and I was able to sit in a large business-class seat. My seat placed me near the stairway and just forward of the bulkhead that separated business class from coach. My partner and I were able to arrange a seat swap, so we ended up seated next to each other (with him seated near the aisle and me seated near the window). After we were airborne, my partner and I talked and watched movies for a few hours, settling into the ten-and-a-half-hour flight. While we talked, we noticed a man from coach class move the curtain next to us and then enter the mid-galley a few times to mix himself a free drink before returning to his seat. This activity went on several times, however, it was not our job to get involved. Instead, we went about our business and talked about what we would do when we landed in Germany. It was Christmas. Frankfurt has a beautiful Christmas market, so we decided to go there after a quick rest at our hotel.

As we flew over Greenland, one of the flight attendants from coach class came running up the aisle. My partner and I knew there was some kind of trouble in the rear of the aircraft. We assumed that the flight attendant was running up the aisle to see the purser in first class. The flight attendant was an inflight mirror for my partner and me, reflecting some type of trouble in the rear of the aircraft. We assumed that the situation probably involved the man who had been serving himself alcoholic drinks in the mid-galley; we knew that passengers who exhibit suspicion indicators are often the passengers who cause problems during a flight. The purser approached me and my partner soon thereafter and said, "A man in the back just jumped on a passenger." The purser told us that the suspect passenger was intoxicated and was now asking where he could smoke a cigarette. By observing activities in the aircraft and watching the flight attendants to determine what was going on in the cabin, my partner and I had a tactical advantage because it allowed us to begin to form our response based on information that would have been impossible to acquire if we were not situationally aware of our surroundings and had not been watching flight attendant activities.

My flight to Frankfurt serves as a good example of how to use flight attendant behavior as an inflight mirror for evaluating inflight security. It allows us to peer into areas we cannot directly see. This true story example of an inflight incident and the actions taken to solve it will be further examined in the section on *pre-incident considerations*. Expanding on the example of my flight to Frankfurt will show you not only the benefits of using flight attendants as inflight mirrors, but will show you what *not* to do when working as part of an inflight security team and explain the actions that can be taken by armed and unarmed first responders to combat an onboard security threat and protect the aircraft from a hijacking or bombing.

9
Passenger Search and Restraint

In this chapter, you will learn how to search and restrain a dangerous passenger. You will also begin to learn procedures and techniques that will teach you what to do in the event of an actual hijacking or attempted bombing. The techniques of restraining and searching a suspect during flight will carry over to those actions that you will learn to perform in the section on aircraft-specific tactics. The inflight environment presents special security considerations that need to be taken into account when searching and restraining a violent passenger, hijacker, or suicide bomber. By the end of this chapter, you will be more prepared to think critically about how the restraint of certain individuals may lead us to perform other actions in the cabin to ensure the safety and security of the aircraft, passengers, and fellow first responders. For law enforcement officers who are reading this, this chapter will teach you to think more critically about the differences between restraining an individual on the ground and restraining a passenger in the aircraft cabin.

UNIQUE ENVIRONMENT

One of the biggest differences between the aircraft and ground environment is that when a passenger is searched and restrained in an aircraft cabin it will always be done in a confined space. On the ground, law enforcement officers can spread out. They can typically use a wide swath of territory to take advantage of unimpeded movement when they approach a suspect. They can even find objects to take cover behind which are able to stop dangerous projectiles, like bullets. These tactical advantages are not present

DOI: 10.4324/9781003336457-12

inside the aircraft cabin. In contrast with the ground, everywhere inside the aircraft cabin is a confined space. There is nothing inside the cabin that can stop a bullet. There is also always a higher probability that you will have a lot of other people within close proximity to you in the air than you will on the ground; people who can create a potential danger to you and themselves in certain situations. For example, when a law enforcement officer is on the street and they approach a suspect to restrain them, this officer will be able to approach the suspect from multiple angles; they will have the option to call for help from other law enforcement officers; and they will have cover and concealment options to help protect them if the suspect is violent. In contrast, when a law enforcement officer is in an aircraft cabin and they approach a suspect to restrain them, this officer will have limited avenues of approach; there will likely be few, or no trained law enforcement officers on board for them to call for help; and if a situation is or becomes violent, there are no options for cover and few for concealment. Law enforcement officers who carry a loaded firearm in aircraft should understand this difference.

Depending on your behavior and actions inside the aircraft, you may be viewed as a threat by other passengers in the cabin. For example, a passenger in the cabin cannot be expected to distinguish between a terrorist and a first responder with a firearm. You should expect a passenger to try to attack you if you take action to stop a hijacking or attempted bombing inside the aircraft. In inflight security parlance, the potential for passengers to revolt during a hijacking is referred to as *"Let's Roll" syndrome*. Although you can use an able-bodied passenger for assistance when you try to restrain a threatening passenger, you should remain aware that you could be viewed as a threat by other passengers whenever you do so. The potential that you could become the target of a passenger revolt should always be kept in the back of your mind. Always remain situationally aware when attempting to restrain a violent passenger inside the cabin. Consider the possibility that one of the suspect's family members, loved ones, or nearby passengers may view your actions as a threat to the suspect individual or to their own protected environment.

RESTRAINTS

The majority of you reading this book will not be carrying handcuffs inside the aircraft. Therefore, it is important for you to think about other restraint devices you can use to restrain a dangerous passenger. A restraint is anything that can be used to restrain a person in a way that immobilizes their hands. The hands are dangerous because they can be used as weapons or to grab weapons and detonate explosives. The hands must be controlled whenever you restrain a dangerous person. Therefore, restraints are used to bind a suspect's hands and wrists so they cannot be used to harm the aircraft, passengers, or crew. Restraints that might be found in the aircraft cabin include traditional handcuffs, flex-cuffs, professionally made shoe-string cuffs, and shoelaces. Many other rudimentary restraints are also available in the cabin. For example, you can use straps taken from your overhead luggage; seatbelt extenders (used for large passengers); or flex-cuffs in the inflight medical kit (the emergency medical kit is typically stored in one of the overhead bins above the first row of seats). Passengers can also use a tie, a sash, or any other long piece of strong fabric which can be used to tie knots. If shoelaces are used as a restraint, you should use the suspect's shoelaces instead of your own.

PREPARING RESTRAINTS

Law enforcement officers are taught to prepare restraints before they approach a suspect who they intend to restrain. The officer typically does this by *pre-loading*, which is to have the restraints in their hand and ready to apply prior to approaching the suspect. This is not a recommended technique in the inflight environment; the close confines of the cabin make having handcuffs that are pre-loaded in your hand (especially metal ones) difficult for you to control a dangerous individual. Instead of having them in your hands, you should have them somewhere on your body (e.g., in a pants or shirt pocket). Restraints should be readily available when needed. If you are an armed law enforcement officer who is carrying a firearm on board, you should always carry restraints on your body and not inside a bag stowed out of reach. As a first responder who is not carrying a firearm, you may decide to carry a restraint device in a bag in the overhead bin, or under the seat in front of you. You should weigh this decision carefully and consider the fact that if a restraint is not carried on your body, it may be difficult to reach in certain situations. Improvising is always possible by using other rudimentary means of restraint; however, it is more efficient and expeditious to carry actual restraints somewhere on your body so that they are readily accessible when needed.

Preparing restraints could mean taking your shoelaces off and putting them in your pocket; pulling handcuffs out of your bag and placing them in your pocket; taking handcuffs from one location on the body and shifting them to another, or a similar type of action that places restraints in a position to be quickly used while keeping your hands free as you approach a suspect. Preparing your restraints is nothing more than the act of placing them somewhere on your body for quick access so that they are ready when you need them after you gain control of the suspect.

HIGH-READY AND UNARMED HIGH-READY POSITIONS

For the unarmed first responder, it is best for you to have your hands free when moving toward a suspect to restrain them. You should walk toward the suspect with both of your hands out in front of you with elbows bent and palms open; this will help protect your face and body from attack and will prepare you to use your hands for grabbing the suspect if they resist you. This *high-ready position*, with hands slightly under your chin to protect your face and avoid blocking your vision, allows you to react quickly to a sudden threat.

For the armed first responder, it is best for you to have a high-ready position with your pistol in-hand when you move toward a suspect to restrain them. The high-ready position for an armed first responder is very similar to that of the unarmed first responder; the major difference is that this high-ready position involves holding the pistol closer to the center of your chest in a thumbs-forward grip, with the pistol oriented directly away from your chest. This high-ready position allows you to point the firearm in whichever direction you turn your body, often referred to as *point-shooting*. This high-ready position will also give you excellent weapon retention; by holding the firearm close to the center of your body, it will give you better weapon retention and more leverage to control the firearm within the close confines of the cabin. In this high-ready position, your finger should always be off the trigger when you are not actively shooting a threat; your finger should rest along the side of the pistol instead. The pistol should also always be held in a high-ready position when moving in the aisles or approaching a suspect for restraint.

STEP #1: EVALUATE THE SITUATION

After you make the decision to restrain a suspect, you should evaluate the safety and security of your immediate environment. To do this, you might ask yourself: Could the suspect be carrying a bomb? (If they do, this could expedite your response.) Should I search the individual's belongings immediately, or can I wait? (If the individual has inferred the possession of a weapon or explosive, then you should search their belongings as soon as safely possible after restraining them.) Are there any other passengers traveling with the suspect who may be a threat? (If so, then you should use able-bodied passengers to help you restrain them.) Are there any impediments located between me and the suspect? (Your angle of approach and the timing of your response will depend on this information.) These are some considerations (among others) which you should think critically about before moving to restrain a dangerous individual in the aircraft or airport. When making a security evaluation inside an aircraft (or airport), the most advantageous position for you to be in is the seated position. From the seated position, you can watch the behavior of people around you more discreetly and can take the time when there is an inflight threat to think about the best way to protect the integrity of the aircraft and the safety of passengers, crew members, and fellow first responders. Your safety should always be your number one priority. You should always consider your personal safety with every decision you make a inside the aircraft (or airport). Preserving your personal safety might mean that it is best to approach the suspect from a particular angle, or it may mean that it is better to retreat, reevaluate, and then attempt to restrain the suspect individual at another time. Understand your physical limitations and do not attempt to exceed them. The totality of circumstances will greatly influence your response to an inflight security threat. For example, it may be more prudent for you to block access to the flight deck than for you to leave a position of advantage to restrain someone. Each situation is unique and will dictate your response. Evaluating a threatening situation carefully will help you to form a plan to restrain a dangerous person.

STEP #2: COMMUNICATE

Once you have decided to act, you should tell a nearby able-bodied person or another first responder (e.g., your partner) about your plans. Communication with other able-bodied passengers or first responders will provide you with security, which is important because your actions are likely to be seen as a threat by other passengers. To do this, you could use nonverbal signals, or you could have a quick conversation with the chosen person to tell them your plan. For example, you might tell a nearby able-bodied passenger: "Watch my back while I go grab this person," or "I'm going to go grab this person. Stop anybody who runs toward me." This type of clear communication tells other passengers in the cabin what you are going to do, it gets them involved in the situation, and it makes them more likely to help you if you are in trouble. This will make a personal connection between you and the other person by simply communicating with them. And when you respond to a time-sensitive inflight security threat, your chances of survival increase substantially with each additional able-bodied passenger or first responder with whom you can make a personal connection with and recruit to help you. If you need to restrain a threatening individual in the aircraft cabin, recruit as many able-bodied passengers as necessary. Communicate your plans by telling them what it is you plan to do and what it is that you want them to do.

An excellent use of able-bodied passengers or other first responders when you are going to restrain a threatening passenger is to have them watch the area in front of and behind you and to protect you if someone tries to rush toward you. This simple act of communication will protect you from sleepers and provide you with freedom of movement. You should also ask for assistance from one or more able-bodied passengers to help you approach, hold, and restrain the suspect; before you take action to restrain a threatening passenger, always make sure that you receive some verbal or nonverbal indication from this able-bodied passenger to let you know that they understand you and are willing to help you.

Law enforcement officers have their own unique form of communication. When they move toward a suspect to restrain them, they often tell their partner, "Moving to secure!" This means that the officer is going to move toward the suspect to place restraints on them. You should use whatever means necessary to communicate your intentions and expectations to an able-bodied passenger. Whenever you are speaking to an able-bodied passenger, simple language is preferred over technical language. Words like *lavatory, forward area,* and *flight deck* should be avoided when simple words like *bathroom, up front,* and *cockpit* can be used. You should also be aware that language barriers may keep your message from being understood by the receiver. Time is precious. Choose your words carefully and know your audience.

Aside from communicating with able-bodied passengers and other first responders, you will also need to communicate with the suspect. You might tell the suspect, "Put your hands on top of your head and interlace your fingers." Or you might tell the suspect, "Put your hands behind your back and touch the back of your hands together." There are many ways to communicate with a suspect, but nonverbal communication will not be a very effective option when you are trying to restrain a threatening individual. You need to be assertive, and this is just not possible through nonverbal means. You have to tell the suspect what you want them to do. You may want them to lie down in the aisle (in the aircraft) or on the ground (in the airport). You may want them in the seated position so that you can strap them to a seat. You can tell a suspect any thing you want which will help to put you in the most advantageous position to restrain them. If your intention is to have a suspect move to a position of advantage (e.g., near galleys and lavatories) where you will have more room to control them, then you need to tell them to move there. Tell the suspect what you want them to do in simple and easy-to-understand terms. Positions of advantage give us more space to work, a better view of the cabin, and provide distance from other potentially threatening passengers. As you communicate with the suspect, you may also need to communicate with nearby passengers. You might need to tell people to "Get back!" or you might need to issue cabin compliance commands to everyone in the cabin, such as telling people to "Slowly place your hands on top of your heads, interlace your fingers, and turn away from the aisles." Or you may need to encourage other passengers to get involved, like telling people to "Grab their arms!" Whichever way you choose to communicate as a first responder will depend greatly on your chosen response to a given situation. Keep your communication simple. Your safety as a first responder in civil aviation depends on clear, concise communication with others.

STEP #3: PLACE YOUR HANDS ON THE SUSPECT

Restraining a passenger is a physical act. You must place your hands on the suspect in order to restrain them. To do this, you need to be assertive with your actions. You cannot be timid. You should approach the suspect quickly and aggressively. You need to be assertive and aggressive in order to maintain control of the suspect because once you have made the decision to stop a violent act inside the cabin, it is important for the integrity of the aircraft and the safety of passengers, crew, and other first responders that you do not lose control. Therefore, once you have decided to restrain a threatening passenger and have evaluated your surroundings and communicated your intentions to an able-bodied passenger or first responder, you should move directly to the suspect and place your hands on them in a way that allows you to control the suspect's hand movement. Regardless of whether you have told the suspect to place their hands behind their back, or to place their hand on top or their head, or to lay down in the aisle (or anything else for that matter),

141

you should always physically grab one of the suspect's hands or wrists when you first make contact with them. This will keep you safe by preventing the individual from using their hands to harm you.

Your goal should be to end up in a position with the suspect's back to you with their hands behind their back, palms out. We always restrain a suspect with their hands behind their back. A suspect with their hands restrained in the front of them is more likely to be able to escape or use their hands to harm others. By placing a suspect's hands behind their back, you put them in a position of disadvantage and restrict their ability to escape and harm themselves or others. If you need to get physical with an unconscious and previously violent suspect, you should apply bone pressure prior to putting your hands on them. This will ensure that the suspect is not bluffing unconsciousness. To check bone pressure, place your foot on the nearest long bone of the suspect and begin applying downward pressure. If the suspect is bluffing, they will show some physical sign of consciousness and have a noticeable physical reaction. In contrast, a person who is truly unconscious will not have any reaction when you apply bone pressure.

If you are an armed law enforcement officer and you pull out your firearm inside the aircraft, you should always apply bone pressure to an unconscious suspect before you holster your firearm, especially if you are alone with no other armed law enforcement support; however, always holster your firearm prior to applying restraints. Whenever you are moving inside the aircraft with a loaded firearm, you should be in the high-ready position with the firearm held near the center of your chest with the front of the barrel oriented away from you.

STEP # 4: APPLY THE RESTRAINTS

Once you have checked bone pressure on an unconscious suspect, or have gained physical control of them, you should apply your chosen restraints. As previously noted, you should always apply your restraint with the suspect's hands behind their back and their palms facing out. Ignore the passenger if they claim to be injured, have a lack of mobility, or any other kind of complaint. You should apply your restraints as tight as you need to make sure they will not come off the suspect. As you are applying the restraints by clasping the handcuffs closed, tying the shoelaces around the suspect's wrists, or applying some other form of restraint to a suspect's wrists, you should always maintain positive control of one of the suspect's hands. If a suspect tries to resist as you are putting restraints on them, you can control them by continuing to hold their other hand or wrist and then use your other hand to push on the elbow of the same arm to lay the suspect down in the aisle (this is called an *arm-bar*). If a suspect resists to the point where the arm-bar technique will not work, you should use whatever means necessary for you to restrain the suspect. Escalate your force if necessary until you can control the suspect and effect the restraint.

You should restrain an unconscious suspect quickly. This is because when you move to restrain someone who is unconscious and laying in the aisle, you put yourself in a vulnerable position. To restrain someone laying in the aisle requires you to kneel down next to them. There are a lot of dangers in the aircraft cabin when you act as a first responder. And even though you can place yourself in an advantageous position by moving other passengers away from the immediate area, or by moving the suspect away from other passengers before restraining them, the kneeling position that you must take to place restraints on an unconscious suspect makes you vulnerable to attack. It is recommended that you always try to remain standing on both of your feet at all times when effecting a restraint, if possible. For your safety, you should always recruit the help of other first responders or able-bodied passengers to provide security for you as you put restraints on an unconscious suspect. For the unconscious suspect, check bone pressure and then restrain them quickly.

After restraining the unconscious suspect, you should place the individual in the *recovery position*. The recovery position is performed by tilting the suspect's head and then moving one of the suspect's knees toward their chest to take pressure off their diaphragm. The recovery position is performed as a precautionary measure, to make sure that the unconscious suspect does not have an unobstructed airway. The recovery position should be used on all suspects who are unconscious and laying in the aisle. If the unconscious passenger has a suspected explosive device attached to their body, there are other safety precautions that you will need to take that will be explained in a later section of this book; however, you should place an unconscious suspect with an explosive device attached to their body in restraints like any other dangerous person.

STEP #5: PERFORM AN EXPEDITED SEARCH

After you have placed restraints on the dangerous passenger, you should search the suspect quickly for weapons and explosives. When law enforcement officers search a suspect outside of the aircraft cabin, they are typically looking for things they can use to charge the individual with a crime (like drugs or other illegal items). In contrast, when you search a dangerous individual in the aircraft cabin, you should be looking for weapons and explosives and other things that can damage the aircraft or hurt passengers, crew, or other first responders. The precarious nature of the inflight environment requires that you focus on finding prohibited items that can harm the protected environment of the cabin. This excess of caution extends to your expedited search for weapons and explosives and allows you to ignore other prohibited items that pose no safety risk.

To perform an expedited search of a dangerous suspect, start at the top of the suspect's head by running your fingers through their hair. Run your fingers through all parts of the hair, especially behind the suspect's ears. If the suspect's hair is tied in a pony tail (or similar fashion), untie the suspect's hair and search it thoroughly. When you are performing your search, you should be feeling for anything unusual or suspicious. As you continue moving your hands down the suspect's head and neck, feeling as you go, you should take a look in the suspect's mouth. After looking in the suspect's mouth, continue feeling down their back and around the front of their chest. Continue your search by feeling under the armpits, around the waist, and in between the groin area. Continue your search by moving down the suspect's thighs, patting them down and sweeping your hands along the outside and inside of each thigh. Move your way toward the suspect's ankles as you search, feeling for anything suspicious. It is good practice for you to remove the suspect's shoes and to visually inspect them for weapons or explosives. (Remember: a shoe could be a disguised weapon.)

An expedited search should only be performed after the suspect is already restrained. The search should be performed quickly, but thoroughly enough that nothing is missed. You may decide to completely remove a suspect's clothes during your search if it is the only way for you to ensure that no dangerous items are missed. If your search process has a systematic approach with a goal to ensure the integrity of the aircraft and the safety and security of passengers, crew and other first responders, then this will provide a safer environment while you work to secure the cabin.

If you ever have to search for a dangerous suspect as a first responder in civil aviation, slow down. Use your critical thinking skills. As a first responder in civil aviation, you have knowledge that others do not have. Use the information in this book and your previous knowledge and experience to figure out what you will do and how you will do it. The lives of passengers, crew and other first responders could depend on your swift and thoughtful actions. Search dangerous suspect's carefully for weapons and explosives and do so in a methodical and thoughtful way.

STEP #6: COMMUNICATE AND MOVE

After you have restrained a dangerous passenger, you should communicate with other first responders or able-bodied passengers by telling them that you are getting ready to move. Your intended movement could be to move the individual who you have just restrained or to move to a position of advantage, for example, the forward area. You should tell people where and when you intend to move. You might say, "I am moving back to you," or "I am moving this passenger to the front row of seats," or "I am moving to the front of the plane." You should not wait for a reply back before you move, because it is safer for you to return to a position of advantage than it is for you to stay with a dangerous passenger who you have just restrained.

If you have just restrained a passenger and you need to move them to another area of the aircraft cabin, it is best for you to put them somewhere where you can observe them. Once you have restrained someone in the aircraft, you have a responsibility to make sure that nobody hurts them and that they do not hurt themselves. There are many options for you to consider when you move a restrained passenger in the aircraft cabin. For example, you can walk the conscious passenger over to a nearby seat, sit them down, and strap them to the seat by using the seatbelt and seatbelt extenders. You can drag the unconscious passenger by their feet to move order them to a few rows away from the forward area. (It is always good to create at least three rows of space between the forward area and threatening passengers.) You can make a conscious passenger kneel and then shuffle order them to a nearby window and make them face the fuselage. There are many options available if you need to move a restrained passenger in the aircraft cabin. Think critically about what is best for your particular situation. Consider the totality of the circumstances and rely on all of your knowledge, training, and experience before you make any decisions. After you have moved the restrained individual (or left them where they are) you should move to the forward area to take an *overwatch position.*

THE OVERWATCH POSITION

An overwatch position is a place where you can watch for threatening passengers. An overwatch position is preferably a place where you can see the entire aircraft cabin. This is not possible in all aircraft, because some aircraft are too large for you to stand in one place and see the entire cabin. Likewise, there are some areas in the aircraft that provide no tactical advantage when you stand there. Consequently, the forward area is the best place for an overwatch position. When standing in the forward area of most aircraft, you can see the majority of the cabin; from the first row to the last row of seats. The forward area is also the portal to the flight deck, and it is the best place for you to be to protect the cockpit if there is a hijacking. From the forward area, you should watch the cabin for color, contrast, and movement. If you are a first responder with security responsibilities in the aircraft (e.g., a flight attendant, federal air marshal, or armed law enforcement officer), there are a few other things that you will be doing in the forward area that will be explained in a later section of this book. The forward area is an excellent overwatch position; it allows you to see the majority of the cabin and makes a hijacker come toward you from one direction if they want to breach the cockpit door.

OTHER RESTRAINT CONSIDERATIONS

If you restrain a dangerous passenger in the aircraft, you may want to consider walking over to their seat so you can search the surrounding area for weapons and explosives. The totality of the circumstances should guide your thinking process and any decision you make to search other areas inside the aircraft. For example, if you restrained an individual because they attempted to hijack the aircraft, it would be prudent for you to perform a search of the individual and all of the areas in the cabin they had access to. When performing a search, you will target the area around the suspect's seat, their carry-on luggage, and any other areas that the suspect may have been in contact with during the flight. If the suspect was seen exhibiting bizarre behavior near the lavatories, then the lavatories should also be searched. If you choose to search the area around the suspect's seat, you should look under the seat cushions, behind all of the magazine holders in the seat-backs of the suspect's row, and inside any overhead bins they may have had access to. Your search in the aircraft should focus on finding weapons and explosives.

If you find an *unattended bag* in the aircraft during your search, you should search it as soon as possible. An unattended bag is a bag that is not claimed by any passengers in the immediate area and that is unknown to cabin crew members. As you already know, an unattended bag is a threat to the integrity of the aircraft. Several aircraft have been blown out of the sky by unattended bags that contained explosives. Detonating an explosive is a known adversarial method of operation in civil aviation; therefore, an unattended bag in the aircraft or airport is an immediate threat that needs to be dealt with. This way of thinking is a threat-oriented approach to security. If an explosive is found inside the aircraft, you should follow protocols to put the explosive in the *least-risk bomb location*. The least-risk bomb location is an area on the aircraft where an explosive device can be placed so that it will cause the least damage possible to the aircraft if it were to detonate. The specific protocols that you should follow to put an explosive device in the least-risk bomb location will be explained in detail in another section of this book.

10

Inflight Medical Response

A commercial aircraft flying over the United States has the capability of landing within 30 minutes or less during an emergency. This is possible because commercial aircraft pilots have specific routes they use to keep an aircraft within reach of airports and other landing zones that they can reach quickly and safely. Certain emergencies in the air could lead a pilot to make an emergency landing. For example, a medical emergency could require an aircraft to make an emergency landing. Most airlines use a contracted service called *MedLink* which puts the first responder in direct contact with a physician on the ground via the cabin interphone. MedLink serves to establish a three-way call between the first responder, the pilot-in-command, and a medical physician on the ground. If you call MedLink, you will likely be asked to provide a description of the symptoms for the sick person for whom you are calling. The physician will then decide the severity of the medical emergency and the pilot-in-command will make a decision as to whether or not the aircraft needs to make an emergency landing. You should use the interphone to contact the pilot-in-command if there is a medical emergency in the cabin; they will call MedLink and establish a three-way call to help you assist with the medical emergency.

Flight attendants are accustomed to dealing with medical emergencies during flight. A flight attendant will attempt to solve a medical problem by recruiting the help of an onboard physician or other medical professional (e.g., a nurse or emergency medical technician). The vast majority of scheduled flights have a passenger on board who can assist in medical emergencies. As a first responder, it is better for you to avoid getting

DOI: 10.4324/9781003336457-13

involved with a medical emergency. If you need something to do, stand in an overwatch position and look for suspicion indicators in the cabin. If there is an inflight security threat during your flight, you should always consider (1) the integrity of the aircraft, (2) the safety of the crew, (3) the safety of others passengers, (4) the safety of other first responders, and 5) the safety of a dangerous individual. This hierarchal guide for your tactical decision making inside the aircraft is referred to as the *tactical mission statement*. The tactical mission statement is one of the tenets of inflight security. You will learn more about the tactical mission statement and the tenets of inflight security in Section IV. First and foremost, you must understand the hierarchy of care for an *inflight medical emergency.*

HIERARCHY OF CARE

There are three types of inflight medical emergencies on board: *medical*, *trauma*, and *psychiatric emergency.* The hierarchy of care for first responders during an inflight medical emergency is (1) self, (2) partner or family, (3) law enforcement officers, (4) pilots, (5) flight crew members, (6) passengers, and (7) suspect. The aircraft environment is an unforgiving one; any mistake you make as a first responder can compromise the safety of everyone on board. You must always consider our own safety and health before anyone else; in this way, you can help others by making sure that you are healthy enough to render aid. Your health and mental acuity will also help you think more critically about your situation and how to improve it.

TACTICAL AND SPECIAL CONSIDERATIONS

Certain special tactical considerations in the aircraft need to be made in order to successfully counter a hijacking or attempted bombing. As a first responder in civil aviation, you should consider the following during an inflight medical emergency: Is the injured person my family member, friend, or a law enforcement officer? Is this person capable of helping me provide physical security in the aircraft? Is the person able-bodied? Should I call the pilot-in-command so I can talk to MedLink? What other medical resources are available on board? Should I ask a flight attendant to make a call on the public-announcement system to see if there are any medical professionals on board? Could this medical emergency be a bluff to prepare for the execution of a hijacking? Remembering to think critically during a medical emergency is important because a medical emergency will divert your focus away from the security of the aircraft. Slow down. Evaluate the security of the aircraft and the security of the forward area before you attend to any inflight medical emergencies. MedLink is a great resource for you to use during an inflight medical emergency, but you should only use it when you have first made sure that the integrity of the aircraft is not at risk. MedLink services can be contacted via the interphone with the help of a flight attendant. If you need medical assistance as a first responder, you should have a flight attendant contact MedLink as soon as possible.

SAMPLE/AVPU

If you contact MedLink, you will first talk to the pilot-in-command and then they will call MedLink and connect you to a physician on the ground. The use of MedLink reduces your liability as a first responder because it allows you to work under the direction (and license) of the on-call physician. The pilot-in-command will decide whether or not the aircraft should make an emergency landing. The decision of the pilot-in-command to land the aircraft may depend on whether it is a medical, trauma, or psychiatric emergency. The on-call physician will typically want a report on the patient which can be remembered by the acronym SAMPLE, or *sex, age, mechanism of injury, past history, last oral intake*, and *events leading to the injury.* The physician may also want someone to provide them information with the patient's chief complaint, any obvious signs and symptoms of injury or sickness, the aircraft tail number, the caregiver's level of medical training, and the patient's *level of consciousness.* Level of consciousness is typically determined by checking the patient to see if they are alert, responsive to your voice, responsive to pain, or unresponsive. This can be remembered by the acronym AVPU: *alert, verbal, pain, unresponsive.* Check the patient to see if they are alert, alert to verbal commands, alert to pain, or unresponsive before talking to the physician so you can have an indication of the patient's level of consciousness beforehand. The MedLink physician may ask other questions about the patient's physical and mental status; however, the information that you can obtain from following the acronyms SAMPLE and AVPU will help you relay a timely report that may help save the patient's life. Time is of the essence during medical emergencies. Gather as much information as possible before using the interphone to call the pilot-in-command.

Listen carefully to what the captain and physician have to say to you. Slow down. If you are not providing security in the forward area, make sure someone stands in the forward area to block access to the cockpit so you can attend to the medical emergency with all of your focus. If you are working in the aircraft with another first responder, one person should be providing security in the forward area while the other person is providing tending to the medical emergency.

11

Inflight Fire Response

An inflight fire is a major threat to passenger safety. An aircraft is most vulnerable to an inflight fire during flight; an inflight fire can destroy an aircraft within 90 seconds at cruising altitude. The results of extensive research by the Federal Aviation Administration on inflight fires caused them to require all commercial airlines to install fire retardant material in their aircraft. Evidence from the investigation of the May 19, 2016, crash of Egypt Air flight 804 suggests that the aircraft may have crashed because of an inflight fire in one of the forward lavatories. We may never know what really happened to cause the crash of this particular flight, but if an inflight fire brought down that particular aircraft then it must have been a particularly violent ending for the passengers and crew on board. An inflight fire is a danger to everyone on board. The destruction that an inflight fire can cause makes it one of the most dangerous threats to an aircraft during flight. You can prepare yourself as a first responder by reading the inflight safety brochure. Make yourself aware of where the emergency exits are located. Understand how to evacuate from the aircraft by paying attention to the preflight safety demonstration. Prepare yourself to fight an inflight fire by understanding what to do if there is a fire in the cabin during flight.

ELECTRICAL SOURCES

An inflight fire that comes from an electrical source can develop from an aircraft's wiring (e.g., electrical component failures), short circuits, or overheated components. These types of inflight fires are more likely

DOI: 10.4324/9781003336457-14

to start out of view, behind a wall or ceiling panel. Entertainment system consoles located in seat-backs can also fail and have the potential to lead to an electrical fire. An inflight fire may be hard to see depending on its location. Any smoke you see or elevated heat you feel in the cabin should be investigated immediately. Your sense of smell could be the first indicator of a fire. The fire axe stored in the cockpit, a pair of keys, a walking cane, or other items can be used to remove wall and ceiling panels if there is smoke seen coming from behind one of them. It may be easier for you to gain access to ceiling panels if you step on a seat. Regardless of method, you should use any means necessary to gain access to the source of the fire as quickly as possible. Work quickly. Time is of the essence. Once you have removed enough panels to locate the source of the fire, use the extinguisher to suppress the fire completely.

Although a fire axe is a great tool for removing panels and finding an electrical fire quickly, new anti-terrorism laws restrict its use and may even prohibit an aircraft from carrying one inside the cockpit. In the event that one is carried on board, pilots may be reluctant to make a fire axe available to the flight crew because of their airline's security protocols or because of a totality of the circumstances. You cannot rely on having a fire axe available if there is an inflight fire. Use whatever means necessary for you to locate the source of the fire so that it can be extinguished quickly and safely.

CIGARETTES ARE A MAJOR SOURCE OF INFLIGHT FIRE

Even though there has been a smoking ban on all flights to and from the United States since April 2000, there are still hundreds of passengers who continue to smoke in lavatories every year. If you see a passenger smoking on board the aircraft, you should tell a flight attendant as soon as possible. The most vulnerable time for an aircraft to an inflight fire is when a smoker extinguishes their cigarette. This is because smokers will often smoke in the lavatory and then attempt to extinguish or dispose of the cigarette in a trashcan. This is unsafe because hot ash from the cigarette can ignite papers inside. The source of an inflight fire will most likely be a cigarette. If you suspect this, you should check the lavatory trashcan by pulling the metal tab located underneath the trash receptacle and then open the panel door to access the can.

OTHER INFLIGHT FIRE SOURCES

There are many potential sources for an inflight fire besides cigarettes. One such source could be an explosive device. On December 25, 2009, a passenger on Northwest Airlines flight 253 attempted to detonate an explosive device that was hidden in the bomber's underwear. Instead of exploding, the explosive malfunctioned and almost started a fire in the cabin. The quick thinking of flight attendants and passengers were the only thing that stopped the fire from spreading. In 1974, Samuel Byck used a canister filled with gasoline to threaten pilots, flight attendants, and passengers as he attempted to hijack Delta Airlines Flight 523. Laptop computers have also been known to have issues with their batteries and chargers, causing many aircraft to make emergency landings because of the grave danger and seriousness of an inflight fire.

FIRE EXTINGUISHERS

Fire extinguishers are typically marked in the cabin or can be found near emergency exits, or along the side of the *auxiliary seat*, or *jumpseat*. Fire extinguishers can sometimes also be found in overhead bins and they will be clearly marked so you can find them easily during an emergency. These fire extinguishers are usually of the halon variety. They commonly have a hose attached to allow you to spray the flame retardant in all directions without the need to tilt the bottle. Halon has excellent firefighting properties. Although there is some risk of skin irritation when halon is used in the aircraft cabin as a fire suppressant, the Federal Aviation Administration claims that it would not be possible to reach harmful levels even if all of the fire extinguishers on board an aircraft were sprayed in the cabin at the same time.

Before you use the fire extinguisher, pull out the small tab in front of the trigger. Once you have removed the tab, point the front of the nozzle in the intended direction and prepare to depress the trigger. When you depress the trigger to begin spraying the fire retardant material, try not to tip the bottle over too much (handheld halon fire extinguishers are bottom-fed through a small hose and can appear empty even when they still have ample halon left inside the bottle). If a hose is attached to the fire extinguisher, the bottle should be held upright while the hose is held in a way to ensure that the halon stream is directed at the base of the fire and moved in a sweeping motion. You should use all of the contents of the fire extinguisher and keep spraying it until the fire is extinguished. Additional fire extinguishers should be brought to the scene of the fire and then be made ready for use by removing the trigger guards. If there are a lot of passengers crowding the aisles, pass the fire extinguishers to the scene of the fire by using the passengers to deliver them in a chain-like fashion. A teamwork approach is the best way to fight an inflight fire. Use passengers, crew members, and other first responders as needed to stop an inflight fire from spreading through the cabin.

FLIGHT ATTENDANTS AS FIREFIGHTERS

Flight attendants are trained to fight inflight fires. They have protocols they follow in the event of an inflight fire, like notifying the pilot-in-command of the situation. Although fighting an inflight fire might sound straightforward, it is not. Training and experience are important factors to successfully fight an inflight fire. A flight attendant's training and experience should be relied on during this kind of life-threatening emergency. If a flight attendant needs your assistance, they will ask for it. Listen carefully to flight attendant instructions. Flight attendants will most likely have more information about the situation and know more about the aircraft configuration and other special precautions than you. Because of their recurrent training, flight attendants should be followed as an example of the best course of action during an inflight fire. But, what happens if an inflight fire is just a bluff to turn your attention away from the real danger? What if the inflight fire you are helping to fight is really just part of a plan to hijack the aircraft? How do you respond? How should you prioritize your actions inside the aircraft? These questions are answered in the next section as you build a more clear understanding of how you can help to prevent and respond to an attempted hijacking or bombing.

Section IV

Tenets of Inflight Security

"Everyone was on edge and my biggest fear was that of being overrun. I went through a mental checklist of my equipment, my 'layered offense' as I termed it, and how I was going to do business if the bad guys came at us in mass."

—MSG Paul R. Howe, US Army Retired

DOI: 10.4324/9781003336457-15

12

The Basic Principles
of Inflight Security

The aircraft-specific tactics for armed and unarmed first responders that we will discuss in this section have four *inflight security principles* that never change. The basic principles of inflight security are that you should (1) *understand the tactical mission statement*, (2) *you should act decisively*, (3) *you should use speed, surprise, and aggressiveness;* and (4) *simplicity should be a primary characteristic of your tactics*. The basic principles of inflight security are the same for all first responders (regardless whether or not you are carrying a firearm) and they never change.

DOI: 10.4324/9781003336457-16   **159**

13

The Tactical Mission Statement

As you already know, air carrier common strategy is a tactical methodology that cabin crew members use to handle inflight security threats. Air carrier common strategy has their own prescription for dealing with potential criminal and terrorist acts on board aircraft. Inflight security officers, in contrast, have the tactical mission statement. The tactical mission statement is a statement that reminds a first responder what they should do if they choose to respond to an inflight security threat. Understanding the tactical mission statement is the first basic principle of inflight security. For first responders in civil aviation, the tactical mission statement and preferred method of securing an aircraft inflight is to (1) *ensure the security of the flight deck*, (2) *ensure the integrity of the aircraft*, (3) *ensure the safety of the crew*, and (4) *ensure the safety of passengers and fellow first responders*. The tactical mission statement has already been mentioned several times in this book. It is important, however, to explore this statement and its priorities here in more detail because it is important to have a clear understanding of the tactical mission statement in order for you to be able to successfully counter an aircraft hijacking or suicide bombing. A deeper understanding of the tactical mission statement will also help you think more critically about how to prioritize your counter-hijack response.

The first inflight security priority is to *ensure the security of the flight deck*. This means that you should always ensure that no unauthorized people enter the cockpit. If you consider what could happen if a dangerous, unauthorized person gained access to the flight deck, it is not hard to imagine that this could easily lead to a loss of control of the aircraft for the legitimate pilots. You can undoubtedly imagine this scenario. You are already familiar with the history of past threats to civil aviation, so it will

DOI: 10.4324/9781003336457-17

not be difficult for you. Individuals have stormed the cockpit in the past to deliberately force a crash, but as you know, a breach of the cockpit is not the only threat to the flight deck. Therefore, to *ensure the security of the flight deck* means that you should also make sure that nothing *harms* it. There are vital aircraft controls inside the cockpit. If the cockpit is destroyed, then the security of the flight deck has been compromised. For example, a bomb that is detonated in the forward area could separate the cockpit from the aircraft; a pilot in the cockpit could conspire to deliberately crash the aircraft; a hijack-team could breach the cockpit and take control of the aircraft by forcing the pilot-in-command to follow another course-heading. Always provide security for the flight deck: this is your first priority as a first responder in the aircraft.

The second inflight security priority is to ensure *integrity of the aircraft*. This is similar to the first priority, though slightly different. If a bomb is detonated on board an aircraft inflight that is powerful enough to damage more than three square meters of the aircraft fuselage, this would affect enough of the structural integrity of the aircraft that it would have a high probability of breaking-up midflight. A criminal who is intent on bringing down an aircraft could also destroy vital hydraulics and other essential aircraft equipment by ripping cabin panels from the walls or ceiling and destroying enough of the essential aircraft wiring that stable flight could be affected. Given that any one of these scenarios would be catastrophic for the aircraft, the integrity of the aircraft is the second priority for inflight security. (Despite popular belief, a bullet that penetrates the fuselage or window of an aircraft during flight will not affect the integrity of the aircraft.)

The third inflight security priority is to *ensure safety of the crew*. Cabin crew member safety is important because these individuals have more emergency training than anyone else on board the aircraft. Off-duty flight attendants who fly on a *buddy-pass*, who *dead-head* during their commute, or who fly for vacation are often on board; flight attendants on these flights are usually readily recognizable because most of them are required to wear their uniforms in order to receive these economic benefits. It is important for you to remember as a first responder that a flight crew's number one priority is the safety of all passengers on board; their priority is not to give passengers refreshments and warm peanuts. Although the safety of the crew is important, it is *third* on the list because the death of any one crew member will not bring about the destruction of an aircraft inflight, nor will it jeopardize the safety and security of other passengers and crew members on board. The only exception to the safety of the crew is the pilots because this particular safety consideration ties into your first priority which is to *ensure security of the flight deck*; therefore, the pilots' safety should always be among your primary inflight security consideration as a first responder.

The fourth inflight security priority is to *ensure the safety of the passengers and other first responders*. Although the safety of the passengers and other first responders is at the bottom of the list of inflight security priorities, in many ways it is just as important as the others. For example, if a hijacking occurs on board and a passenger is killed as a way for the hijackers to send an intimidating message to the passengers or crew (as a means of cabin compliance), the death of the passenger is not a high-consequence event if a first responder like you successfully stops the hijacking and regains control of the aircraft. Albeit, if all of the passengers are in danger of being flown into the ground by a hijacker-pilot, then the safety of all passengers quickly becomes the number one priority. This is especially important to consider during a suicide terrorist hijacking attempt that escalates quickly; these circumstances may require passengers to use a *Hail Mary*-type of aircraft-specific tactic, similar to that which was reportedly enacted during the passenger revolt on United Airlines flight 93.

The safety of passengers and other first responders is not very high on the list of inflight security priorities because it is the ultimate responsibility for each and every first responder to ensure that the aircraft lands safely. This also means that passengers and first responders are ultimately all responsible for their own safety and security. This last point is one of the main reasons why you, as an armed or unarmed first responder in the aircraft, should always communicate with another first responder (e.g., your partner) or another able-bodied passenger before you respond to a threat in the aircraft cabin. The precarious nature of the seemingly benign importance of the safety of passengers and other first responders is sometimes hard to understand. To provide another example, imagine if another inflight security officer was shot or killed in the aircraft during the process of stopping a hijacking; that officer's death it will not affect the safe landing of that aircraft. The job of an inflight security officer is a selfless one. Another inflight security officer will stand up behind the first, ready to finish the job. Inflight security officers place themselves in potential harm's way each and every day. As a first responder in civil aviation, this selfless philosophy should be adopted by you as well. Any response to a hijacking or attempted suicide bombing in the aircraft must be swift. The response must be violent. Your response must always consider the safety of *all* passengers, crew, and first responders, not just the safety of one individual.

14

Act Decisively

The second principle of inflight security is to *act decisively*. This principle urges you, as a first responder in civil aviation, to determine a counter-hijack strategy quickly and to follow that course of action without hesitation. Hesitation kills. When a split-second response is needed, you should decide on your response as quickly as possible and then rapidly act on that decision. You will need to use all of your critical thinking skills when you respond to an inflight security threat. You can incorporate your decisive action into your response by visualizing your actions in advance. When you practice visualization techniques to improve your critical thinking skills in civil aviation security, you can do this by brainstorming the different ways attacks against airports and aircraft could potentially be used by terrorist organizations. Furthermore, the fact that a hijacking or bomb attempt will likely be especially violent is something sobering that you as a first responder in civil aviation must come to accept. If the safety and security of not only passengers and crew on board but people on the ground is to be preserved you must be able to act in a decisive manner. This is only possible if you are able to predict and detect an adversary method of operation. Practice visualization techniques by brainstorming adversary methods of attack so you can be a better predictor of attacks against civil aviation. Once you have formulated your response plan, act decisively. For your safety and the safety of those around you, communicate with a nearby first responder or able-bodied passenger by telling them your plans and what you are preparing to do in the cabin (or airport). The inflight environment is a precarious one. Act decisively.

DOI: 10.4324/9781003336457-18

15

Use Speed, Surprise, and Aggression

The second principle of inflight security is to *use speed, surprise, and aggression* during your response. This means that any counter-hijack action that you take should be done as quickly, aggresively, and with as much surprise as possible. By using speed, surprise, and aggression, you will have a better chance of success with your chosen counter-hijack response and will create a tactical advantage over your adversary. This advantage can be improved if you can move to the forward area within 3–5 seconds from the time you begin your counter-hijack response. Thus, the surprise stage starts once you make a movement to stop a dangerous individual from compromising any of the four inflight security priorities, as per the tactical mission statement. Surprise may mean using concealment of the passenger sitting in front of you to ambush an adversary in the aircraft during your counter-hijack response. Surprise could also involve establishing a position of concealment prior to your response, for example, inside a lavatory, or behind a bulkhead, galley, or the curtains that divide cabins by travel class. By using surprise, you can use speed to your advantage when you are ready to respond. Your readiness to respond may depend on things like the readiness of your partner or able-bodied passenger(s), the position of the adversary relative to yours, the timing of your counter-hijack response, and a number of other factors. You should plan your action at a time that gives you the best chance of success, that allows you to surprise your adversary, and which uses speed and aggression

DOI: 10.4324/9781003336457-19

to dominate the adversary. Aggression is important because, as a first responder, you must act with more aggression than the adversarial threat. Civil aviation cannot afford another September 11 attack. Speed, surprise, and aggression is the recommended tactic for you to use as a first responder when you act to stop an attempted aircraft hijacking or suicide bombing, or mass shooting or suicide bombing in an airport.

16

Simplicity of Tactics

The fourth principle of inflight security is that *simplicity must be a primary characteristic of all tactics*. When you have simple tactics, you will be able to apply them more easily during a stressful situation. As will be discussed in further detail in a forthcoming chapter on stress management, stress causes certain physiological changes to the body like increased heart rate, pupil dilation, and deterioration of fine and gross motor skills. The amount of psychological change that a first responder will experience when they try to stop a hijacking or attempted suicide bombing will be dependent on their level of civil aviation security training and experience. An attempted inflight hijacking or bombing makes for a stressful environment in the cabin. You should attempt to manage your stress as well as you can. By keeping your tactics simple and easy to remember, you can give yourself an advantage when you apply them under stress.

DOI: 10.4324/9781003336457-20

17

Techniques Versus Principles

As you already know, the basic principles of inflight security never change. The basic principles of inflight security are *understand the tactical mission statement, act decisively, use speed, surprise, and aggressiveness,* and *simplicity should be a primary characteristic of your tactics.* Contrary to these principles, techniques *can* be changed to help you adapt to a given situation. Techniques should be thought of as your particular way of performing counter-hijack activities (e.g., applying aircraft-specific tactics, restraining a violent passenger, blocking the forward area, building a least-risk bomb location shelter, providing medical aid to an injured crew member) that help you as a first responder to adhere to the tactical mission statement. The basic principles always remain the same, because they provide you with an advantage that you can leverage against a threat. By varying the way you apply certain techniques when you use the tactics described in the following section of this book, you will have many more response options to choose from. The tactics described in this book have been used by hijackers for decades. Adapting techniques while adhering to the basic principles of inflight security can enhance your tactical response and make it less predictable. Therefore, techniques will vary by each individual first responder and be fluid with the situation; aircraft-specific tactics stay the same but have variance through technique; and the basic principles of inflight security never change.

DOI: 10.4324/9781003336457-21

18

Communication

The aircraft-specific tactics that are described in the following section of this book can only succeed if you work as a team with other first responders and able-bodied passengers. To ensure your safety, you must communicate with other passengers, crew members, and first responders (in the aircraft or airport) when you respond to a threat. To increase your chances of success when you respond to a threat in civil aviation, it will be helpful for you to recruit the assistance of another able-bodied passenger or first responder. To do this, you must communicate with whoever it is you want to help you. This person could be a law enforcement officer, an able-bodied passenger, or another first responder. Communication does two important things. First and foremost, it makes conditions safer for you as a first responder. Secondly, it helps reduce the possibility that a revolt will take place by creating a buffer of security for you with the use of other passengers and crew members in the cabin. If a passenger on board knows that you are *there to help*, they can communicate this with other passengers and help mitigate the possibility of *Let's Roll-syndrome* in the cabin.

It can be helpful for you to have a basic way of communicating with other first responders during a counter-hijack response. This is done by using simple words like *moving, move, cover, up, status,* and other basic words that communicate your intentions and actions. For instance, if you are in the aircraft and you tell someone that you are *moving*, this means that you are going to move up or down the aisle. If you carry a firearm in the aircraft (or airport) as a first responder and are preparing to make a tactical movement, you should tell someone you are *moving* to deconflict potential fields of fire with other armed first responders. You may be preparing to move to

DOI: 10.4324/9781003336457-22

the forward area, to move down the aisle to restrain a violent suspect, or to move to secure some other area of the aircraft (or airport) that needs an immediate response. Regardless of where and why you intend to move, always communicate this intention to those around you. This is a simple way to help keep you safe. And although you will always communicate your intention to move during a threat-response by saying *moving*, it is important for you to understand that this is *not a request*, it is a signal of intent that does not require a reply.

Another first responder might reply to you by telling you to *move*. However, they may not say anything at all; the other first responder may not have read this book and may not be trained at the same level as you. When first responders work together as a pair, they increase their security if one is the *watcher* and the other is the *worker*. The roll of watcher and worker can switch between two first responders, but there may be times when both first responders must work. Your goal as a first responder in the aircraft should be to form a partnership with another first responder which promotes the *worker and watcher* role. If you view this partnership through the lens of tactical mission statement and principles of inflight security, a first responder who tells their partner to *move* means that they have taken an overwatch position in the cabin and it is safe for the worker to move to the forward area.

Problems often arise when we least expect them. Whenever you are acting in the capacity of a watcher or worker, there could be a problem that requires you to deal with something unexpected and also require you to signal to your partner that you need them to take an overwatch position. For example, while standing in the forward area in an overwatch position, you may feel the need to draw your firearm (or find a weapon to use, such as a wine bottle or seat belt extender). This need may arise from the nature of the threat inside the aircraft that caused you to move to the forward area, or it may simply be that you are nervous and would feel better with a weapon in your hands to help you defend yourself and the cockpit. You would communicate this to your partner by telling them *cover*. The word *cover* means that there is something you need to do that requires your partner to watch the cabin to provide *security*, or *cover* for you. If you are an armed first responder, telling your partner *cover* might mean that you have a malfunction with your firearm and you need some time to fix it, or that you are actively shooting a threatening individual in the cabin and you need your partner to provide security and overwatch of the cabin while you assess/handle the threat. If you need to respond to a threat in the aircraft or airport and you find yourself needing to become the worker, think about your own safety and security. You will need someone to provide security, or cover for you while you are working. When you find yourself in need of cover in the aircraft or airport, communicate this with other first responders so they can help you. Depending on the training and experience of the first responder with whom you communicate, they may tell you *covering* to let you know that they are providing security for you and overwatch. Once you have finished handling the situation for which you needed cover, it is always good to let your part-ner know that you are *Up*. The word *up* means that you have finished your work and that you are back in an overwatch position.

If there is a situation that requires you to react to a threat in the aircraft or airport, it is important for you to let other first responders know how you are doing. This is also be referred to as your *status*, or your physical *status check*, of wellbeing. It is equally important for you to know the sta-tus, or wellbeing of the first responder with whom you are partnered. If you wanted to ask your partner for the state of their wellbeing, you would ask them by saying *Status* or you would tell them you need a *Status check*. Your partner would reply that they are okay by saying *Up*. If you use the word *up*, this means that your well-being is fine, that you are in an over-watch position, and that you are ready to respond to threats. If you are a law enforcement officer who asks your partner for *Cover* so you can reload your firearm, you would say *Up* when you have reloaded your firearm and have resumed an overwatch position. Although reloading a firearm may not require you to take your eyes off the cabin, it *is* work. This means that, as first responders, you and your partner must provide one another cover when one of you is working during a threat-response. Your partner needs to cover you when you work and you need to cover your partner when they are working. Use simple language to communicate with other first respond-ers whenever possible to avoid confusion and to make your response safer for you and others around you.

If you are an armed law enforcement officer who is working in the avia-tion sector or just happen to be traveling through an airport or sitting inside an aircraft, you will want to identify your law enforcement status if there is a threatening situation in which you need to respond with your firearm. This can be done by saying, *Police, police, don't move!* You should also announce your presence whenever you discharge your firearm in an airport or air-craft. The word *Police* is similar in many languages and, if you respond to a threat in civil aviation, these words will be understood by the vast major-ity of people around you. For example, the English word *Police* is *Policia* in Spanish and Portuguese, *Policija* in Croatian, *Policie* in Czech, *Politi* in Danish, and *Politie* in Dutch. The words *Police, police, don't move* are used to get the attention of those around you in the cabin or airport who can hear you. If you are an armed law enforcement officer and you have a firearm in your hands while you are wearing plainclothes, you should consider wearing a tactical badge around your neck and carry a vest which can be worn in case of an emergency that will help identify you as a law enforcement officer. You always need to be aware of the chance for *blue-on-blue scenarios*, where another law enforcement officer mistakes you for a threatening individual instead of as another first responder like them. If you are a law enforcement officer, it is important for you to speak loudly in order to command the cabin with your presence, however, you should also speak slowly. It is important to say the words *Police, police, don't move* slowly, because some people may hear *Please, please* instead of *Police, police*. If you are an unarmed first responder, you may also decide to use this statement in the form of a question. You might, for instance, ask for police assistance and request that they make themselves known by saying, *Police? Police? Don't move.* This statement can be used to help you gain control of the aircraft cabin. You do not want people to move in an emergency situation. Instead, you want them all to be uniformly situated and seated so that you can look for other threats by looking for color, contrast, and movement. As you already know from previous sections, cabin compliance can often be had by telling people to *Slowly place your hands on top of your head, interlace your fingers, and turn away from the aisles.* The combination of these two cabin compliance statements and commands will ease your control of the cabin and help you to move to the forward area where you can provide better security of the aircraft and watch for any movement that would indicate an imminent threat to the integrity of the aircraft and the safety of the crew, passengers, and fellow first responders.

If you are a trained law enforcement officer who is also a first responder in civil aviation (e.g., a federal air marshal), you may have ample training in stressful situations. Many of you, however, do not have this level of training. Some of you will be highly stressed if you have to respond to a threatening situation in the aviation environment. It is important for you to try to remain as calm as possible at all times. During a hijacking, bombing, mass shooting, or other violent event, many people around you will be notably stressed. You will need to take control and also help to calm people around you when you are responding to a threatening situation that may endanger their lives. In these kinds of situations, you can tell the people around you to *Remain calm*. When you tell people *Remain calm*, it will put them at ease and show them that you are in control of the situation. You may be just as anxious or nervous as those around you, but it is important for you to show poise and remain in control whenever you respond to a threat in civil aviation. In the forward area of an aircraft, your actions will be on full-display. In the middle of an airport, you will be seen by others when you respond to a threat. Remain calm. Show confidence by giving clear commands to those around you. Use simple language to tell others what it is that you intend to do and what it is that you want them to do. This will help you gain control of your environment during a threatening situation without having to be too aggressive or overbearing to those in the immediate area. If your behavior is not calm, then it is unlikely that your language will be able to persuade others to be calm.

As was previously mentioned, it is important for you to gain cabin compliance in the aircraft as quickly as possible during an onboard threat. This puts passengers in the cabin in a uniform position, making it easier for you to see color, contrast, and movement from potential threats. As you already know, you can easily achieve cabin compliance by standing in the forward area and telling people to, *Slowly, place your hands on top of your head, interlace your fingers, and turn away from the aisle.* If you are a first responder who is carrying a firearm in the aircraft, you will typically give cabin compliance commands from the forward area, in the *high-ready position* (the high-ready position was explained in Section II). However, you might also give cabin compliance commands from another position within the cabin; for example, from your seat. It depends on the situation. There may be times when you cannot move from your where you are and instead, you may take a position of overwatch from your seat as your partner moves to the forward area. This situation is an example of where giving cabin compliance commands from your seat, through the use of simple, easy-to-understand language, would be a good use of communication for you to apply while you cover your partner's movement to the forward area. Once you have gained cabin compliance, it will be easier for you to tell people to *Remain calm*, or something to that effect in order to calm those around you. You may also choose to reassure people in the cabin by telling them, *If everyone remains calm and stays in their seats then we should all be safely on the ground soon.*

177

19

Six-Check

During the initial stages of the hijacking of American Airlines Flight 11, reports to the ground suggest that passenger Daniel Lewin was killed because he had attempted to stop the hijacker seated in front of him. He was reportedly unaware that there was a hijacker seated just behind him. This event serves as a reminder to the importance of making a *six-check*, or quick glance behind you before you move from your seat. The six-check is as important inside the airport as it is inside the aircraft. By making a six-check (taking a quick glance to the rear) before you leave your seat, you will be able to see if there is anyone behind you who may try to prevent your counter-hijack response. Therefore, a six-check is meant for you to ensure that there are no threats behind you prior to your movement in the cabin. It is a safety precaution. Always perform a six-check by looking behind you (down the aisle) prior to moving toward the forward area. This small safety measure is a great way for you to ensure the security of not only yourself, but of those around you as well.

DOI: 10.4324/9781003336457-23

20

Aggressive Mindset, Stress, and Motor Skills Management

From a tactical standpoint, the close-quarters environment of an aircraft cabin is unique. The tight confines make movement difficult. Options for the defense of positions of advantage and dominance are few. The airport is not much different. The violent aggression that a first responder can expect to encounter during a terrorist attack inside of an aircraft or airport is that of up-close, bloody, and intimate hand-to-hand combat. An understanding of how to have an aggressive mindset and manage stress during violent confrontations can help you to be more present to the tasks you need to accomplish.

The study of killing, a term coined *Killology* by author Lieutenant Colonel Dave Grossman (the leading recognized authority on the subject), is that killing another human in hand-to-hand combat is not an easy thing to do psychologically. Killing another person is not a natural human response. Grossman suggests that there is "psychological protective power" for the aggressor when "1) hitting a precise, known objective, 2) conducting such exact rehearsals and visualizations prior to combat (a form of conditioning), and 3) attacking an enemy who is caught by surprise" (Dave Grossman, *On Killing*, 98). As you will learn, these "psychological protective powers" have been directly integrated into the response strategies that you will read about in the forthcoming section. Grossman refers to the *bulletproof mind*, a way of inoculating yourself from violence. This inoculation can be acquired through the previously discussed visualization techniques and by understanding potential adversary methods of attack and vulnerabilities in civil aviation.

DOI: 10.4324/9781003336457-24

Hitting a precise known objective should be the goal of any deployment strategy. This is the approach taken for those strategies outlined in the following section of this book. The rehearsals that most inflight security officers perform during their training prepare them for a real-world hijacking or suicide-bomber attempt. These counter-hijack rehearsals can also be conducted by first responders like you. By following the visualization guidance described in the following section, you can go through the mental steps to prepare yourself to stop a hijacking or suicide-bombing attempt. One of the most powerful tools you can use to practice aircraft-specific tactics is your mind. Visualization techniques can be used in the comfort of the sofa your own home, or the seat on your next flight. Visualization will allow you to continue to build on what Grossman refers to as "psychological protective powers" (Dave Grossman, *On Killing*, 98). Grossman's words connect with the basic principles of inflight security, one of which is to *act with speed, surprise, and aggressiveness.*

THE BULLETPROOF MIND

People who have been in combat often refer to the need for a *bulletproof mind*, a term used by Dave Grossman in his lectures on killology. Having a bulletproof mind means that, instead of having a defensive mindset you have an *offensive mindset.* You do not react to a threat, you attack it. Retired Master Sergeant Paul R. Howe wrote about the layered offense in his book *Leadership and Training for the Fight.* When describing combat for which he and his team were preparing, he writes, "Everyone was on edge and my biggest fear was that of being overrun. I went through a mental checklist of my equipment, my 'layered offense' as I termed it and how I was going to do business if the bad guys came at us in mass." Having an offensive mindset helped Howe think clearly under stress, allowing him to prepare mentally and physically for the fight ahead. An aggressive mindset can do the same for you as a first responder. Master Sergeant Howe writes that a layered offense will help you to find your own "personal beast." Everyone has a personal beast inside of them. During times of danger, some people rise above the fear and unknown. They dig down deep to find their inner beast. Instead of just sitting there doing nothing, these people act. Some people will do this out of fear for their own personal safety, while others will do this to protect the themselves and those around them. Regardless of your own personal motivations for stopping a hijacking or suicide-bombing attempt, as a first responder, you should practice inoculating yourself from violence by adopting a bulletproof, aggressive mindset.

An aggressive, bulletproof mind will help you manage stress in situations that will make most people freeze or react in an inappropriate way. Having a bulletproof mind is a type of mindset in which one sees themselves as the *hero* in a given emergency situation, like a hijacking or suicide bombing attempt. This visualization helps inoculate us from violence because it prepares us with mental images of a violent situation prior to us being involved in the real-life incident. By having a bulletproof mind, you will already have several solutions to potential onboard threats because you will have already rehearsed these situations in your mind through the use of visualization. When you brainstorm potential situations in which you are the first responder, you should always visualize yourself as the hero who saves the aircraft and passengers (or those in transit in an airport) from harm. This is important because it will reinforce positive feedback in your mind that will cause an imprint to be made in your aggressive mind that. There is no type of violent scenario inside the aircraft (or airport) that you cannot handle. If you use this approach to your visualization techniques while you also attempt to predict new adversary methods of operation, you will be able to become a very effective first responder to threats against civil aviation.

Once you have finished reading this book, you will have all the information you need to begin thinking about hijack and suicide-bomb scenarios and your response to them. You will be able to use *simplicity of the tactics* to adapt to a wide-range of scenarios, giving you the ability to think more critically and to predict adversary methods of operation a terrorist might use to attack a civil aviation target. The opposite of the bulletproof mind is a weak mind. A weak mind makes a person more vulnerable to an emergency situation. For example, there are reports of people who were trapped in burning buildings who failed to escape because they continued to pull the emergency exit door closed instead of just pushing it open. People may even follow the ineffective actions of others during stressful situations. Stress often causes some people to repeat the same behavior, even though it may not be doing anything to help their situation. Therefore, it is important that you think clearly when you are under stress. In this way, we can make logical decisions and take intelligent steps to ensure the safety of us and others inside the aircraft (or in the surrounding area of the airport).

HEART RATE AND DEGRADATION
OF GROSS AND FINE MOTOR SKILLS

Fine motor skills are tactile tasks that are performed with the use of small muscle groups. Fine motor skills start to diminish at a heart rate of above 115 beats per minute. Fine motor skills are used to perform tasks like using a key to open or manipulate and engage the double-lock feature on traditional metal handcuffs. Fine motor skills are also used to pull the trigger and manipulate the slide-lock on a firearm. Fine motor skills are essential for you to perform many tasks as a first responder, like dialing the number for the cockpit on the cabin interphone. Fine motor skills begin to diminish at a lower heart rate than does the deterioration of gross motor skills.

Gross motor skills are tactile tasks that are performed with the use of large muscle groups. Gross motor skills start to diminish at a heart rate of above 175 beats per minute. Gross motor skills are used to perform tasks like, holding and manipulating a firearm and grabbing a suspect's wrists. Your ability to operate the slide on a semiautomatic pistol, grab a hijacker's arm to control a knife, or to bend a suspect's arm behind their back in order to apply restraints will be affected if your heart rate reaches 175 beats per minute. When our heart rate gets so high that you begin to lose gross motor skills, you may also lose the ability to think clearly about the situation in front of you. Your elevated heart rate will cause you to lose your ability to think critically, and you will rely more on instinct and training than you will on any innate ability to survive. You must be able to control your stress because stress is what will cause the physiological responses that will either hamper or help your counter-hijack response.

PHYSIOLOGICAL EFFECTS OF STRESS

Stress comes in many forms, both good and bad. *Eustress* (often referred to as *good stress)* can induce many of the same physiological responses in humans as *distress* (often referred to as *bad stress).* An example of *eustress* is the happy yet stressful feelings of planning a wedding. In contrast, an example of *distress* is the feeling you would likely have if you witnessed the suspicion indicators, or execution phase of an aircraft hijacking or suicide bombing. The way you perceive a threatening situation will depend on your level of training and the amount of past experience you have working in

184

stressful situations. The amount of exposure you have to the event through visualization will also have an effect on how you will perceive a threat and how your body will react to it. Distress and eustress cause certain physiological changes in the human body, such as the production of adrenaline. Adrenaline causes an increase in heart rate, which leads to diminishing fine and gross motor skills.

When the heart rate increases and the body begins sending blood to the areas of the brain and body that are most important for survival, the brain begins relying more on an instictual part of the brain, the midbrain. Grossman's research on killology suggests that "During times of extreme stress, cognition tends to localize in [the midbrain]." This *mammalian reflex* preserves blood because the brain needs a lot of it, and it also diverts the blood to certain areas of the body like the heart, lungs, and muscles in order to give the body the best chance of fending off an attack or to prepare for an offensive posture toward a threatening adversary. By practicing visualization, you can train yourself how to react in a way during emergency situations which accounts for the security of the aircraft (or airport) and the safety of yourself and those around you.

PSYCHOLOGICAL EMPOWERMENT

Some of the things you might find yourself doing as a first responder to secure the aircraft, like using a food cart to block an aisle, can give you the "psychological protective powers" that Grossman refers to in his book *On Killing*. When you put objects like a seat, an overweight passenger, a food cart, or other physical object between you and an adversary, you establish a mental advantage. In his book *Leadership and Training for the Fight*, Master Sergeant Paul R. Howe wrote about the need to put things between "you and your objective," thus "denying [the adversary] the physical and mental advantage." Even though a cabin curtain will not stop a butter knife and is a poor physical barrier, it still works as a psychological barrier that can help to inoculate you from violence. (You should use caution when considering a cabin curtain as a psychological barrier because it can also block your vision and cause you to have a delay when reacting to a threat if one blitzes the forward area.)

Psychological empowerment can be acquired during a threatening onboard incident by asking passengers for cabin compliance. It also helps to correct any problems early on if there are certain passengers who do not want to place their hands on their head and interlace their fingers. As MSG

Paul R. Howe intelligently points out in his book *Leadership and Training for the Fight*, "If you educate the problem child as fast as possible, especially in front of their peers, you will make believers of non-believers." This can be translated as: If you come across a problem-passenger who is not following your cabin compliance commands, you may need to teach them a lesson by using language that helps them understand the seriousness of the situation inside the aircraft, or by getting physical with them. For example, you might tell a passenger, "Put your hands on top of your head, interlace your fingers, and turn away from the aisle, or I am going to come down there and smack some sense into you." This may be the only message you need to send to an unruly passenger in order for you to gain cabin compliance; however, there may be times when you need to get physical with a passenger. For the more rambunctious and troublesome passenger, you may need to physically push them into their seat, physically restrain them, or otherwise "educate" them, as Master Sergeant Howe points out. This kind of controlling behavior by you as a first responder will send a message to other passengers who may be thinking of getting unruly, too. Your aggressive actions could even serve to deter a secondary sleeper hijack team on board from acting. You must be aggressive and act as if your life and the lives of those around you depends on it when you respond to an attack against civil aviation, because ironically, it will.

VISUALIZATION AS A TOOL

To further expand on the discussion previously discussed visualization techniques, it is important for you to first undertake a quick mental exercise. Imagine you are walking down a dark alley when a large person suddenly jumps out of the shadows and swings a baseball bat at your head. What do you see yourself doing to counter this attack? You might imagine yourself raising your hand up to block the bat from hitting your head. Most people will visualize themselves in this type of defensive posture, and they will be prepared to try to block or shrink away from a violent confrontation like this. An individual with an aggressive mindset, however, will be prepared for this situation before the attack occurs. They will have performed visualization techniques beforehand in order to try to inoculate themselves from future violence and prepare themselves by thinking critically in advance about their response to this kind of violent attack. Instead of mentally picturing yourself shrinking away from the attack, or assuming a defensive posture, visualize yourself moving toward the

186

threatening individual and confronting them head-on. In your mind, it is not them attacking you; you are attacking them. This is an example of the offensive mindset in action. This example of meeting aggression head-on is a much more advantageous mindset for you to have during a violent encounter than the defensive posture that would be expected of someone with a weak mindset.

Visualization is important because it prepares you, the practitioner to deal with a variety of threatening situations in the civil aviation environment. If you have already used visualization to solve a potential inflight emergency in your mind, putting that action into practice during a real-life situation will be that much easier and will give your counterhijack response a greater chance of success. The use of these visualization techniques is like that which was used by prisoners of war during the Vietnam War. These prisoners played golf in their minds during their captivity and, when they were released from captivity and returned to the United States, many of these men ended up playing some of the best golf of their lives even though they had not played a real game of golf in several years. Visualization helped these prisoners of war play better golf just like it can help you to more calmly handle threats on board and allow you to think more critically about the totality of the circumstances of your emergency situation.

By visualizing violent scenarios and attacks in the civil aviation environment, first responders like you can better prepare yourselves for a violent attack in an airport or aircraft. Visualization techniques will help you to think more critically and allow you to implement a more intelligent response during a threatening encounter, helping you to deal with stressful events by inoculating you to violence. A lower stress level will help you to maintain a lower heart rate, which will in turn help you to better control your fine and gross motor skills and greatly enhance your chance of survival during a hijacking or inflight bombing attempt.

Section V

Counter-Hijack Response Strategies

"Slow is smooth, smooth is fast."

—Sergeant Major Kelly Venden, United States Army (Ret.)

In this section, you will be introduced to aircraft specific tactics and learn how to apply them in the aircraft environment. It is important that you approach the study of counter-hijack deployment strategies by thinking of this subject as a synthesis of all of the previous lessons in this book. A few other special topics you will learn about in this section will complement those lessons. As you read this section, it will help if you seek the tactical logic within each of the tactical scenarios that are presented. This will greatly enhance your critical thinking skills. You should seek to understand how the tactics explained within this section might be applied to any of the unlimited number of possible hijack and suicide bomber scenarios that your training, knowledge, and experience allow you to consider. It will be helpful for you to use visualization exercises to predict future adversary methods of operations as you read this section. As will become quickly apparent during your study of the various deployment strategy options, there are many possible counter-hijack response options at your disposal. Many potential counter-hijack responses are possible through a variation in technique which will make your tactical response unpredictable. By understanding the principles and reasons for each specific tactic and then practicing these tactics in a slow, smooth, and consistent

DOI: 10.4324/9781003336457-25

manner (either mentally or physically), you will be able to establish muscle memory for your counter-hijack response. Slowly and expeditiously practicing the lessons of this section will psychologically empower you to stop a hijacking or suicide bombing attempt with the same ease as a trained inflight security professional. (Training can be performed by law enforcement officers who fly armed by contacting your local federal air marshal field office for use of their aircraft simulator, or by hiring an outside contractor versed in inflight security to help you setup a mock aircraft at the firing range.) Regardless of how you choose to train, slow, smooth consistency is the key to success for your approach. If you pursue the subject of counter-hijack deployment strategies in this manner, you will be much more effective and more apt to respond in an advantageous way when you need to react to a civil aviation threat.

Many of the things you will learn about in this section will be unfamiliar to you because the information within has not previously been made public until the publication of this book. The subjects in this section are seldom taught to armed law enforcement officers and unarmed first responders, unless you are a federal air marshal who was provided with aircraft specific tactical training. This section not only teaches you the steps you need to follow if there is a hijacking or attempted suicide bombing on your next flight, but it also examines the tactical forethought you should have when traveling inside the cabin, dealing with specific medical emergencies, and performing an emergency evacuation in single- and multi-level aircraft, and teaches you how to prepare yourself for an outside breach of the aircraft. These subjects will demand all of your critical thinking skills to help you understand why and when certain actions should be taken and how it is that these actions can be improved and adapted during an inflight security incident. The information in this section is best viewed through an ultra-critical lens; one that sees aviation security as a culmination of the past, present, and future. A threat-oriented security approach will help bring this critical lens into focus. You may find yourself reading this section several times. But that is okay. Take your time. Learning the information in this section is important. And when you finish reading this section, pat yourself on the back, because by then you will know more about inflight security than 99.9% of the general population and you will be better prepared to ensure the security of the flight deck, the integrity of the aircraft, and the safety of crew members, passengers, and fellow first responders during an inflight security threat.

21

OODA-Loop Theory

Before reading the following chapters, you need to understand OODA-loop theory, as proposed by United States Air Force fighter pilot Colonel John Richard Boyd. OODA is an acronym for *observe, orient, decide*, and *act*. OODA-loop theory is often explained as a watered-down version of what Boyd actually meant when he developed it. In all fairness, however, Boyd only wrote one official document about it and he otherwise avoided writing down many of his theories. OODA-loop theory ultimately took Boyd over two decades to conceptualize. To understand the theory and how it relates to aircraft-specific tactics, it is important to have an understanding of who Colonel Boyd was and how he came to introduce a theory that would go on to change not only aerial combat, but would find tactical applications in military and law enforcement groups around the world.

Colonel John R. Boyd was an expert fighter pilot and instructor at the prestigious Fighter Weapons School at *Nellis Air Force Base* in Southern Nevada. As an instructor at the Fighter Weapons School, and before writing the first and only guide on aerial tactics, Boyd had a standing bet with instructors and other students that he could go from a position of disadvantage (the lead position in a dogfight) to a position of advantage (behind the other aircraft) within 20 seconds. This was so radical and unheard of that fighter pilots from around the United States Air Force and other branches of the military took him up on his "Twenty-seconds for twenty-dollars" bet. Later, Boyd would change the bet to "Forty-seconds for forty-dollars," but even that was considered impossible. Because of his fame from this challenge and the widespread rumor that Colonel Boyd was the best fighter pilot in the Air Force and perhaps the entire military, he became known as "Forty-seconds Boyd."

DOI: 10.4324/9781003336457-26

After working as an instructor at the Fighter Weapons School for over five-and-a-half years, Boyd prepared for his next assignment which included higher education and the study of engineering at the *Georgia Institute of Technology* as part of an Air Force scholarship program and in response to a need for engineers during the space race against the USSR that was occurring in the late 1950s. But before Boyd went on to further his education, he wrote an official United States Air Force white paper titled "Aerial Attack Study" which was the first scholarly publication on the art of aerial combat. This paper was later adopted as an official guide for aerial combat tactics for the United States Air Force and the United States Navy. After completing his study in engineering, Boyd began working on other important projects which would lead him to study a history of the past thousand years of ground tactics. This then caused him to begin studying the classic tactician's Sun Tzu and Carl von Clausewitz. During his study of these great tacticians, Boyd expanded on his former tactical theories and aerial combat training accomplishments and white papers and further molded them into the OODA-loop theory.

COMPRESSING TIME

For our purposes, the OODA-Loop theory explains how the first responder will physically react during a hijacking or bombing attempt. The basic premise of the OODA-loop theory is that a person must first (1) *observe* a threat or emergency, then (2) they must *orient* themselves toward it, then they must (3) *decide* what to do, and finally (4) they must *act* based on their decision. OODA-loop theory states that it takes approximately *three to five-seconds* for a normal person to complete the OODA-loop cycle. Thus, a hijacker or suicide bomber may be startled when they first sense movement from you during a counter-hijack deployment scenario, but it will take them between three to five-seconds to react to your movement. This was almost an expansion of a tactic that Boyd used when he would "pull the brakes" on his jet, thus sending the other jet past. When Boyd performed this maneuver, the second fighter pilot could not anticipate when Boyd would act and thus, they were always behind in the OODA-loop. Boyd called this "compressing time," the advantage of which went to whoever could move through the loop the quickest. This is the general idea behind the tenets of inflight security because these tactics use speed, surprise, and aggression to get inside of the adversary's OODA-loop process and therefore, operate at a faster tempo than they do. The OODA-loop theory implies that whoever can go through the loop the fastest will have a tactical advantage.

The OODA-loop is important because it directly influences a tactical response in the aircraft. Its principles are woven into the aircraft-specific tactics that you will learn about in this section. First responders like you can use the OODA-loop to your advantage, because when you respond quickly to a threat, the adversary will need to complete the OODA-loop cycle before they can react. An example of the OODA-loop in action would be the following: A criminal points a pistol at a victim's head and tells them "Don't move." If the victim was trained in weapon-takeaways, applying the OODA-loop principle would allow the victim to take the criminal's firearm before they can pull the trigger. Action *trounces* reaction. If you learn how to use the OODA-loop in your favor, you can gain an immediate advantage over an adversary in the civil aviation environment.

22

Positions of Dominance
and Advantage

As you already know, the *forward area* (or *position of dominance*) is the area inside the aircraft cabin that is located aft of the flight deck door and forward of the first row of seats. The forward area is the most important *position of advantage* in the aircraft cabin. Aside from other positions of advantage like *in and around galleys, in the mid-cabin area above the wings,* and near the *rear lavatories,* the forward area is the most important of these positions of advantage because the flight deck is located forward of that area. An adversary must transit through the forward area to reach the flight deck and therefore, special precautions must be taken to ensure the security of the forward area.

If there is an inflight security threat that requires you to react, you should plan on moving up to the forward area as quickly as possible. As you move up and through the forward area you should (1) check all forward lavatories to ensure they are cleared of prohibited persons and then (2) take an overwatch position in the forward area overlooking the cabin. You should allow flight attendants to remain in the forward area if they are not a security threat to you, the aircraft, or other passengers and crew. If you are an armed first responder, you should acquire a guns-up, high-ready overwatch position in the forward area if there is a life-threatening person or situation in the cabin. Regardless of whether you have a firearm, you should always stand in a position of advantage by orienting yourself toward passengers in the cabin; in this way, you can give cabin compliance commands more easily and watch for threatening activity in the cabin. You are already familiar with cabin compliance commands, such

DOI: 10.4324/9781003336457-27   **195** as telling people to *Slowly place your hands on top of your head, interlace your fingers, and turn away from the aisle.* This command puts passengers in a position of disadvantage and makes the cabin uniform where it is easy to observe color, contrast, and movement. By telling passengers to *turn away from the aisle*, you will make it easier for you to move in the aisles; passengers' elbows, hands, and other body parts will be less of an impediment with passengers in this position. An overwatch position in the forward area gives a first responder a lot of control in the cabin and allows them to see any adversarial threats that are moving toward the front of the aircraft.

You will first acquire a high-ready position after clearing the forward area lavatories. You will then make passengers aware that there has been an incident in the cabin. Lastly, you will ask passengers to sit down and stay in their seats. Obviously, passengers may decide not to follow your directions. You can do all of this by saying, "There has been an emergency in the cabin. Please stay in your seats and remain calm." If you are an unarmed passenger with no law enforcement authority, it would be hard for you to make passengers do what you say. And, even though you may be an armed first responder who is pointing a firearm at passengers while you tell them to *Remain calm and stay in your seats,* you cannot assume that passengers will just sit still and do as they are told, especially during a life-threatening incident. With the help of other able-bodied passengers and by using communication during your response, however, you can gain control of the aircraft and garner more cooperation from other passengers fellow first responders, and crew members.

If you are a first responder with law enforcement or military training, you may find it easier to gain cabin compliance and to harden a position of advantage than first responders without this experience. If you are a first responder with law enforcement or military experience who is on the aircraft during an inflight security incident, you should make yourself known to on board law enforcement officers if they request volunteers to help and you should follow their commands if you decide to help. If you are unarmed, it is critical that you try to wait as long as possible before you attempt to counter an aircraft hijacking, move to the forward area, or harden a position of advantage, because there may be an armed law enforcement officer on board who could view your actions as a threat. Time is often on your side during a hijacking, because hijackers will typically spend some time in the main cabin to intimidate passengers before they move to the forward area to breach the cockpit. However, an attempted suicide bombing is typically handled much differently.

A suicide bomber is especially dangerous, and any threat (real or inferred) of an explosive device inside an aircraft must be stopped immediately. If there is an explosive device found inside the aircraft, you will need to move it to the least-risk bomb location as soon as possible. Finding the least-risk bomb location in the aircraft can be done quickly by simply asking a flight attendant. (Protocols for moving an explosive to the least-risk bomb location are discussed in detail later in this section.) You should restrain the hands of a suspected suicide bomber before you attempt to move to, or harden a, position of advantage. If the threat inside the aircraft is not imminent, that is, a suicide bomber, you should try to determine if there are any armed law enforcement officers on board before you implement a tactical plan to stop the threat. All of these things must be taken into consideration before you decide to move to a position of advantage.

SECURING A POSITION OF ADVANTAGE OR POSITION OF DOMINANCE

Providing security at a position of advantage is easy. Most of these positions are located near lavatories because bathrooms are typically found in the rear, middle, and front of a commercial aircraft (the same places where you will find a *position of advantage*, an area that provides you time-distance separation from potential threats). Therefore, to provide security of your chosen position of advantage, you will (1) clear the lavatories, (2) stand in an overwatch position, (3) issue cabin compliance commands, and (4) look for color, contrast, and movement. If there is a threat in the cabin while you are in your position of advantage, you should deal with the threat and tell your partner *Cover* so they can provide security for you.

HARDENING POSITIONS

You already know that a position of advantage is ideally located in an area near the galley or a cluster of lavatories because these areas often offer the most space from which to maneuver as a first responder. When you establish an overwatch position in a position of advantage, you will eventually need to harden these positions, or reinforce the area around the position of advantage in a way that will slow an adversary down if they try to move through that position. You can harden a position of advantage by moving a service cart, luggage, or an unconscious (restrained) suspect

197

to block the aisles. You might also use other able-bodied passengers or first responders by positioning them in front of the position of advantage in order to deny access to the area. Or you may decide to use one, or several seatbelt extenders to block a position of advantage. You can do this by tying one end of a seat belt extender to the seat posts on each side of the aisle and then stretching them across, buckling them together, and tightening as necessary. Due to the forward area's vulnerability to attack during a hijacking or suicide bombing, the use of seat belt extenders is a good option if you need to harden it from adversary intrusion. You may also decide to stack luggage in front of the forward area if the threat is especially serious, to completely block access to it during the remainder of the flight. The decision to completely seal the forward area from the rest of the cabin should be made after considering all options available to you and after consultation with the pilot-in-command.

The forward area is the most vital and important position of advantage because it is the area through which a person must move inside the aircraft in order to gain direct access to the cockpit. By positioning yourself in the forward area, you can watch the entire cabin and protect the flight deck from an attempted breach. Common air carrier strategy protocols dictate that you should protect the forward area if you need to respond to an inflight security threat. Protection of the cockpit is an essential part of first responder tactics. You should always consider hardening the forward area if you find yourself standing in the position of dominance in an overwatch position. A totality-of-the-circumstances-approach should guide your decision.

23

Considerations for Armed First Responders

If you carry a firearm inside the aircraft, you need to take certain safety precautions. Carrying a loaded firearm in a commercial aircraft is a huge responsibility. You need to protect the firearm from being physically taken away from you; you need to make sure that you do not leave the firearm somewhere inside the aircraft where another person can gain access to it; and you need to make sure that you are always concealing it from view so that you do not become a target for attack. For reasons of passenger safety, you need to understand how to properly carry and use a firearm in the aircraft environment before you can successfully respond to a hijacking or other inflight security threat.

HIGH-READY POSITION

As previously discussed in Section III, the high-ready position with a firearm involves holding the pistol up in front of the center of the chest with the pistol oriented forward. This high-ready position allows the armed first responder to point the firearm wherever their body faces, also known as *point-shooting*. This puts the first responder an excellent position for weapon-retention; by holding the firearm near the center of the body, you will be able to pull it close to your chest and are more likely to remain holding on to it if someone tries to take it away from you. While you are holding your firearm in the high-ready position, your trigger finger should always be off the trigger and resting alongside the

DOI: 10.4324/9781003336457-28

trigger-guard whenever you are not actively shooting, or preparing to shoot a threat. Your grip on the pistol should be a thumbs-forward grip, with your hand seated high up on the pistol's back-strap.

CARRYING A FIREARM IN AN AIRCRAFT OR AIRPORT

The following should serve as a review for those of you whom are law enforcement officers and have training with firearms from a law enforcement academy, especially if you have further training on basic and advanced pistol marksmanship and tactics. If the following material is too advanced for you, it is recommended that you consider other avenues of training (e.g., on the range with firearms instructors) that can bring you to an appropriate level of readiness for close-quarters shooting.

DOWNRANGE VERSUS INSIDE THE AIRCRAFT

Shooting a firearm at a life-threatening person inside an aircraft is not much different from shooting a firearm at a life-threatening person on the ground. (We will refer to the life-threatening individual as a target for simplicity.) In many ways, shooting a firearm at a target inside the cabin of an aircraft inflight is much more simple than shooting at a target while on the ground; however, in other aspects, it can be much more difficult. The aircraft environment is a linear one. The aircraft cabin is essentially a long, hollow, aluminum tube. The muzzle blast inside of an aircraft cabin will certainly be more noticeable and louder in this confined space than it will be on the ground; however, the principles of pistol shooting remain the same. In many respects, it is easier to shoot targets inside an aircraft because the majority of the threats in the cabin can be channeled in one direction. In fact, as long as you make it up to the forward area in three to five seconds, the only threats that will not be channeled in one direction will be those you will find during your clearing of the forward area and lavatories. It is especially possible for you to acquire a favorable shooting position when you acquire a position of dominance in the forward area. This positioning in the cabin will allow you to turn the environment into a *turkey-shoot* of sorts, by channeling adversarial threats from one direction. Although you may have been taught to acquire a particular shooting stance during previous firearms training, it is best for you to use an *isosceles shooting* stance when you are in the aircraft. The isosceles shooting stance is better than others because it is more stable and will provide more balance for you as a shooter during normal aircraft movement and times of turbulence. The inflight environment is much different from the ground because it is an unstable and unpredictable shooting platform. The isosceles shooting stance is the preferred shooting method if you are standing in the cabin. Whenever possible, however, it is preferred for you to shoot from the seat, because it will help you retain the element of surprise and is a more stable shooting platform than standing.

ISOSCELES SHOOTING STANCE

The isosceles stance is the best shooting stance to use in the aircraft cabin when standing because it facilitates better stability and ease of movement in the aircraft cabin. The isosceles stance can be acquired by standing with your feet shoulder-width apart and pointed-forward, as if you were a snow skier preparing to ski down a hill. You will be in the guns-up, high-ready position, in an isosceles stance whenever you are standing in an overwatch position. If you need to shoot a target from the isosceles stance, you will push your firearm out with a thumbs-forward grip and acquire front-sight focus to paste the front sight on your intended target. The isosceles stance, in the high-ready position gives you the best stability as a shooter to handle normal aircraft movement and turbulence, and it allows for a quick transition from the in the high-ready, guarded position, to the fully extended, sighted, and on-target position. If you need to move from your shooting position, the isosceles stance will give you a wider range of possible movement than other shooting stances that position the shooter with one leg back and the other leg forward. The added mobility of a shoulder-width stance gives armed first responders like you an advantage of quick, unrestricted movement in the aircraft.

FIREARM PRESENTATION, STANDING

Presenting your firearm in a standing position (also known as the *standing draw*, or *standing firearm presentation*) should be performed with the least amount of movement possible. With your hands tight against your body, you should brush aside whatever cover garment is concealing your pistol and then immediately assume a grip high up on the back strap of the pistol. After assuming a solid and high grasp on the pistol grip, the firearm should be immediately removed from its holster by pulling it straight up (so that the barrel can clear your holster) and then should be rotated so that the barrel is facing forward by pushing the elbow toward the ground as you bring the firearm up to the high-ready position close to the center of your chest.

WEAPON RETENTION

Weapon retention is important on the aircraft, because if a hijacker or other dangerous individual is able to get a hold of your firearm then they will be much harder to control them than an unarmed individual. You should always guard your firearm carefully and consider the need to retain your weapon if someone tries to grab ahold of it. Retention of your firearm can be accomplished by pulling the firearm close to your chest; this is the reason a high-ready position is so effective in the aircraft environment. The high-ready position places the firearm close to the center of the body where large muscles can be used to control it. If an adversary tries to grab a weapon from your hands, it will be more difficult for them to gain physical control of the firearm because it is easier for you to retain control of the weapon close to your body than it is for an adversary to control it from afar. This is because you can keep the firearm close to your body and use large muscles (pectorals, biceps, and deltoids) and the leverage of your bodyweight to your advantage. Weapon retention can also be accomplished by using speed, surprise, and aggression. For example, if someone tries to grab your firearm while you are in the high-ready position, you can act with speed, surprise, and aggression by keeping the firearm tight to your body, and then extend your elbow while twisting your body to strike the adversary in the face. This action uses the principles of inflight security and weapon retention in a way that will deter the adversary from trying to take your firearm again. Any attempt to take your firearm in the aircraft should be considered a life-threatening situation. You should use your critical thinking skills by evaluating the totality of the circumstances before you decide what to do if someone attempts to physically take your firearm from you while you are acting in an armed first responder role. The nature of the threat and level of violence inside the aircraft should determine your response.

MOVING IN THE AISLE WITH A FIREARM

The isosceles stance facilitates movement in the cabin. Other things you do can also help you move in the cabin with your firearm without hindrance from obstacles or other impediments that could be overlooked without prior consideration and training. The cabin is a tight, confined space. You will have a less amount of movement possible to you in the aircraft cabin than you will on the ground. This means that you will want to make decisions in the aircraft that will facilitate your ease of movement if you need to respond to an inflight security threat with your firearm. Many of the decisions that you will want to consider making as an armed first responder will also need to be considered by you as an unarmed first responder for the same reason, that is, for ease of movement in the aircraft. For example, you should always consider restraining people who are a threat to the aircraft and place them in a seat so they do not block the aisle(s). You would also want to move an unconscious body out of the aisle if possible, in order to ease your movement in the aircraft; this would also be helpful for an unarmed first responder, and therefore, many of the tactical decisions that you will make as an armed first responder will also be helpful for you to make as an unarmed first responder. You will also want to choose a position of advantage that facilitates your movement. Communicating with your partner (or an able-bodied passenger or crew member) will be important if you are moving in the aisle with a firearm because it will let them know your intentions and provide you with some security in *Let's roll-syndrome* scenarios. When you move with a firearm inside an aircraft, the high-ready position can be used to ensure that you have weapon retention and it gives you the ability as a shooter to extend your firearm and put your front sight on a target faster than other shooting methods or positions allow. The high-ready position also places you in a position as an armed first responder where your elbows are tucked inward, further facilitating ease of movement in the tight confines of the aircraft and reducing your profile to provide you with extra security.

When you are moving in the aircraft cabin with a firearm, you should acquire your high-ready position in a slightly hunched-over position, in order to lower one's profile. This is sometimes referred to as a *turtle back*, or often times someone is said to be *turtle-backing* when they are in this slightly hunched-over shooting position. A reduced profile in the aircraft will allow you to use the OODA-loop theory to your advantage and to compress time in a more efficient manner by making your movement in the aircraft less noticeable. When you move with a firearm in the aircraft, hold the firearm in the high-ready position, crouch down as low as you can while still allowing yourself the ability to reach the forward area in three to five seconds if starting from the tenth row of seats. (You should be able to move at least ten rows in three to five seconds in the cabin while holding a firearm in the high-ready position.) When you move with your firearm in the cabin, you should try to take small steps, with your feet facing directly forward as if they were on snow skis. Your feet should be kept close together so that your knees will not strike the seat frames in the aisle as you move. As you walk toward your objective, you should scan the cabin for threats by looking at passengers' hands as you move up or down the aisle. Always perform any movement in the cabin as quickly and safely as possible. Your main goal should be to avoid being detected within the timeframe of the OODA-loop cycle; however, your safety should always be your number one priority. You can be much safer while moving in the aircraft with a firearm if you do not run. Never run in the aisle, unless there is an imminent threat to the security of the aircraft that can only be reached if you run. Running with a loaded firearm is particularly dangerous because the close proximity of passengers in the cabin can lead to an unintentional discharge. You should only move as fast as safely possible when you are moving in the aircraft with a loaded firearm, and you should do so in a way that allows you to simultaneously scan for threats, evaluate the security of the cabin, and maintain retention of your firearm.

FIREARM PRESENTATION, SEATED

If you are an armed first responder traveling in a commercial aircraft, then you will be seated for the majority of your time in the cabin. If you need to shoot your firearm, try to do so from the seated position. You will have lower profile shooting posture when you are seated, making your initial actions (like removing your firearm from its holster) less likely to be seen by an adversary. The seated firearm presentation is preferred to the standing firearm presentation because it will allow you to surprise an adversary in the cabin and will make it difficult for other adversaries in the cabin to locate you in the crowd. If you identify a threatening individual in the cabin which requires you to remove your firearm from its holster, you should (1) sink as low in the seat as possible with your elbows tucked tight to your body, (2) make a discreet scan of the cabin for threatening passengers, (3) sweep aside clothing that is covering your firearm and acquire a tight grasp high up on the back-strap of the pistol grip, and (4) pull the firearm straight up into the high-ready position while you rotate the barrel into a point-shoot orientation.

24

Considerations for Unarmed First Responders

Unarmed first responders have slightly different tactics than do those who are armed. As an unarmed first responder, you must consider the fact that you will have less control over other passengers because you will not have a weapon to use for intimidation and cabin compliance purposes. You will only be able to rely on the use of your body (or any weapon you can find) to stop a violent passenger. You may need to use your hands and feet, or even your head to stop a hijacker or suicide bomber from causing harm to the aircraft or jeopardizing the safety of passengers, crew, and fellow first responders. Although in many circumstances you will need to take a more aggressive approach than an armed first responder, in others you will need to use softer techniques to get other passengers to follow your lead and listen to your requests. As an unarmed first responder, you will need to rely more on fellow passengers than first responders who are armed. For example, if you needed to try to subdue a violent passenger in the aircraft, an armed first responder could simply shoot the individual whereas as an unarmed first responder you would be better off recruiting the help of able-bodied passengers and other first responders to help you. Therefore, an unarmed response to an inflight security threat takes more of a collective tactical approach than the more individualistic approach of an armed tactical response.

A firearm and police badge immediately and definitively display authority for those who present them. An unarmed responder will not have the ability to command this kind of authority by, for example, standing up and telling people *Please, remain in your seats.* Therefore, the main difference between unarmed and armed aircraft specific tactics is how much authority and control the first responder can expect to attain in the aircraft during a threat response. An armed first responder will not have as much of a need to communicate with an able-bodied passenger or other first responders, because they have the ability to shoot a violent individual inside the aircraft; they do not need to recruit the help of others in order to restrain a violent person. Unarmed first responders are at a disadvantage in this respect; however, as an unarmed first responder you can use the previously mentioned collective approach to be just as effective, if not more, than an armed first responder. The armed first responder relies on an individualistic approach, but this will only provide them a limited amount of security inside an aircraft filled with potentially hundreds of passengers. A collective approach to inflight security is, therefore, a more favorable approach for both armed and unarmed first responders.

UNARMED HIGH-READY POSITION

As discussed in Section III, as an unarmed first responder, you should acquire an unarmed high-ready position whenever you are moving into the cabin. In the unarmed-high-ready position, your hands are held up in front of your chest with your palms facing forward. You will also use the unarmed high-ready position when you are standing in an overwatch position and when preparing to move from your seat. This high-ready position, and its use in your tactical response, should closely mimic that of an armed first responder; the only difference is that you will not have a firearm in your hands. This position makes your hands readily available near the front of your body where they can be used to grasp and restrain the hands of a violent passenger, or to strike and defend. As an unarmed passenger, it is best for you to have your hands free when you are moving toward a suspect who you intend to restrain. The high-ready position will allow you to react quickly to a violent individual. For these reasons, you should use the unarmed high-ready position whenever you are moving up or down the aisles and while approaching a suspect person. The high-ready position will allow you as an unarmed first responder to be better able to react to a sudden threat in the close-quarters environment of the aircraft cabin and will shorten your reaction time.

KILLING WITH THE HANDS

In inflight security training, or *defensive measures training* teaches students how to *counter* attacks like punches, kicks, jabs and slashes (from a knife), and grapples. The name *defensive measures* suggests that the student should have a defensive mindset instead of the aggressive one, which you already know is a far more advantageous mindset to have as a first responder in civil aviation security. It is a reality that, during a hijacking or suicide bombing attempt, as an unarmed first responder you may need to kill a violent passenger adversary with your hands in order to maintain the security of the flight deck, the integrity of the aircraft, and the safety of the crew, yourself, passengers, and other first responders. You should be mentally prepared for this possibility if it arises, and you should inoculate yourself from potential violence through the use of visualization techniques.

If you need to control someone physically, it will be easier for you if you try to acquire control of their hands or head. Restraining the hands will keep the person from hurting you and others. And if you push under the person's chin, then you can direct their head wherever you want them to go. This may be preferred over breaking their neck. If a person tries to get physical and you need to control them by their head, try pushing up from under the bottom of your adversary's chin to guide their head back and push them over on to their heels and then onto the ground. The individual will fall back naturally to protect themselves from injuring their own neck. If the situation dictates, however, you may need to use your hands on a violent individual in an attempt to bring about unconsciousness in that person. This should be used as a last resort and should only be used if the violent individual will not cooperate with the use of other physical means. It takes only a small amount of force to break a person's neck. By using a tight grip on the back of a person's head with one hand and the other hand under the person's chin, you can use a slight twisting motion to render them unconscious. If the situation dictates, you should use whatever means are necessary to stop a suicide bomber or hijacker from causing death and destruction on board (or in the airport). If the totality of the circumstances requires you to take a fork from the galley and stab a suicide bomber through the eye (or to use your hands to break a violent individual's neck), then that is what needs to be done. An aggressive mindset and the tactics and techniques presented in this section should serve as your guide to ending a violent onboard threat as swiftly and as safely as possible.

25

Least-Risk Bomb Location

In the year 2014, the release of an action movie called *Non-Stop* caused a lot of intrigue over the subject of the *least-risk bomb location*. The least-risk bomb location is an area inside the aircraft where an explosive device can be placed so that it has the least risk of bringing about a crash if the explosive detonates. The least-risk bomb location is typically one of the emergency exits on either the left or right side of the aft area of the main cabin. As noted earlier in this section, it is important for you to determine the location of the least-risk bomb location after you have restrained the hands of a suicide bomber. The safe movement of an explosive device to the least-risk bomb location will be one of the first things you will need to do after a suicide bomber's hands have been restrained. The hands of a suicide bomber should be restrained regardless of whether or not the individual responds to bone pressure. Of course, there may not be any suicide bomber at all; an explosive device may simply be discovered inside the aircraft. The only difference with how you deal with these two situations is that, if the explosive device is attached to a person's body then you will move both the person's body and the explosive to the least-risk bomb location after you have restrained the individual's hands. (You should not attempt to remove the explosive device unless you are instructed to do so by the pilot-in-command; this will most likely be done in conjunction with a call to the ground to an explosives expert who can provide guidance.) If you do need to restrain a suicide bomber's hands, you should make sure that the restraints are especially tight. If there is any possibility that the individual who is wearing the explosive device will regain consciousness, or may be able to regain consciousness access an explosive device for which they are responsible for bringing on board then you should ensure

DOI: 10.4324/9781003336457-30

that the individual is rendered unconscious or that their unconsciousness is assured by any means necessary. Flight attendants will know the exact location of the least-risk bomb location. They can also assist you with building a shelter for housing the explosive device. The bomb shelter will be need to be constructed in order to surround the explosive to help contain an inadvertent explosion. Any rumor or indication of an explosive on board the aircraft during flight should be taken seriously. If an explosive device is discovered on board, flight attendants should be questioned as soon as possible in order to determine the location of the least-risk bomb location. If a suicide bomber is involved in the threat, you will need to subdue and restrain the individual as quickly as possible before you move them and the explosive to the least-risk bomb location.

Once an explosive has been found inside the aircraft, you must tell the pilot-in-command of the situation. It is important for pilots to know about the presence of an explosive device on board the aircraft because they will need to descend below 9,000 feet above sea level. Descending below 9,000 feet above sea level puts the aircraft at the safest altitude possible in the event of an explosive detonation. The *first notification* to the pilot-in-command on the interphone should be as follows: *This is law enforcement officer/first responder/flight attendant (your full name). There has been a situation on board and we have found an explosive device. We are going to build a least-risk bomb location. We will notify you when we are ready to move the explosive.* This notification allows pilots to prepare for the aircraft's descent and gives them an opportunity to try to find a patch of smooth air before the explosive device is moved in order to make the movement of the explosive safer for first responders. After your notification to the pilot-in-command, one of the pilots will alert the respective law enforcement agency on the ground that will have jurisdiction where the aircraft is scheduled to make an emergency landing and which will be able to coordinate with any other federal, state, local, or emergency agencies on the ground that may need to know. When you notify the pilot-in-command of a threatening situation in the aircraft, you make it possible for the pilots to initiate their own set of safety procedures so that they can ensure the best chance of survival for everyone on board. The pilot-in-command is ultimately responsible for the safety of everyone in the aircraft. You should always notify the pilot-in-command if there is a dangerous situation on board, and this is especially important prior to moving an explosive device in the cabin during flight.

The least-risk bomb location is nearly always centered around one of the rearmost emergency exits. Emergency exits have weak points around their edges. Federal Aviation Administration test trials have verified that the force from an explosive blast inside of a properly built least-risk bomb location shelter will push with the majority of its force against the emergency exit door, causing failure at the weak points and less damage to structural components inside the surrounding fuselage. When an explosive device has been properly placed inside of the least-risk bomb location, with a shelter built around it with the help of luggage and wet blankets, then the detonation of the device will essentially blast open the emergency door. The negative pressure outside of the aircraft compared to the positive pressure inside the cabin will essentially extract any surrounding material out of the aircraft (like blankets and luggage), with minimal damage caused to the aircraft fuselage.

HOW TO BUILD AN LRBL AND MOVE AN EXPLOSIVE DEVICE

After first notification has been made to the pilot-in-command, you will need to begin building a *least-risk bomb location shelter* at the least-risk bomb location. A least-risk bomb location shelter is constructed from various items found inside the aircraft which are then used to surround the explosive device at the least-risk bomb location. We begin by building the base of the shelter to provide a platform on top of which the explosive device will be placed. You can do this by gathering luggage from overhead bins and stacking it around the base of the least-risk bomb location (this is usually the right-rear emergency exit door; however, you should verify this by asking a flight attendant). You can facilitate the movement of luggage by recruiting passengers to help open overhead bins, remove luggage, and pass it back to the least-risk bomb location. You should build the base of the least-risk bomb location shelter until the luggage stack is just below the emergency exit window. Once the stack has reached a point just below the emergency exit window, you should begin gathering blankets in the cabin and then wet them by using water bottles or by putting them in the lavatory sink. Blankets can be found by asking a flight attendant or by searching the first-class cabin. You will find it helpful to have other first responders or able-bodied passengers wet the blankets and then bring them to to you in order to finish building the least-risk bomb shelter as expeditiously as possible. When you have the first wet blanket in your hands, spread it out over the luggage stack. Try to spread at least one or two more wet blankets over top of the first; this is where the explosive

211

device will be placed and you want to make sure there is a thick layer of wet blanket material underneath the explosive before you place the device on top of the least-risk bomb shelter luggage stack.

Prior to moving the explosive device to the least-risk bomb location, you should communicate with the pilot-in-command a second time. The *second notification* to the pilot-in-command by interphone should be as follows: *This is law enforcement officer/first responder/flight attendant (your full name). We are ready to move the explosive device.* With this information, the pilots may be able to stabilize the aircraft, for example, by finding smooth air, so you can move the explosive more comfortably and without fear of dropping it. Once the pilot-in-command has given the okay to move the explosive, it (or the body and the explosive that it is strapped to) should be moved extremely carefully. Depending on the situation, the pilot-in-command may decide during the second notification that they want to connect you via a three-way call on the interphone with an explosives expert on the ground who can help determine the best way for you to move the explosive device.

When the explosive device is in the process of being moved, you should provide security in front of and behind the device. If you are an armed first responder, you should walk in front of the device with your firearm in the high-ready position; if there are two of you who are armed, one of you should walk behind the device and the other in front. Unarmed responders can also help provide security when an explosive device is being moved. You can do this as an unarmed first responder by walking in front of and behind whoever is carrying the device; however, you should remain especially vigilant in the cabin when moving the explosive and you should consider recruiting others to help you. Once the device has been moved to the least-risk bomb location, it should be placed on top of the first layer of wet blankets on the luggage stack. The device itself should be centered on the emergency exit window as much as possible. The least-risk bomb location stack can easily accommodate an explosive-strapped body if needed; simply place the body on top of the stack with the explosive and center it as close to the emergency exit window as possible. The face down position will be the easiest position to place a body in the least-risk bomb location. Once you have placed the explosive device in its proper position, you should spread out several more wet blankets and place them on top of the explosive device. The wet blankets should be tucked into every possible crevice to ensure a tight, wet capsule around the explosive. After you have put additional wet blankets in place, the least-risk bomb location shelter can continue to be built. You can do this by continuing to stack additional luggage around and on top of the explosive device. You should continue stacking luggage on and around the explosive until the luggage stack reaches the ceiling of the aircraft cabin. Wedge the luggage in place as necessary to ensure a tight fit. After the least-risk bomb shelter is finished, you should clear the last three rows of the aircraft and move the passengers to seats more than three rows forward of the least-risk bomb location to help ensure the safety of passengers in the immediate area.

The last step in the process of preparing the least-risk bomb location is to communicate with the pilot-in-command. The *third notification* to the pilot-in-command should be as follows: *This is law enforcement officer/first responder/flight attendant (your full name). The least-least bomb location is complete and the explosive device is in place. Passengers have been moved away from the immediate area of the least-risk bomb location.* Depending on the circumstances, the pilot-in-command may require you to perform other actions inside the cabin to further ensure the integrity of the aircraft. Listen to the pilot-in-command carefully and follow the instructions of the pilot exactly as you are directed.

26

Suicide-Bomber Response

The suicide-bomber response for responders in civil aviation first responder is at the heart of aircraft-specific tactics. The suicide bomber represents one of the most dangerous threats to civil aviation, both inside and outside the aircraft. As an armed first responder, you will typically deal with a suicide bomber in the same way in the airport as you will in the aircraft: You will shoot the suicide bomber in the ocular triangle in order to keep them from detonating their explosive device. As an unarmed first responder, you will need to control the suicide bomber's hands as quickly as possible to stop them from detonating their explosive; you may also consider this option as an armed first responder if the suicide bomber is close enough to grab without jeopardizing the security of the aircraft. Law enforcement officers are taught to shoot a life-threatening suspect in the *center mass* area, or chest region. This is because, statistically speaking, police officers are terrible marksman. By teaching officers to aim at the center mass of their target, it will give the officer the highest potential hit ratio. This type of training is not helpful to an armed first responder in civil aviation, because the response that you should have to a suicide bomber as an armed first responder is to shoot the suicide bomber in the *ocular triangle*, or the triangular area centered around the eyes and bridge of the nose. Law enforcement officers do not typically train to shoot with this precision, and therefore, as an armed first responder you should self-evaluate your shooting abilities and consider training to a higher standard if you are authorized to carry a firearm inside the cabin of a commercial aircraft inflight. Unfortunately for innocent bystanders, statistics consistently show that police only hit their intended target three times for every ten bullets they fire. Few officers are taught what to do when they are confronted with a suicide bomber; however, far

DOI: 10.4324/9781003336457-31

fewer receive the training with their firearm to be able to safely use this response inside of a crowded aircraft cabin.

On June 28, 2016, three suicide bombers entered Istanbul International Airport by taxi. The individuals walked unchallenged to prearranged locations in the airport parking area and international arrivals hall. The suicide bombers then attempted to herd people into a group before detonating their explosives. A video surfaced on the Internet shortly after the attacks which showed one of the suicide bombers at the moment they were shot by a security officer. The suspect can be seen falling to the ground and dropping what appears to be an assault rifle. The security officer approaches the suspect, looks at them carefully, and then runs quickly toward the nearest exit. The suspect moves around on the ground and then reaches for something in their pocket. Although the suicide bomber was shot numerous times in the torso by security personnel, they were eventually able to detonate their explosive device. Unfortunately, the security officer who initially incapacitated the suicide bomber failed to shoot them in the ocular window while the terrorist was down on the ground; this simple action would have ended that particular attack by making it impossible for the suicide bomber to detonate their explosive device.

As previously noted, the *ocular triangle*, or *ocular window* is located in the triangular area that is formed by the suspect's eyes and the bridge of their nose. By placing a bullet in this area, you can take away a life-threatening suspect's ability to control their motor skills. In essence, they will be incapable of physically detonating an explosive device. The only way that an explosive device can be detonated after a suspect is incapacitated would be if the explosive had a timer-, pressure-, or remote-controlled detonator. Therefore, shooting a suicide bomber in the ocular triangle is the preferred method to incapacitate and prevent them from consciously detonating an explosive device.

As an unarmed passenger, you do not have the aforementioned option. Instead, you need to immediately control the suspect's hands so they cannot physically detonate their explosive device. If you need help holding the life-threatening individual's hands, have another first responder or able-bodied passenger help you. After the life-threatening individual has been restrained, they can be incapacitated if needed by using your hands. This could involve breaking the suspect's neck by twisting their head sideways, or by pushing your thumbs through the suspect's eye sockets. You should use any means possible to incapacitate a suicide bomber if circumstances require; however, your main goal should be to restrain the suicide bomber's hands in a manner that keeps them from detonating their explosive device. This can be done by simply restraining the individual. Through consultation with an explosives expert on the ground, the pilot-in-command may decide to have you remove the explosive device from the suicide bomber; an explosive device should only be removed from a suicide bomber if you are ordered to do so by the pilot-in-command.

27

Aircraft-Specific Tactics for Armed First Responders

When you respond to an inflight security threat, the number one rule is: Get to the front of the aircraft as quickly as possible, where you can protect the flight deck from breach and channel threats in the cabin. Aircraft-specific tactics are built around these principles. There are some differences with how an armed and unarmed first responder can apply these tactics, and it is for this reason that this subject has been split between this and the following chapter to explain the differences between *armed* and *unarmed* aircraft specific tactics for first responders. The four tactics for armed first responders are the (1) *Responder-Rush*, (2) *Covered-Movement*, (3) *Modified Rush*, and (4) *Bounding-Overwatch*. These tactics can be applied by the lone-first responder or by a team of two or more first responders.

RESPONDER-RUSH

The *responder-rush* is a blitz to the forward area. As you already know, this a tactic that has been used by hijackers since the dawn of hijackings. The goal of this tactic is to reach the forward area within three to five seconds. You can do this easily by taking a quick glance to the rear to check for threats (six-check) and then, in a low, crouched manner, move up the aisle to the forward area. To reinforce this idea, imagine you are an armed first responder who is sitting in the cabin of a single-aisle aircraft en route to one of your favorite destinations. There are no other armed first responders inside the aircraft.

DOI: 10.4324/9781003336457-32

A person suddenly stands up in the back of the cabin and says: *I have a bomb! Everyone stay in your seats or I will blow up the plane!* You understand that this a signal for a terrorist attack, so you begin to slide down in your seat as you discreetly scan the cabin for other threats. You remove your firearm from its holster and pull it into a high-ready position, continuing to scan the cabin. After a quick glance up and down the aisle, you spring from your seat and move down the aisle toward the threat. When you have reached a satisfactory distance from the threatening individual, you shoot them in the ocular window. You then perform another quick glance around the cabin as you begin to repeatedly tell passengers: *Police! Police! Don't move!* You turn to face the forward area and then move in a low, crouched manner as quickly as possible toward the cockpit while you repeat your mantra: *Police! Police! Don't move!* When you reach the forward area, you open the lavatory door(s) and clear the bathroom(s) of any prohibited persons by telling them to leave the forward area and return to their seats. After the bathroom(s) and forward area are clear, you acquire an overwatch position in front of the first row of seats by facing the passengers in the cabin. There in the forward area, you tell passengers: *We are the police! Remain calm. Slowly place your hands on top of your head, interlace your fingers, and turn away from the aisle.* Once all passengers are in compliance, you call the pilot-in-command on the interphone to let them know that there was a life-threatening incident in the cabin.

In contrast to the lone-first responder response, a team response would be as follows: You are an armed law enforcement officer sitting inside an aircraft en route to one of your favorite destinations. There is another armed security officer inside the aircraft who is sitting a few rows away from you. A person suddenly stands up in the back of the cabin and says: *I have a bomb! Everyone stay in your seats or I will blow up the plane!* You begin to slide down in your seat while you discreetly scan the cabin for threats. The other armed first responder in the cabin is doing the same. You remove your firearm from its holster and pull it into a high-ready position as you continue to scan the cabin. The other first responder does this, too. After a quick glance up and down the aisle, you spring from your seat and move down the aisle toward the threat. The other first responder sees this, so they spring up from their seat after a quick six-check and then move up to the forward area in a low, crouched manner, clear the forward area of prohibited passengers, and acquire an overwatch position of the cabin. When you are close enough to make an accurate shot, you shoot the suicide-bomber threat in the ocular window. You then perform another quick glance around the cabin as you begin to repeatedly tell passengers in the cabin around you: *Police! Police! Don't move!* The other first responder begins telling passengers in front of the aircraft: *Police! Police! Don't move!* You turn to face the forward area and in a low, crouched manner, you move up the aisle as quickly as possible while you repeatedly tell people: *Police! Police! Don't move!* When you reach the forward area, you acquire an over-watch position behind the other first responder. The other first responder is now *the watcher* and you are *the worker*. The watcher begins to give cabin compliance commands by telling passengers: *We are the police! Remain calm. Everyone slowly place your hands on top of your head, interlace your fingers, and turn away from the aisle.* When passengers are in compliance, the worker tells you: *Call the pilot and tell them what happened.* You then turn around, pick up the interphone, and call the pilot-in-command to let them know that there was an incident inside the aircraft.

If you take some time to consider the previous examples, you can exercise your critical thinking skills. For instance, you can probably already think of other ways to apply the responder-rush tactic with the help of able-bodied passengers. Or you may have considered that the second first responder in the team response could have waited in the cabin to provide overwatch and provide better safety for their partner. Exercising your critical thinking skills and using visualization techniques like this are important because they will imprint tactics like the responder rush in your mind, making them easier to access during an emergency. A totality-of-circumstances approach should be taken when you are responding to an in-flight security threat. When you read the tactical examples through-out this book, use your critical thinking skills to ask yourself questions like: Did the first responder(s) follow the principles of inflight security? Did the first responder(s) adhere to the tactical mission statement? What would I have done differently? Is there something else I could do during my tactical response to help improve the security of the aircraft and the safety of myself, passengers, and other first responders?

COVERED-MOVEMENT

The aircraft-specific tactic of *covered-movement* is a controlled responder-rush to the forward area made by a first responder who first needs to cover their partner, or avoid an obstacle that is blocking their movement prior to their rush to the forward area. Although this tactic is most com-monly used when there is an obstacle blocking your path from rushing up the aisle, it can be used as a standalone tactic to give you variety in your tactical response. You may also decide to use this tactic if you are seated near a window and cannot immediately move from your position. To acquire an overwatch position in the cabin from the seated position, a good option is to pop up in your seat to better observe the cabin around you. (If you decide to do this, be careful not to hit your head on the overhead bins.) A standing position in the aisle may or may not be safer than a seated or crouched position; the totality of the circumstances will dictate how you will respond and how you will acquire your overwatch position. (Circumstances may require you to abandon the covered-movement tactic and immediately move whatever is blocking your path in order to perform a responder-rush to the forward area instead.) Whenever possible, you should seek to reach the safety of the forward area and issue cabin compliance commands from there. Consequently, the covered-movement tactic can be viewed as a tactical action that will eventually lead to a responder rush to the forward area.

If you were to apply the covered-movement tactic in the aircraft, it might look something like this: You are an armed law enforcement officer sitting inside an aircraft that is en route to one of your favorite destinations. There is another armed security officer inside the aircraft who is sitting a few rows away from you. A person suddenly stands up in the back of the cabin and says: *I have a bomb! Everyone stay in your seats or I will blow up the plane!* You begin to slide down in your seat while you discreetly scan the cabin for threats. The other armed first responder in the cabin is doing the same. You draw your firearm and pull it into a high-ready position and continue to scan the cabin. The other first responder does this, too. After a quick glance up and down the aisle, you spring from your seat and move down the aisle toward the threat. The other first responder sees this and, as the watcher, they decide to spring up onto their seat to get a better view of the cabin and acquire an overwatch position where they provide security for you as you move toward the threat. When you are close enough to make an accurate shot, you shoot the suicide bomber threat in the ocular window. You then perform another quick glance around the cabin as you begin to repeatedly tell passengers: *Police! Police! Don't move!* The other first responder then also begins to tell people in the cabin: *Police! Police! Don't move!* You turn to face the forward area and move in a low, crouched manner as quickly as possible as you continue to repeatedly tell people: *Police! Police! Don't move!* When you reach the forward area, you open the lavatory door(s) and clear the bathroom(s) of prohibited persons by telling them to leave the forward area and return to their seats. After the bathroom(s) and forward area are clear, you acquire an overwatch position in front of the first row of seats by facing the passengers in a high-ready position where you begin to give cabin compliance command by telling passengers: *We are the police! Remain calm. Everyone slowly place your hands on top of your head, interlace your fingers, and turn away from the aisle.* When all passengers are in compliance, the other first responder who is still in the main cabin communicates with you by saying: *Moving.* Although you know that this first responder is not making a request, nor waiting for a reply, you tell them: *Move.* After the first responder has moved to the forward area, they acquire an overwatch position behind you. Finally, you tell the other first responder to contact the pilot-in-command and let them know that an incident has occurred in the cabin.

Would you have done anything differently in the previous scenario? It was not altogether necessary for the first responder to tell the other that they were "moving," especially when they were moving from the rear of the aircraft where their voice may not even be heard. As a first responder, you should always try to communicate with other first responders because it is the safest thing to do. Our voice may not be heard by the other first responder(s), but we should always try to make ourselves heard because this will provide us with as much security inside the aircraft as possible. Are there any other inflight security considerations that the first responders in this scenario should have made? Can you think of other inflight security threat scenarios to which this tactic might be applied?

If you take the time to think critically about what has already been discussed, you will quickly realize that these tactics can be applied in countless different scenarios. They can be applied to attempted suicide bombings, hijackings, and a number of other life-threatening scenarios. As an armed first responder, you can apply the techniques of your chosen tactical response and protect the aircraft from the forward area where you can best observe life-threatening individuals and prevent the cockpit from being breached.

MOVEMENT FROM THE REAR OF THE AIRCRAFT

If you need to move from the rear of the aircraft as a first responder, you should apply the aircraft specific tactics of the (1) *Modified Responder-Rush* or the (2) *Bounding Overwatch.* Your response may also include some combination of the two. The modified responder-rush and bounding-overwatch take into account that moving to the forward area within three to five seconds will not be possible in some of the larger aircraft configurations. Your seating assignment will also affect whether you can reach the forward area in three to five seconds. These two tactics are especially useful when you are sitting in the last rows of the aircraft cabin and when normal activities in the cabin create obstacles in the aisles. When there is an inflight security threat in these particular situations, you should first seek a position of advantage in the area near the rear galley before preparing to use one of these two tactics (modified responder-rush and bounding-overwatch) as described below in order to move to the forward area. Movement to the forward area should be coordinated with your partner or other first responder, if one is available.

MOVEMENT FROM THE REAR OF THE AIRCRAFT

If you ever end up on an aircraft that has been hijacked and the aircraft is able to land safely on the ground, an assault team will eventually breach the aircraft and walk the aisles to ensure there are no more threatening individuals on board. The tactical team will typically employ the use of *aisle runners, aisle walkers,* and *aisle watchers.* After entry or breach of one of the emergency exits, aisle watchers will enter the aircraft at the rear, neutralize threats with their rifles, and then acquire an overwatch position. Two pairs of aisle runners will typically enter the aircraft from the mid-doors at the same time as the aisle watchers. The aisle runners will button-hook upon entering the aircraft and one pair will move up the aisle(s) to the forward area and the other pair will move down the aisle(s) toward the rear of the aircraft. Aisle walkers move slowly and methodically, watching passengers' hands closely. If you close your eyes and visualize this dynamic entry, it will become apparent to you that this ground-based dynamic entry is similar to the responder-rush tactic. Aircraft-specific tactics are based on this dynamic ground-based response; however, aircraft specific tactics have been adapted to consider the limited number of first responders that can be expected to be on board an aircraft inflight. By looking at aircraft-specific tactics in this way, it will help you to better understand the modified responder-rush and bounding overwatch tactics. You will want to move slowly and methodically from the rear of the aircraft. The tactics are a modified version of the rush because you will not be able to reach the forward area in three to five seconds. Take your time and be slow and methodical in your approach when you move from the rear of the aircraft. Watch the hands of passengers closely while you are scanning the cabin for threats. And as you review each of the following tactical responses, it is important for you to think critically about how you can use your newfound knowledge of ground-based dynamic entry techniques and your understanding of the added security that aisle walkers, runners, and watchers add to inflight security when you need to respond to an inflight security threat.

MODIFIED RESPONDER-RUSH

The modified responder-rush is similar to the responder-rush; however, there are some slight differences. If there is an inflight security threat and you are near the rear of the aircraft, it is best for you to first move to the area near the rear galley as quickly as possible to establish a position of an advantage there. When you move to the rear galley, use the same low, crouched profile as you do when you are moving to the forward area with the responder-rush tactic. Once you are in the rear galley, you can prepare to move toward the forward area by communicating with your partner (if you have a partner with you). If you are alone, you will move to the forward area only when you are ready. If you are moving from the rear of the aircraft to the forward area with a partner, one of you will need to walk in front of the other while the person in the rear holds on to their pants, belt, or shirt. If you are working as part of a larger security team with one pair of first responders working in the front and the other pair working in the rear of the cabin, call the forward area via the interphone to let the other team know you are preparing to move to the forward area. Once you are ready to move, the first responder in the lead position will begin moving up the aisle in the (armed or unarmed) high-ready position while they look for threats in front of them; as the first responder in the rear, you will hold on to the shirt of the first responder in front of you and maintain security behind you by glancing backward and scanning for threats as you are led up the aisle by the other first responder. If you are armed, you should communicate with passengers as you move up the aisle by telling them: *Police! Police! Don't move!* If you are a lone-first responder, you can perform the modified rush by yourself by glancing behind you periodically as you are moving slowly and methodically toward the forward area.

BOUNDING-OVERWATCH

The bounding overwatch is another tactic that is used when a first responder must move to the forward area from the rear of the cabin. You can perform the bounding-overwatch tactic by first moving to the rear galley area to establish an overwatch position. You will then communicate with the team in the forward area (if needed) in order to tell them that you are preparing to move up the aisle. Once you are ready to move, one of you will move to an overwatch position further up the aisle (three to four rows) while telling passengers in the cabin *Police! Police! Don't move!* When the overwatch position has been established three to four rows ahead, the watcher will cover the worker as they move up the aisle. This first responder will keep moving past the position of the other and establish an overwatch position three to four rows ahead. As they move up the aisle toward their overwatch position, the worker will tell passengers: *Police! Police! Don't move!* The two responders can communicate with one another by using the words *moving* and *move*. You may also perform this tactic alone by moving to an overwatch position, watching the cabin for a brief period, and then moving up the aisle to repeat the process once again until you reach the forward area. This slow, methodical movement is preferred (to the modified responder-rush) when you are moving from the rear of the aircraft because it gives you time to evaluate threats in the cabin and respond to them if needed.

The bounding-overwatch tactic can be used by itself or in conjunction with the modified responder-rush. A given threat scenario will determine what types, or combinations of tactics you will use to respond. The bounding-overwatch tactic gives you yet another option when responding to a threatening situation inside the aircraft. For example, an obstacle may block your path in the aisle and you might decide to use the bounding overwatch tactic instead of the responder-rush in order to pause in the cabin to evaluate threats. You can switch from the bounding overwatch to the modified responder-rush tactic whenever it is advantageous to your particular situation.

THE WATCHER & THE WORKER

Your tactics as a lone armed first responder will be very similar to your tactics you apply when you are working as part of a team; the main difference is the way with which you perform the roles of the watcher and the worker. A first responder is considered to be applying team tactics and a team-oriented approach when there are at least two of them coordinating a tactical response inside the aircraft. Aircraft-specific tactical duties can be split into two categories: watching and working. Your duties as a watcher include acquiring a position of overwatch of the cabin to watch passengers in the cabin for color, contrast, and movement. Your duties as a worker might include restraining a life-threatening passenger, moving up the aisle to the forward area, or clearing the lavatories, among others.

Your goal as a first responder, regardless of whether you are carrying a firearm or not, should always be to reach the forward area as quickly as possible when there is an inflight security threat. This should be done in three to five seconds. As you already know, you want to reach the forward area as quickly as possible because that is where you can protect the cockpit from being breached and where you can channel adversarial threats in the cabin. In the forward area, you can acquire an overwatch position in a single-aisle cabin by standing in the middle of the aisle slightly forward of the first row of seats; or you can stand in the left aisle of a double-aisle aircraft configuration just forward of the first row of seats. As noted previously, double-aisle aircraft configurations are typically *left-side vulnerable* because most of the flight deck doors that are installed in the cabins of wide-body aircraft are offset and in line with the left aisle. This left-side vulnerability should be taken into account when you acquire an overwatch position in the forward area of a double-aisle aircraft as an armed first responder. If you are alone on a wide-body aircraft, it is preferred that you acquire an overwatch position in the left aisle, just forward of the first row of seats.

Whenever you respond to a threat inside the aircraft, acquire an overwatch position after clearing the forward area and forward area lavatories. Because this may not always be possible, especially if you are a lone-first responder, you should always attempt to use a flight attendant to make notifications to the pilot-in-command and to help clear the forward area. An able-bodied passenger can be used for these tasks, too; however, the use of a trusted flight attendant helps to ensure your safety and the safety of other passengers and crew. An inflight security threat will always require a close overwatch of the cabin in order to ensure cabin compliance and to monitor passenger activity for active threats. Lone-first responders are more vulnerable to attack and you must divide your time as a watcher and a worker whenever you are acting in the lone-responder role. You must also rely more on the help from able-bodied passengers and cabin crew members. You should consider these things carefully and think critically about your particular situation and tactical response if you ever find yourself acting as a lone-first responder during an aircraft hijacking or attempted suicide bombing.

The first person who acquires the overwatch position during the application of team tactics is referred to as the *lead overwatch officer*. The lead overwatch officer will typically stay in the overwatch position until the aircraft lands. This is because the lead overwatch officer will have the best understanding of what is occurring in the cabin; the lead overwatch officer is the first person to assume the overwatch position, is the first person who gives cabin compliance commands, and is the person who will know who in the cabin may pose a potential problem later during the flight. Your goal is to make sure that the pilot-in-command can safely land the aircraft after an inflight security incident; the lead overwatch officer can help satisfy this goal through their keen observation of the cabin. In team-oriented tactics, a second first responder would typically take a position just behind the lead overwatch officer in a single-aisle aircraft, or a position just forward of the front row of seats on the right-side of the aisle when responding to a threat in the cabin of a wide-body aircraft.

The worker in team-oriented tactics should remain ready to move up and down the aisle to handle threats, or to help to act as a physical and psychological barrier to the flight deck by restricting access to the forward area. The lone-first responder, however, must approach their tactics in a more broad way by acting as both the worker and the watcher if needed; you can enhance inflight security by recruiting others to help with one or both of these roles. You should remain in the overwatch position until the aircraft is safely on the ground.

CLEARING TECHNIQUES

When you react to a threat in the aircraft, you will eventually move to the forward area or other position of advantage so you can acquire an overwatch position. Before you take a position of advantage, however, you will need to remove prohibited persons, or *unknowns,* from the area. This is often referred to as *clearing* a position of advantage. A position of advantage needs to be cleared of unknown persons because they may be a threat to us, the aircraft, or other passengers. Aside from the need to clear a position of advantage of unknowns, you should also consider the need to evaluate passengers in the cabin as you are moving up and down the aisle. You do not need to physically remove passengers from their seats like you do when you clear a position of advantage (unless they are a threat), but you *do* always need to scan the cabin for threatening passengers from the moment you respond to an inflight security threat until the moment the aircraft is safely on the ground. Therefore, for our purposes, *clearing techniques* are techniques that you can use as a first responder to maintain and evaluate the security of the aircraft as you are moving in the cabin, acquiring an overwatch position, or establishing security of the forward area or other position of advantage. To do this while you are moving in the aisle to a position of advantage, use your peripheral vision, move in a methodical manner, and clear all unknowns from the position of advantage before you acquire an overwatch position.

When a worker moves toward a position of advantage when implementing team tactics, they may announce to their partner that they are *Going deep* in order to avoid confusion over which one of them will assume the worker role. Confusion can arise on double-aisle aircraft when two first responders rush up the aisle at the same time, creating a situation where both officers reach the first row of seats (or other boundary to a position of advantage) at the same time. By announcing *Going deep* first responders can avoid this confusion. Upon hearing this, the other first responder will acquire the overwatch role. The first responder who goes deep will clear the forward area (or other position of advantage) to create a zone of security there; this would entail ensuring that any lavatories are clear of unknowns and that area within the position of advantage is clear of persons who may present a potential security concern. After this safety buffer zone has been established, both responders will assume an overwatch position and focus their full attention on passengers in the cabin.

The lone-first responder has a more challenging job when responding to a threat in the aircraft cabin than a first responder who is responding with a partner. To perform inflight security duties alone, a first responder must perform both the watcher and the worker roles simultaneously. This is difficult because the brain can only concentrate on so many activities at once. For example, a first responder will typically attempt to clear the forward area before acquiring an overwatch position; however, there are times when this is not possible. Of course, you can always use the help of other first responders or able-bodied passengers to do this for you, but this also may not be an option. The reason an armed first responder always attempts to clear the forward area before establishing an overwatch position is that, even though the lone-first responder can use a flight attendant or able-bodied passenger to clear the forward area under special circumstances, the lone, armed law enforcement officer is best equipped to deal with a threat who may be hiding in the lavatory or other area of the forward area. Clearing the forward area before the lone-first responder assumes an overwatch position can be performed hastily by entering the forward area in a high-ready position and scanning around bulkheads, opening the forward lavatory, or lavatories while using your eyes to scan at a waist-high level scanning where hands would be expected to be seen by a passenger hidden inside and by quickly removing any unauthorized passengers or unknowns from the forward area.

Single- and double-aisle aircraft configurations do require some special attention when you clear the forward area. A single-aisle configuration, for example, is easier to clear than a double-aisle configuration because the forward area is typically small; by moving directly toward the forward lavatory while using peripheral vision to ensure there are no threats hiding behind bulkheads, by opening the lavatory door from the outside if it is locked, or by simply pulling or forcing the lavatory door open with your foot, you can expeditiously clear a lavatory and then move around to an overwatch position to finish clearing the forward area. Double-aisle aircraft typically have two lavatories located in the forward area. You should begin clearing the forward area from the respective aisle of the cabin from which you enter the forward area and then work your way around to the other side while you search each of the lavatories (removing or neutralizing unauthorized or threatening passengers as you go). Your goal should be to ultimately end up in the overwatch position in front of the aisle that gives the quickest access to the cockpit; in double-aisle configurations, it is preferred that you start clearing the forward area from the right side and then work your way over to the left aisle to acquire an overwatch position there since the left-side aisle is typically in-line with the cockpit door.

A final consideration for you is to evaluate the manner in which the lavatory doors are opened. Lavatory doors may be a single door panel that opens outward by pulling a handle on the right side of the door, or they consist of a double-panel door with a split down the middle that can be pushed inward at the fold by using your foot or hand. Regardless of type, all lavatory doors will have a lock mechanism that can be opened from the outside; this is a common feature that allows flight attendants and other first responders to open the door in an emergency. To unlock a lavatory door, use your finger to flip up the small cover that says No Smoking in order to access the lock mechanism so you can grasp and slide it with your thumb and forefinger to the Open position.

The small size of an aircraft lavatory makes it possible to clear if you simply open the door and look inside. Regardless of how many lavatories are in the forward area, they should be cleared as quickly as possible in order for you as a lone-first responder or as part of a first responder team to move as quickly as possible to the safety of an overwatch position. From an overwatch position (especially in the forward area), you can gain cabin compliance, funnel adversarial threats in a linear direction, and communicate with the pilot-in-command by interphone.

NOTIFICATIONS TO THE PILOT-IN-COMMAND

If you are an armed first responder and you unholster your firearm to respond to a threat while you are in the cabin of an aircraft inflight, you should notify the pilot-in-command about this security incident as soon as possible. The *first notification* to the pilot-in-command is typically given after you have cleared the forward area and gained cabin compliance. You should also make sure there are no other *threatening individual*(s) in the cabin prior to the first notification. A threatening individual is any person who is an immediate threat to the integrity of the aircraft, or the safety of the crew, passengers, or other first responders. If you are a lone-first responder, you should use a flight attendant to make the notifications to the pilot-in-command so you can remain in an overwatch position.

The *first notification* is as follows: *This is law enforcement officer/first responder/flight attendant (your full name). There has been an incident on board. We are securing the cabin. I'll get back to you.* Once you have restrained all threatening individuals in the cabin and you are satisfied there is no immediate threat to the integrity of the aircraft, you should make the *second notification* to the pilot-in-command as follows: *This is law enforcement officer/first responder/flight attendant (your full name). The cabin is secure. Are any pilots injured? How long until we are on the ground?* The first notification serves to inform the pilot-in-command that there has been a security incident, that the cabin is under the control of a first responder, and that there are no more visible threats in the cabin. The second notification seeks to ensure the pilot-in-command that the cabin is secure and to answer questions related to the safety of the pilots and that seek to determine how much time it will take to land the aircraft. In the event that a passenger, crew member, or first responder is injured during an inflight emergency it is important for you to know how long the aircraft will take to reach medical personnel on the ground who can assist. If there is an injury on board, you may want to have a flight attendant contact MedLink so they can coordinate an emergency medical response with the pilot-in-command.

231

28

Multi-Level Aircraft Considerations

If you need to respond to an inflight security threat in a double-decker aircraft, your tactical response will change in a few small ways. If you recall our previous study in Section I, double-decker aircraft can have double-aisle configurations on both the top and bottom decks, as is the case with the Airbus A380. Aircraft can also have a double-aisle configuration on one deck and a single-aisle configuration on the other deck, as is the case with the Boeing 747. The positioning of the flight deck and how it is accessed is the single most important thing to consider for your tactical response. The manner in which the aisles are arranged inside the aircraft will determine how a hijacker can move if they want to breach the flight deck and control the aircraft. You should plan your response accordingly.

For example, if you are traveling on a Boeing 747 as a first responder, you will want to get to the upper deck as quickly as possible during an inflight security incident because that is where you will be able to protect the forward area. In contrast, the cabin of an Airbus A380 aircraft has access to the flight deck door from both decks. The Airbus A380 introduces special security challenges for first responders because of this dual-access forward area configuration. These types of differences should be investigated whenever you step on board an aircraft which has a configuration with which you are not readily familiar. You should plan your inflight security response to adapt to an aircraft's configuration.

29

Emergency Evacuation

There is a high probability that an aircraft will crash if it is under the threat of a hijacking or bombing during flight. This is one of the main reasons why understanding what to do during an emergency evacuation is important for you to understand as a first responder. You should read the inflight safety brochure prior to take-off to familiarize yourself with your aircraft's emergency evacuation procedures. These small pamphlets have important safety information. The information inside includes: where emergency exit lighting is located, how to remove an emergency exit door, how to exit the aircraft, and when to inflate your life vest. You should understand your role as a passenger during an emergency evacuation. As a first responder, you may be required to help cabin crew members during the evacuation process. It is important that you follow flight crew members' instructions as directed. When the door opens for an emergency evacuation, you should no longer concern yourself with providing security for the flight deck or ensuring the integrity of the aircraft. Providing security for the aircraft is essentially over once the aircraft is evacuated (or in the process of being evacuated). Your personal safety should be your number one priority during an evacuation.

On November 23, 1996, a Boeing 767 (Ethiopian Airlines Flight 961) was hijacked by three Ethiopian citizens seeking asylum in Australia. The hijackers eventually forced a crash of the aircraft. Many passengers drowned when they became trapped in the cabin after the aircraft flipped over during impact with the ocean surface. Unfortunately, many of these passengers died because they inflated their life vests before they had safely exited the aircraft. During the accident investigation into the Ethiopian Airlines flight 961 crash, it was learned that many of the passengers inside the cabin who survived the crash had heard others inflating their life vests and decided it was a bad idea to do the same; these passengers survived. These passengers understood proper safety procedures after reading and watching the inflight safety brief and it saved their lives. This incident underscores how important it is for you to understand safety procedures before an emergency happens and to listen carefully to the instructions of the flight crew during an emergency evacuation.

30

Outside Breach of Aircraft

The few brief scenarios you read about in the chapter on aircraft-specific tactics did not mention what happens when the aircraft lands on the ground. In a real-life hijacking or bombing attempt, you should expect a breach of the aircraft by rescue personnel once the aircraft is safely on the ground. Depending on where in the world the aircraft lands, a breach of the aircraft will typically be performed by security, law enforcement, or military personnel. A breach of the aircraft requires its own specialized tactics through the use of aisle walkers and aisle runners. As a first responder, your behavior may be similar to that of a hijacker and could be seen as a threat by rescue personnel when they enter the aircraft. It is important for your safety that you are prepared for a breach of the aircraft and that you make sure you do not appear threatening. If you are a first responder who is carrying a firearm in the aircraft, your safety will be at greater risk than unarmed first responders when the cabin is breached by rescue personnel.

In 1985, Egypt Air flight 648 was hijacked by three Abu Nidal hijackers. The aircraft ultimately landed at an airport on the small island of Malta. A standoff between security personnel and the hijackers began shortly after the aircraft landed. Soldiers from a US Army special operations detachment were sent to the island and began preparing for an assault with Egyptian commandos. Maltese authorities reportedly refused to allow the US soldiers to assist with the rescue operation, however, and when the Egyptian commandos breached the aircraft during their rescue attempt they shot and killed a number of passengers. The lack of training and experience of the rescue team ended up costing many lives. This example highlights the fact that it is not only the armed first responder who needs to be concerned about the dangers associated

DOI: 10.4324/9781003336457-35

with a ground breach; the unarmed first responder and passenger must be especially on guard during this time as well. As Egypt Air flight 648 shows, the dangerous part of an attempted hijacking or suicide bombing may not be in the air; it may be when the aircraft is already safely on the ground.

In the event of an outside breach of the aircraft, you should immediately fall on your weapon (if you are an armed first responder) with your hands away from any threatening objects. You should make your hands readily visible to rescue personnel. When rescue personnel respond to a hijacking situation, they will be searching for threatening individuals. If a threatening individual is seen by a rescue team member, it is highly likely that they will shoot that threat. Unarmed first responders should also make their hands visible to rescue personnel for this reason. Avoid standing in the aisle when the aircraft is breached. Lay down on the ground instead and spread your hands out so they are clearly visible. If you are seated, acquire a position with your hands placed on top of your head and fingers interlaced. You should avoid bending over when you are in the seated position; this could give rescue personnel cause to believe you are hiding something or acting decepitvely. Always refrain from making any quick movements when possible. If you are an armed law enforcement officer, you may find it helpful to identify yourself by saying, "Police! Police! Police!" and by having your credential at the ready or on display.

In the event of the breach of an aircraft, it is extremely important for you to follow the directions of rescue team members. The rescue team will operate under the same principles of speed, surprise, and aggression, and any refusal to obey their orders will be seen as a potential threat. Do not draw attention to yourself. Instead, keep your hands visible, do as you are told, and move only when you are told to move. By folllowing these few basic rules, you will help ensure the safety of yourself and those around you after the flight has landed.

31

Post-Incident Stabilization

Post-incident stabilization refers to those actions which occur after the hijacking or suicide bombing situation has been dealt with. This may mean, for example, that all of the hijackers are dead or restrained; that all bomb-strapped bodies or explosives have been placed in the least-risk bomb location; and that the cabin is secure, or free from threats. Technically, the post-incident period begins when the second notification has been made. The second notification as explained in this section should not be confused with the second notification to the pilot-in-command when an explosive device has been found on board or ready to be moved to the least-risk bomb location. The post-incident timeframe and second notification begin only when the cabin is secure and when it is safe and feasible for you to make as a first responder. Therefore, when there are no more immediate threats present or visible in the cabin and all threatening individuals have been restrained, then the pilot-in-command can be notified and the post-incident period can begin.

COMMUNICATION CONSIDERATIONS

If you need to respond to an inflight security threat, internal agency protocols may require you to contact a dedicated watch-desk or call-center. If this is the case, it would be best for you to make this notification as quickly as possible once post-incident stabilization has begun. This will give first responders on the ground ample warning ahead of time before the aircraft lands. Some call-centers act as a type of fusion center, where various government agencies can be contacted by talking to one central command. These fusion centers will direct the appropriate federal, state, and

DOI: 10.4324/9781003336457-36

local emergency agencies to respond wherever the aircraft lands. Quick coordination and communication is the key to ensuring the safety of the aircraft after it lands. Notification to the respective agency responsible for aviation security in the country where the aircraft is flagged should be a priority of all first responders, regardless of your law enforcement status.

You can talk to the respective call center, fusion-center, or watch desk in your geographic area by calling the pilot-in-command on the cabin interphone. A three-way call can be established between you, the pilot, and rescue personnel on the ground at the designated airport where you will make an emergency landing. If you are armed, this will be the best time to notify the rescue team on the ground that there is an armed first responder on board. You should also tell the rescue team about any additional threats that are still active on board the aircraft and where those threats are located. You will also want to tell the rescue team if any other passengers, law enforcement officers, or crew members are injured, and you should request any assistance you might need on the ground, including medical services or the need for a diplomatic officer's presence.

The acronym TAPS should be used when you communicate information to the pilot-in-command or to rescue personnel during the post-incident stabilization process. The TAPS acronym symbolizes *threats, attendants, passengers, status*. Threats are those threatening individuals who are (1) remaining in the cabin and (2) those who have been neutralized or restrained; *attendants* are any crew members or flight attendants who are injured; *passengers* are any passengers who are dead or injured, and the location where a passenger death or injury has occurred in the aircraft cabin; and *status* refers to the status of the first responder, such as any injuries or other noteworthy things which could affect their ability to perform security in the aircraft. The main point of communication in the post-incident environment (besides relaying the aforementioned security information) is to keep your speech as short and simple as possible. The ability to be understood is important, especially when the aircraft is landing in a country where it is not flagged and when you are trying to communicate with people with whom you do not share a common language.

MEDICAL CONSIDERATIONS

For post-incident medical considerations, you should first concern yourself with those injuries in the cabin which could affect the safety or security of the aircraft. This might include the injury of another armed law enforcement officer or first responder, which would require you to make a decision as to whether you should secure that individual's firearm. You should ask a crew member if your aircraft uses MedLink. MedLink should be contacted as soon as possible after you begin the post-incident stabilization process. You should be especially aware of exactly *what* medical emergencies are present on board and *where* those injured people are located in the aircraft. You should be prepared to relay this type of information to medical professionals on the ground when you speak to MedLink. Flight attendants and able-bodied passengers can help relay information to MedLink on the cabin interphone. Flight attendants and able-bodied passengers should be used to conduct these communications whenever you need them to, especially when the totality of the circumstances require you to remain in the forward in an overwatch position to ensure security of the flight deck. Most commercial flights have medical doctors, paramedics, or emergency medical technicians on board who can help during a medical emergency. As a first responder, you should use all of the resources available to you inside the aircraft in order to ensure that any and all passenger, crew, and first responder injuries are treated.

EMERGENCY EVACUATION

We have already touched on the subject of emergency evacuation, if only briefly toward the end of the previous section. A post-incident emergency evacuation can be *crew-initiated* or it can be *passenger-initiated*. A crew-initiated post-incident emergency evacuation can be expected to be more orderly than a passenger-initiated post-incident emergency evacuation. As a first responder, you should be prepared for a sudden post-incident emergency evacuation whenever the aircraft lands after a hijacking or attempted suicide bombing. If there is a post-incident emergency evacuation, you should consider whether or not the pilots are still inside the flight deck. Even though the activation of any of the emergency exits will disable the aircraft's ability to fly, the pilots may not have been able to escape the cockpit and may be injured and unable to respond. Always make sure to check on the status of the pilots as soon as possible after an emergency landing has been made after a hijacking or bombing attempt.

You may be asked to help during an emergency evacuation. It is important for you to understand how to operate emergency exits and how to exit an aircraft during an emergency. As a first responder in civil aviation, the ability to understand post-incident emergency evacuation procedures means that you should also be able to explain to passengers how to safely evacuate the aircraft. If you ever find yourself in this position, you should keep your communication with passengers calm, direct, and as short as possible. For example, if you want passengers to wait as the slide inflates you should tell them: *Stay Back!* Or, for example, when it is safe to go down the slide you should tell them: *Go!* Short, concise, calm, and simple communication is important during emergencies. This can help save lives. You can also direct passengers where you want them to go by using hand movements, such as waving and pointing. By remaining calm and confident during an emergency, you will help ease the stress of passengers in the cabin, facilitate evacuation of the aircraft, and prevent needless injury.

COORDINATING EFFORTS WITH OUTSIDE AGENCIES

When there is an inflight security incident on board an aircraft, the pilot-in-command will contact the respective local law enforcement agency as per their airline's security protocol. The type of security protocol that the pilot will follow is highly dependent on the laws of the country where the aircraft they are flying is flagged. If you are an armed first responder, you will have your own security protocols to follow if you need to respond to an inflight security incident. You can call the pilot-in-command on the cabin interphone to contact any necessary outside agencies per your agency or company protocol. If you do need to contact an outside agency per your protocol, you should do this as soon as possible after beginning the post-incident stabilization process.

On a US-flagged aircraft, it would probably also be a good idea to contact the Transportation Security Operations Center (TSOC) in Virginia. If you are an armed first responder on a US-flagged aircraft who needs to respond to an inflight security incident, you should ask the pilot-in-command to connect you with the Transportation Security Operations Center, or TSOC. Other countries have their own dedicated inflight security call centers. The pilots of these countries will have information on who to contact if there is an inflight security incident in their aircraft. As an armed first responder, you should be prepared to relay information like (1) whether or not the security situation is stabilized, (2) how many threats are still active in the cabin, (3) a brief description of the security incident, (4) whether or not the crime scene has been preserved, (5) whether or not there are injured crew members or passengers, and (6) if there has been any contact made with emergency services or other law enforcement agencies on the ground. Certain situations on the aircraft may make it difficult for you to contact an outside law enforcement agency or inflight security call center like the TSOC. If this happens, you should maintain the security of the aircraft by maintaining an overwatch position in the forward area and then wait until the aircraft lands to make contact with federal, state, and local officials on the ground. *Remember!* Make your empty hands visible when the aircraft is breached. You do not want to be viewed as a threat by rescue personnel.

CONCLUSION

This book has hopefully helped you to think a little more critically about civil aviation security. As a first responder in civil aviation, you have a unique ability to have a positive effect on the international effort to secure the transportation sector and protect the lives of air travelers. Your understanding of the aviation sector and access to it make you an indispensable person to the safety of those around you. As you travel to your next destination or continue with yet another day's work in civil aviation, enjoy the smiling faces of those around you. By maintaining security awareness and thinking critically about civil aviation security, you can help to make the aviation sector safer and keep those passengers smiling and looking forward to a bright future. Fly safe.

GLOSSARY

ABP: Able-Bodied Passenger

Adversary: any person who threatens the aviation environment; an adversary can be a suicide terrorist such as a suicide bomber, a hijacker, a hijack team, a lone gunman, or any other person who attempts to kill or injure people within the aviation environment.

Air Piracy: the unlawful seizure of an aircraft within the special aircraft jurisdiction; *see* **hijacking**.

Aisle: the walkway or pathway passengers and crew use to move within the aircraft cabin.

AMO: Adversary Method of Operation

Annex 17: ICAO annex which was adopted as the standard for civil aviation security.

ASO: Aviation Security Officer

Attempted Bombing: an attempt to detonate an explosive device on board an aircraft inflight with the purpose of destroying the aircraft.

Aviation Environment: this refers to the environment within the aviation travel system. In some airports, the aviation environment may also include an airport transportation system, such as an air train, bus service, airport hotel shuttle, or other transportation service used within close proximity to an airport. In an aircraft, the aviation environment includes the various travel class cabins, lavatories, galleys, and other accessible areas inside the aircraft.

AVPU: medical evaluation for alertness; stands for Alert, Verbal, Pain, and Unresponsive.

Back-strap: the rear or upper part of the grip on a handgun which lies beneath the heel of the hand when gripping the firearm.

BDO: Behavioral Detection Officer; used by the Transportation Security Administration at select airports in the United States.

Bone Pressure: technique applied by placing one's foot on an unresponsive suspect's bone and putting downward pressure to attempt to provoke a response.

Cabin: area within the aircraft where passengers sit; the cabin consists of a single lavatory or several lavatories, aisle(s), deck(s), galley(s), and a forward area.

Cabin Compliance: the control of passengers and crew in the cabin by forcing them into a position of disadvantage (i.e., with hands on top of their head and fingers interlaced).

Captain: the captain is legally responsible for the safety and operation of the aircraft. The captain is also known as the *Pilot-in-Command,* or PIC, by first responders in civil aviation.

CBP: Customs and Border Protection

CFR: Code of Federal Regulations

Chief Steward: *see* **Purser.**

Cockpit: *see* **Flight Deck.**

Cockpit Door: *see* **Flight Deck Door.**

Commandeering: the unlawful seizure of an aircraft; includes traditional acts of air piracy and also when an aircraft is not yet considered *inflight,* such as when not all external aircraft doors have been closed.

Concealment: a barrier that helps conceal movement but does not provide any ballistic resistance.

Co-Pilot: also known as the first officer, the co-pilot is considered the second-in-command of the aircraft to the authority of the captain. The captain and co-pilot typically share the role of piloting the aircraft during commercial flight.

Cover: a barrier that provides ballistic resistance. The only cover on an aircraft is the hardened cockpit door.

Cover Story: role-playing, during which the actor gets to assume a new identity. A cover story is often used by inflight security professionals and terrorists for operational security purposes.

Covered: concealed, as in "he has a covered (concealed) firearm."

Cross-Pollination: sharing of information between terrorist organizations; an example of this would be the Lod Airport Bombing during which the terrorist groups PFLP and Japanese Red Army shared information on targets to avoid detection during their planned attacks.

Deck: the floor of an aircraft upon which seats are placed in the aircraft cabin and passengers and crew walk during flight.

Deployment Strategies: the specific strategies used to counter an aircraft hijacking or suicide bombing attempt. These strategies mostly remain the same, although techniques can be used to vary a given deployment strategy in order to add variety and unpredictability.

Dirty Airport: an airport with lax security procedures; these airports are often used as the initial portal for attacks against the aviation domain since, by definition, it is easier to bring weapons and explosives through the checkpoints of these aviation portals.

Double-Decker: aircraft configuration with two decks. The respective decks are typically referred to as the main deck and upper deck.

FAA: Federal Aviation Administration

FAM: Federal Air Marshal

FBI: Federal Bureau of Investigation

FFDO: Federal Flight Deck Officer

First Notification: typically made from first responder to the pilot-in-command to notify them that there has been a security incident on board and that a first responder is handling it.

First Officer: *see* **Co-Pilot**.

First responder: any person who assists to stop a hijacking or inflight bombing on board an aircraft inflight; typically a flight attendant or armed law enforcement officer.

Flag: this is a violation of the second of the four basic firearm safety rules, which is *never point a firearm at someone you do not intend to shoot*.

Flight Attendant: member of an aircrew who performs duties of comfort and safety for passengers on board commercial aircraft. The number one responsibility for a flight attendant is to ensure the safety of all passengers on board.

Flight Deck: the area where the pilots sit and control the aircraft; commonly referred to as the *cockpit*.

Flight Deck Door: the door which leads from the forward area of the cabin into the flight deck. Flight deck doors were hardened on most commercial aircraft after the September 11 hijackings.

Flying Armed: a class given by the Transportation Security Administration for sworn United States law enforcement officers who have a need to carry a firearm on commercial aircraft. The class teaches a law enforcement officer to stay in their seat if an inflight security team is on board and to use their best judgment to solve an inflight problem if an inflight security team is not on board but fails to give them the tactical knowledge offered in this book.

Forward Area: the area aft of the cockpit and forward of the first row of seats; sometimes referred to as the Position of Dominance, or POD.

FSD: Federal Security Director

Galley: food preparation area inside a commercial aircraft cabin; this area is most susceptible to inflight fire due to the large amount of high

249

amperage wiring in these areas. The galley can also be used as a position of advantage for a first responder.

Hard Target: a target with few security vulnerabilities; an example would be the secure environment, or *sterile area* of an aircraft.

High-Ready Position: places the hands near the chest at the ready position and may be incorporated with a firearm (armed high-ready position) or as an unarmed high-ready position.

Hijacker: an adversary within the aviation environment who seeks to hijack an aircraft.

Hijacker-Pilot: an adversary who is also a trained pilot; the hijacker-pilot has been used on numerous occasions throughout history and is a more common hijack tactic for today's would-be hijacker.

Hijacking: also known as *air piracy*, a hijacking is the unlawful seizure of an aircraft within the special aircraft jurisdiction by an individual or group.

ICAO: International Civil Aviation Organization

IFSO: Inflight Security Officer

Inflight: the point in time when all external aircraft doors have been closed until the point when at least one of the aircraft's doors has been opened for passenger disembarkation.

Inflight Medical Kit: a medical kit typically carried on board commercial aircraft; the inflight medical kit is commonly found in one of the forward most overhead storage bins.

Isosceles Stance: preferred shooting stance for an armed law enforcement officer in the aviation environment; performed by standing with feet shoulder-width apart and by squaring up your body with the adversarial threat. This stance provides the most stability during normal aircraft movement and turbulence.

JTTF: Joint Terrorism Task Force.

Jumbo Jet: a name that was historically used as an alternate name for the Boeing 747. The title of *Jumbo Jet* has more recently been applied as an alternate name for many other wide-body, double-aisle aircraft.

Lavatory: the bathroom located inside an aircraft cabin.

Lead Overwatch Officer: the first individual to assume an overwatch position during a team-based, or tandem aircraft specific tactical response during most counter-hijack responses.

Left-Side Vulnerable: most double-aisle aircraft have a flight deck door that is in line with the left-side aisle, making the left side of the aircraft slightly more vulnerable to hijacker movement than the right.

Let's Roll Syndrome: named after the counter-hijack actions of passengers on United Airlines Flight 93, *Let's Roll Syndrome* acknowledges that passengers may revolt against anyone who poses a threat to their protected environment inside the aircraft cabin. In light of this reality, a first responder may be viewed as a threat to other passengers on board. This is why armed first responders should always announce their law enforcement or official status when they respond to an onboard incident.

Least-Risk Bomb Location: the least-risk bomb location in an aircraft where an explosive device can be placed if it is found during flight.

MedLink: operated by *MedAire*, this medical advisory service can be used via any cabin interphone. The PIC can assist with a connection to MedLink which gives the caller access to a physician who can assist with diagnoses of onboard medical problems and help the caller solve medical emergencies.

Micro Expressions: facial expressions which occur within microseconds. These expressions change involuntarily and techniques for detecting them during proactive profiling can be used as a tool to help identify deception.

Mixed Surveillance: a mixture of all types of surveillance, including mobile, static, and technical.

Mobile Surveillance: a type of surveillance that is carried out on foot, vehicle, or other transportation method and used by a surveillance operative to surveil a target.

Narrow-Body Aircraft: *see* **Single-Aisle Aircraft**.

No Fly List: a special list maintained by the United States government which identifies certain people who are prohibited from traveling on commercial aircraft to or from the United States.

Non-Sterile Area: the area of an airport that is not subject to security screening of people or vehicles; this area typically includes the curbside area outside of departure and arrival terminals, air trains, ticket counters, passenger screening cues, and other common public areas of an airport.

Ocular Triangle: the triangle area formed by a suspect's eyes and the bridge of their nose. This area is considered the accepted target for an armed law enforcement officer when confronted with a suicide terrorist; shooting a suicide bomber in this region causes a supect to lose motor function.

OODA: Observe, Orient, Decide, Act.

OPSEC: Operational Security; refers to adhering to certain operational protocols in order to keep an adversary from learning important information that could lead to a security vulnerability

Pilot-in-Command: the captain of an aircraft; the PIC is legally responsible for the safety and operation of the aircraft.

Position of Advantage: minimizes the distance that a first responder needs to move to the forward area, channels threats into a linear direction, and facilitates communication between the first responder and flight crew. A position of advantage is ideally located in the forward area, in an aircraft galley, or near a cluster of lavatories.

Position of Dominance: also known as the POD; see *Forward Area*.

Post-Incident: defined as when the captain has been given second notification; this is typically after all threats have been neutralized and when injuries within the cabin are being stabilized.

Principles: basic truths which never change and include, understanding the tactical mission statement; acting decisively; using speed, surprise, and aggressiveness; and having simplicity as a primary characteristic of all tactics.

Proactive Profiling: the combination of two successful deceptive behavior detection methods (the behavioral detection method and the predictive profiling method) which is used when searching for deceptive, criminal, or terrorist behavior in the protected environment.

Proactive Security Process: defined as detecting suspicion, determining the threat, and deploying against the threat after identifying the AMO.

Protected Environment: the specific environment within which we want to deny the threat of an adversary.

Purser: the lead flight attendant and supervisor for all other flight attendants on board; typically works in the first class cabin section of the aircraft and makes on board announcements during flight. The term purser originated from maritime transport and is used interchangeably with *chief steward*.

Reasonable Suspicion: a legal standard of proof in United States law that is based on "specific and articulable facts." Because the aviation environment is so different from the ground-based environment and reasonable suspicion can be mistaken, this is one of the most important reasons why inflight security training is so vitally important and essential for all *Flying Armed* trained law enforcement officers.

Restraints: anything which can be used to bind a suspect's hands and wrists so they are immobilized.

SAMPLE: an easy way to remember the basics of taking a patient history during a medical emergency; this acronym stands for *signs/symptoms, allergies, medications, past illnesses, last oral intake,* and *events leading up to present illness/injury.*

Second Notification: this is typically made from the first responder to the pilot-in-command in order to let the captain know that the cabin is secure, and also seeks to ensure that the pilots are safe and determine how long until the aircraft lands. The second notification is typically only given when all threats in the cabin have been neutralized and there are no further visible threats remaning. Only after the second notification is made does the *post-incident* stabilization period begin.

Single-Aisle Aircraft: those aircraft configurations which have only one aisle in the cabin; these are sometimes referred to as narrow-body aircraft, but the term single-aisle aircraft is preferred for first responders in civil aviation.

Situational Awareness: having an awareness of the behavior of those around you, even when you are carrying out normal daily tasks.

Six-Check: a term used to describe the action of looking behind oneself prior to moving from the aircraft seat and after discharging a firearm. Used as a safety check of your surrounding area.

Sleeper Agent: a member of a hijack team who does not immediately join the initial execution of the hijacking; also known as a *sleeper hijacker* but typically referred to as *sleeper* for brevity.

Soft Target: a target with numerous security vulnerabilities; an example would be the non-secure area of an airport.

Special Aircraft Jurisdiction: refers to the special jurisdiction of the country from which the aircraft is flagged. When a commercial aircraft is inflight, it is subject to the laws of whatever country that aircraft belongs to, or *special aircraft jurisdiction.* Some countries have certain criminal codes or statutes which apply specifically to special aircraft jurisdiction, such as Title 18 of the United States federal code for criminal violations.

Static Surveillance: surveillance of a target which is performed by a surveillance operative who acquires a static position as an observation post, such as an aircraft seat, the rear galley of an aircraft, the hotel shuttle waiting area of an airport, etc.

Sterile Area: the area of an airport where passengers have already passed through security screening for explosives and weapons. In some respect, the term sterile area is a misnomer because attacks have taken place within the sterile area before. Sterile area attacks include past aircraft hijackings and suicide bombings.

Suicide Bomber: a terrorist or criminal who deliberately detonates an explosive device to kill or injure people and whom dies during the act.

Suicide Terrorism: suicide is used as a perceived means to serve some greater cause. Suicide terrorism has been used for centuries, making it one of the oldest forms of terrorism.

Super-Jumbo Jet: a name commonly used to refer to the Airbus A380.

Surveillance Detection: the practice of spotting surveillance operatives within the immediate area of a potential criminal or terrorist target of interest.

Surveillance Operative: lone-criminal, terrorist, or third-party contracted operative who performs surveillance on a target.

Suspicion Indicators: an indication based on known or predicted terrorist or criminal methods of operation or a deviation from a typical profile that may lead a reasonable person to believe that an observed situation (person and/or object) may have the potential for harming the protected environment.

Tactical Mission Statement: acts as a hierarchy of priorities for inflight security, and reads "Ensure security of the flight deck, the integrity of the aircraft, and the safety of the crew, passengers, and fellow team members."

Tactics: *see* **Deployment Strategies.**

TAPS: used when communicating the post-incident situation to outside agencies; stands for *threats, attendants, passengers,* and *status.*

Technical Surveillance: involves the use of special equipment which monitors a target's use of technology, such as internet, phone, and credit card use. This type of surveillance is typically applied when the target of the surveillance is a person and not an object or common terrorist target such as an airport or aircraft.

Techniques: these vary with each individual and are fluid with the situation.

TEDD: used as an acronym and teaching tool for surveillance detection; stands for *time, environment, distance,* and *demeanor.*

Title 18 USC: title within the United States federal code which covers most crimes committed inside the special aircraft jurisdiction.

Title 49 USC: title within the United States federal code which covers transportation and aviation security programs.

TSA: Transportation Security Administration

TSOC: Transportation Security Operations Center

Unknowns: passengers who are unknown and untrusted; all passengers who are unknown to us personally are considered unknowns, with the exception of flight attendants.

USC: United States federal code

Visualization: a form of daydreaming during which the practitioner can visualize responding to an emergency situation, such as day-dreaming about using aircraft specific tactics to save a hijacked aircraft.

Watcher: may also be referred to as the *Lead Overwatch Officer*; this is one of the first responder roles which is used in conjunction with the role of the *worker*. The watcher's role involves watching the cabin for color, contrast, and movement of potential adversarial threats.

Weapon Retention: techniques used to retain a holstered or unholstered firearm.

Wide-Body Aircraft: *see* **Double-Aisle Aircraft**.

Worker: one of the roles played by the first responder and used in conjunction with the role of the *watcher*. The worker role is used by the first responder whenever they are involved in duties other than those performed by the watcher; this may involve performing tasks like restraining a suspect, searching lavatories, applying bone pressure, shooting a suspect, etc.

INDEX